THE
SETTLEMENT OF ILLINOIS

1778–1830

THE
SETTLEMENT OF ILLINOIS

1778–1830

BY

ARTHUR CLINTON BOGGESS

A THESIS
PRESENTED TO THE FACULTY OF PHILOSOPHY OF THE UNIVERSITY
OF PENNSYLVANIA IN PARTIAL FULFILLMENT OF THE
REQUIREMENTS FOR THE DEGREE OF PH. D.
1906

BOOKS FOR LIBRARIES PRESS
FREEPORT, NEW YORK

First Published 1908
Reprinted 1970

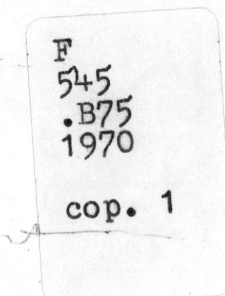

INTERNATIONAL STANDARD BOOK NUMBER:
0-8369-5493-9

LIBRARY OF CONGRESS CATALOG CARD NUMBER:
71-128873

PRINTED IN THE UNITED STATES OF AMERICA

CONTENTS.

	Page.
Author's Preface,	5

Chapter I.
The County of Illinois,	9

Chapter II.
The Period of Anarchy in Illinois,	40

Chapter III.
I. The Land and Indian Questions,	71
II. Government Succeeding Period of Anarchy,	82
III. Obstacles to Immigration,	90

Chapter IV.
I. Illinois During the Territorial Period,	99
II. Territorial Government of Illinois,	111
III. Transportation and Settlement,	118
IV. Life of the Settlers,	128

Chapter V.
The First Years of Statehood; The Indian and Land Questions,	134
The Government and Its Representatives,	145
Transportation,	153
Life of the People,	165

Chapter VI.
Slavery in Illinois as Affecting Settlement,	176

Chapter VII.
Successful Frontiersmen,	191
Works Consulted: I. Sources,	213
II. Secondary Works,	234
Index,	257

MAPS.

	Page.
Indian Cessions, 1795–1809,	72
" " 1809–1818,	104
" " 1818–1830,	136
Chart of Vote for and against a Convention to revise the Constitution, 1824,	184

PREFACE.

IN the work here presented, an attempt has been made to apply in the field of history, the study of types so long in use in biological science. If the settlement of Illinois had been an isolated historical fact, its narration would have been too provincial to be seriously considered, but in many respects, the history of this settlement is typical of that of other regions. The Indian question, the land question, the transportation problem, the problem of local government; these are a few of the classes of questions wherein the experience of Illinois was not unique.

This work was prepared while the writer was a student in the University of Wisconsin. The first draft was critically and carefully read by Prof. Frederick Jackson Turner, of that University, and the second draft was read by Prof. John Bach McMaster, of the University of Pennsylvania. In addition to suggestions received from my teachers, valuable aid has been rendered by Miss Caroline M. McIlvaine, the librarian of the Chicago Historical Society, who placed at my disposal her wide knowledge of the sources of Illinois history.

The omission of any reference in this work to the French manuscripts, found by Clarence W. Alvord, is due to the fact that at the time they were found, my work was so nearly completed that it was loaned to Mr. Alvord to use in the preparation of his article on the County of Illinois, while the press of professional duties has been such that a subsequent use of the manuscripts has been impracticable.

ARTHUR C. BOGGESS.

Pacific University,
    Forest Grove, Oregon.
    September 14, 1907.

SETTLEMENT OF ILLINOIS

CHAPTER I.

THE COUNTY OF ILLINOIS

AN Act for establishing the County of Illinois, and for the more effectual protection and defence thereof, passed both houses of the Virginia legislature on December 9, 1778.[1] The new county was to include the inhabi-

[1] "Jour. H. of Del.," Va., Oct. Sess., 1778, 106-7; "Jour. of Senate," Va., Oct. Sess., 1778, 52.

Erroneous statements concerning the time of the formation of the County of Illinois have been made by Winsor, "Westward Movement," 122; Poole, in Winsor, "Narrative and Crit. Hist. of Am.," VI., 729; Thwaites, "How George Rogers Clark Won the Northwest," 64; Boyd, in "Am. Hist. Rev.," IV., 623; Mason, in "Chicago Hist. Soc. Coll.," IV., 286; Pirtle, "Clark's Campaign in the Ill.," 5; Moore, "The Northwest Under Three Flags," 220; Wallace, "Hist. of Ill. and La. Under French Rule," 402; Butler, "Hist. of Ky.," 1836 ed., 64; and others. Roosevelt's indefinite statement that the county was formed "in the fall of 1778"—"Winning of the West," II., 168—is technically correct. Kate Mason Rowland truthfully says—"George Mason," I., 307, 308—that a committee was ordered to prepare a bill for the formation of the county, on November 19, 1778, and that such a bill was presented on November 30. Butterfield says—"George Rogers Clark's Conquest of the Ill.," 681-6—that the Act was passed between the 19th of November and the 12th of December, 1778. It is true that the bill in its final amended form passed both houses on December 9, was signed by the Speaker of the Senate on December 17, and subsequently, if at all, by the Speaker of the House of Delegates. On the 12th of December, Governor Patrick Henry issued three important sets of instructions in accordance with the provisions of the Act creating the County of Illinois. As the signing of the bill by the Speakers was mandatory after its passage, it is easy to understand the issuance of these instructions previous to the signing. It is almost impossible to conceive that Governor Henry, who showed marked interest in the Western frontier, should first have begun to issue orders at least six weeks after the county was formed, as is implied by the date commonly given for its formation. For the legislative history of the act, see "Jour. H. of Del.," Va., Oct. Sess., 1778, 65, 72, 79-80, 91, 96, 106-7; "Jour. of Senate," Va., Oct. Sess., 1778, 48, 49, 51, 52, 53, 70-1.

tants of Virginia, north of the Ohio River, but its location was not more definitely prescribed.¹

The words "for the more effectual protection and defence thereof" in the title of the Act were thoroughly appropriate. The Indians were in almost undisputed possession of the land in Illinois, save the inconsiderable holdings of the French. Some grants and sales of large tracts of land had been made. In 1769, John Wilkins, British commandant in Illinois, granted to the trading-firm of Baynton, Wharton and Morgan, a great tract of land lying between the Kaskaskia and the Mississippi rivers. The claim to the land descended to John Edgar, who shared it with John Murray St.Clair, son of Gov. Arthur St.Clair. The claim was filed for 13,986 acres, but was found on survey to contain 23,900 acres, and was confirmed by Gov. St.Clair. At a later examination of titles, this claim was rejected because the grant was made in the first instance counter to the king's proclamation of 1763, and because the confirmation by Gov. St.Clair was made after his authority ceased and was not signed by the Secretary of the Northwest Territory.² In 1773, William Murray and others, subsequently known as the Illinois Land Company, bought two large tracts of land in Illinois from the Illinois Indians. In 1775, a great tract lying on both sides of the Wabash was similarly purchased by what later became the Wabash Land Company. The purchase of the Illinois Company was made in the presence, but without the sanction, of the British officers, and Gen. Thomas Gage had the Indians re-convened and the validity of the purchase expressly denied. These large grants were illegal, and the Indians

1. "Jour. H. of Del." Va., Oct. Sess., 1778, 72; "Hening's Statutes," IX., 553.
2. "Public Lands," II., 204, 206–9.

were not in consequence disposessed of them.[1] Thus far, the Indians of the region had been undisturbed by white occupation. British landholders were few and the French clearings were too small to affect the hunting-grounds. French and British alike were interested in the fur trade. A French town was more suited to be the center of an Indian community than to become a point on its periphery, for here the Indians came for religious instruction, provisions, fire-arms, and fire-water. The Illinois Indian of 1778 had been degraded rather than elevated by his contact with the whites. The observation made by an acute French woman of large experience, although made at another time and place, was applicable here. She said that it was much easier for a Frenchman to learn to live like an Indian than for an Indian to learn to live like a Frenchman.[2]

1. The Illinois and Wabash Land companies, which had several members in common, united in 1780. After a long series of memorials to Congress, the Supreme Court of the United States, in 1823, decided that "a title to land, under grant to private individuals, made by Indian tribes or nations, northwest of the river Ohio, in 1773 and 1775, can not be recognized in the courts of the United States"—8 "Wheaton," 543-605. In general see: "Pub. Lands," I., 24, 27, 72, 74, 160, 189, 301; II., 108-20, 138, 253; "Sen. Jour.," 1793-99, 317, 326; *Ibid.*, "2d Cong.," 165; "Va. Calendar State Papers," I., 314; "Jour. of Cong.," III., 676-7, 681; IV., 23; "An Account of the Proceedings of the Ill. and Ouabache Land Companies," 1-55, Phil'a, 1796; "Memorial of the Ill. and Wabash Land Company," 1-26, Phil'a, 1797; "Memorial of the Ill. and Ouabache Land Companies," 1802, 1-20; "An Account of the Proceedings of the Ill. and Ouabache Land Company," 1-74, Phil'a, 1803; "Memorial of the United Ill. and Wabash Land Companies," 1-48, Baltimore, 1816. For a map of the claims, see "Map of the State of Ky. with the Adjoining Territories," 1794, pub. by H. D. Symonds; also a copy of the same published by Smith, Reid and Wayland, in 1795; and "States of America," by J. Russell, London, C. Dilly and G. G. & J. Robinson, 1799. The last map gives the claims of the Ill., Wabash, and N. J. companies, respectively, the others, the claims of the last two only. All references here given are to material to be found in the libraries of the Chicago Historical Society and of the State Hist. Soc. of Wis.

2. Mother Mary of the Incarnation, of Quebec, in 1668. In "Glimpses

SETTLEMENT OF ILLINOIS.

In point of numbers and of occupied territory, the French population was trifling in comparison with the Indian. In 1766–67, the white inhabitants of the region were estimated at about two thousand.[1] Some five years later,[2] Kaskaskia was reported as having about five hundred white and between four and five hundred black inhabitants; Prairie du Rocher, one hundred whites and eighty negroes; Fort Chartres, a very few inhabitants; St. Philips, two or three families; and Cahokia, three hundred whites and eighty negroes. At the same time, there was a village of the Kaskaskia tribe with about two hundred and ten persons, including sixty warriors, three miles north of Kaskaskia, and a village of one hundred and seventy warriors of the Peoria and Mitchigamia Indians, one mile northwest of Fort Chartres. It is said of these Indians: "They were formerly brave and warlike, but are degenerated into a drunken and debauched tribe, and so indolent, as scarcely to procure a sufficiency of Skins and Furrs to barter for clothing," and a pastoral letter of August 7, 1767, from the Bishop of Quebec to the inhabitants of Kaskaskia shows the character of the French. The French are told that if they will not acknowledge the authority of the vicar-general—Father Meurin, pastor of Cahokia—cease to marry without the intervention of the priest, and cease to absent themselves from church services, they will be abandoned by the bishop as unworthy of his care.[3] Two years earlier,

of the Monastery." "Scenes from the Hist. of the Ursulines of Quebec,"——, 1639–1839, "by a Member of the Community," 90. Charlevoix, "Histoire de la Nouvelle-France," III., 322, expressed a similar opinion in 1721, and Collot, "Journey in N. A.," I., 232–3, shows that the Illinois French of 1796–7 were a case in point.

1. Pittman, "European Settlements on the Miss.," 55. See pp. 42, 44, 45, 47, 48, for the settlement in detail.
2. Hutchins, "Topographical Desc. of Va.," 36–8.
3. "Mandements des Evêques de Quebec," II., 1741–1806, 205–6.

THE COUNTY OF ILLINOIS. 13

George Croghan had visited Vincennes, of which he wrote: "I found a village of about eighty or ninety French families settled on the east side of this river [Wabash], being one of the finest situations that can be found. . . . The French inhabitants, hereabouts, are an idle, lazy people, a parcel of renegadoes from Canada, and are much worse than the Indians."[1] Although slave-holders, a large proportion of the French were almost abjectly poor. Illiteracy was very common as is shown by the large proportion who signed legal documents by their marks.[2] The people had been accustomed to a paternal rule and had not become acquainted with English methods during the few years of British rule. Such deeds as were given during the French period were usually written upon scraps of paper, described the location of the land deeded either inaccurately or not at all, and were frequently lost.[3] Land holdings were in long narrow strips along the rivers.[4]

The country was physically in a state of almost primeval simplicity. The chief highways were the winding rivers, although roads, likewise winding, connected the various settlements. These roads were impassable in times of much rain. All settlements were near the water, living on a prairie being regarded as impossible and living far from a river as at least impracticable.[5] The difficulties of

1. Thwaites, "Early Western Travels," I., 141, reprint of Croghan's Jour.
2. "Chicago Hist. Soc. Coll.," IV., 165; "Ind. Hist. Soc. Pub.," II., 513–4.
3. "Public Lands," I., 10.
4. Two of the many maps illustrating this are in "Pub. Lands," II., facing 183, 195. A number of maps in Hopkins', "The Home Lots of the Early Settlers of the Providence Plantations," especially the one following page 17, show that the same form of holdings existed in Providence, R. I. For reasons for this form, see the note by Emma Helen Blair, in Thwaites', "Jesuit Relations," IV., 268–9. Stiles, "Ancient Windsor," I., 149, has a map showing such holdings in Windsor, Conn., 1633–1650.
5. Monroe, "Writings," I., 117; "Ind. Hist, Soc. Pub.," II., 483–92;

George Rogers Clark in finding his way, overland, from the Ohio River to Kaskaskia and Vincennes on his awful winter march, are such as must manifestly have confronted anyone who wished to go over the same routes at the same season of the year.

Wild animals were abundant. A quarter of a century after the Revolution, two hunters killed twenty-five deer before nine in the morning near the Illinois settlements.[1] In 1787, the country between Vincennes and Kaskaskia abounded in buffalo, deer, and bear.[2] For years, the chase furnished a large part of the provisions. The raising of hogs was rendered difficult by the presence of wolves. Game-birds were plentiful, and birds were sometimes a pest because of their destruction of corn and smaller grains and even of mast.

An early traveler wrote in 1796: "The province of the Illinois is, perhaps, the only spot respecting which travelers have given no exaggerated accounts; it is superior to any description which has been made, for local beauty, fertility, climate, and the means of every kind which nature has lavished upon it for the facility of commerce."[3] The wide-spreading prairies added to the beauty of the country. Land which now produces one hundred bushels of corn to the acre must have been capable of producing wonderful crops at the beginning of its cultivation. Coal was not known to exist in great quantities in the region nor was its use as a fuel yet known.

Hutchins, "Topographical Desc. of Va.," map facing 41; Collot, "A Journey in N. A.," I., 239-42, describes the roads in Illinois in 1796, and plate 28 of the accompanying atlas gives an excellent map, *q. v.* in pocket.

1. "Draper Coll., Ill. MSS.," 99.
2. Harmar to Sec. of War from Fort Harmar, Nov. 24, 1787—"St. Clair Papers," II., 30-1.
3. Collot, "A Journey in N. A.," I., 233.

THE COUNTY OF ILLINOIS.   15

Such was the country and such the people now organized into the County of Illinois.[1] The Act establishing the county provided that the governor and council should appoint a county-lieutenant or commandant-in-chief, who should appoint and commission as many deputy-commandants, militia officers, and commissaries as were needed. The religion, civil rights, property and law of the inhabitants should be respected. The people of the county should pay the salaries of such officers as they had been accustomed to, but officers with new duties, including the county-lieutenant, were to be paid by Virginia. The governor and council might send five hundred troops, paid by Virginia, to defend Illinois. Courts were to be established with judges elected by the people, although the judges of other county-courts of Virginia were appointed by the governor and council.[2]

While Gov. Patrick Henry was writing instructions concerning the organization of government in Illinois, the British general, Hamilton, was marching to take Vincennes. Henry did not know this particular fact, but he had a keen perception of the difficulties, both civil and military, which awaited the county. On December 12, 1778, without waiting for the formal signing of the act creating the county, he wrote instructions to George Rogers Clark, to Col. John Todd, jr., and to Lieut.-Col. John Montgomery. Clark was instructed to retain the command of the troops, then in the Illinois country, and to assume command of five other companies, soon to be sent out.[3] Col. Todd was appointed county-lieutenant or

---

[1]. At the November session of 1738, Virginia had formed the County of Augusta, which technically included the Illinois country—"Hening's Statutes," V., 78–80. For a map, see Waddell, "Annals of Augusta Co., Va.," frontispiece.

[2]. "Hening's Statutes," IX., 117, 552–5; V., 489, 491.

[3]. Henry, "Life of Patrick Henry," III., 209–18.

commandant. His instructions contained much wise direction. He was to take care to cultivate and conciliate the affections of the French and Indians, to coöperate with Clark and give the military department all the aid possible, to use the French against the British, if the French were willing, but otherwise to remain on the defensive, to inculcate in the people an appreciation of the value of liberty, to see that the inhabitants had justice done them for any injuries from the troops. A neglect of this last instruction, it was pointed out, might be fatal. "Consider yourself as at the head of the civil department, and as such having the command of the militia, who are not to be under the command of the military, until ordered out by the civil authority and act in conjunction with them." An express was to be sent to Virginia every three months with a report. A letter to the Spanish commandant at Ste. Genevieve was inclosed, and Todd was told to be very friendly to him.[1] Col. Montgomery, then in Virginia, was ordered to recruit men to reënforce Clark. "As soon as the state of affairs in the recruiting business will permit, you are to go to the Illinois country & join Col. Clarke. I need not tell you how necessary

[1] "Cal. of Va. State Papers," I., 312-14.

Col. John Todd, jr., was born March 27, 1750, in Pennsylvania. He was well educated by his uncle in Virginia, in which state young Todd practised law for some years. In 1775, he was one of the representatives chosen at the call of the proprietors of Transylvania to form an ultra-constitutional government for that new settlement. In 1777, he was one of the first two burgesses from the county of Kentucky. He was killed at the Battle of the Blue Licks, August 19, 1782. For biographical sketches see John Mason Brown, "Oration at the Centennial of the Battle of the Blue Licks," 27-31; "Chicago Hist. Soc. Coll.," IV., 285-8; Green, "Historic Families of Ky.," 211; White, "Descendants of John Walker," 56; "Filson Club Pub.," VI., 27-8; Morehead, "Settlement of Ky.," 174. Morehead's facts were from R. Wickliffe, Todd's son-in-law, but this fact loses its significance from the circumstance that Todd's only living child was of posthumous birth.

the greatest possible Dispatch is to the good of the service in which you are engaged. Our party at Illinois may be lost, together with the present favorable Disposition of the French and Indians there, unless every moment is improved for their preservation, & no future opportunity, if the present is lost, can ever be expected so favorable to the Interest of the commonwealth." Montgomery was urged not to be daunted by the inclement season, the great distance to Illinois, the "want of many necessaries," or opposition from enemies.[1] Gov. Henry deserves much credit for his prompt and aggressive action at a time when Virginia was in the very midst of the Revolution.

Col. Clark was much pleased with the appointment of Col. Todd, both because civil duties were irksome to the conqueror and because of his confidence in Todd's ability.[2] Upon the arrival of the new county-lieutenant, Clark called a meeting of the citizens of Kaskaskia to meet the new officer and to elect judges. He introduced Col. Todd as governor and said that he was the only person in the state whom he had desired for the place. The people were told that the government, Virginia, was going to send a regiment of regular troops for their defense, that the new governor would arrange and settle their affairs, and that they would soon become accustomed to the American system of government. In regard to the election of judges, Clark said: "I pray you to consider the importance of this choice; to make it without partiality, and to choose the persons most worthy of such posts."[3] The nine members of the court of Kaskaskia, the seven members of the court of Cahokia, and the nine members of the court of Vincennes, as also the respective clerks were French. Of the three sheriffs, Richard Winston, sheriff

[1]. Henry, "Life of Patrick Henry," III., 216-18. [2]. *Ibid.*, 237.
[3]. "Draper Coll., Clark MSS.," XLIX., 43, original MS. in French.

of Kaskaskia, was the only one who was not French.[1]

Military commissions were promptly made out, those of the districts of Kaskaskia and Cahokia being dated May 14, 1779. So many of the persons elected judges were also given military commissions that it seems probable that the supply of suitable men was small. No fewer than fourteen such cases occur. Of the militia officers appointed at Vincennes, P. Legras, appointed lieutenant-colonel, had been a major in the British service, and F. Bosseron, appointed major, had been a captain in the British service.[2]

The position of Illinois among the counties of Virginia was necessarily anomalous. All counties, except the County of Illinois, were asked to furnish one twenty-fifth of their militia to defend the state. Illinois county was omitted from the western counties enumerated in "An act for adjusting and settling the titles of claimers to unpatented lands under the present and former government, previous to the establishment of the commonwealth's land office." Settlers northwest of the Ohio were warned to remove. No settlement would be permitted there, and if attempted, the intruder might be removed by force— "*Provided*, That nothing herein contained shall be construed in any manner to injure or affect any French,

[1]. "Chicago Hist. Soc. Coll.," IV., 295.

[2]. "Chicago Hist. Soc. Coll.," IV., 294-6, 418; "Mich. Pioneer Coll.," IX., 498.

A Mr. Winston, probably Richard, was in Illinois in 1770, and was regarded as an authority on the prices of cattle, as is shown by the court records. In 1773, upon the occasion of the purchase of land from the Kaskaskia Indians, by the Illinois Land Company, Richard Winston was at Kaskaskia, and interpreted in French to the illiterate Indian interpreter of His Majesty what the company desired to say to the Indians—"Chicago Hist. Soc. Coll.," IV., 435; "An Account of the Proceedings of the Ill. and Ouabache Land Companies," 1796, 14. Richard Winston was one of the riginal Indiana Company—"Cal. of Va. State Papers," VI., 18, 35.

Canadian, or other families, or persons heretofore actually settled in or about the villages near or adjacent to the posts reduced by the forces of this state." These exceptions were made at the May session of 1779. At this session, there was passed an act for raising one troop of cavalry, consisting of one captain, one lieutenant, one cornet, and thirty-two privates to defend the inhabitants of Illinois county. All officers were to be appointed by the governor and council. The men were to receive the same pay as Continentals. Any soldier who would serve in Illinois during the war should receive a bounty of seven hundred and fifty dollars and a grant of one hundred acres of land.[1]

Acting upon the policy that caused Virginia to warn all intruders not to settle northwest of the Ohio, Todd issued a proclamation warning all persons against such settlement, "unless in manner and form as heretofore made by the French inhabitants." All inhabitants were ordered to file a description of lands held by them, together with a deed or deposition, in order to be ready for the press of adventurers that was expected.[2]

Some of the incidents of the summer of 1779 indicate difficulties of the new government. When the governor was to be absent for a short time, he wrote to Winston, who as commander of Kaskaskia would be acting governor, telling him not to impress property, and by all means to keep up a good understanding with Col. Clark and the officers. The judges of the court at Kaskaskia were ordered to hold court "at the usual place of holding court...any adjournment to the contrary notwithstanding." Richard McCarty, of Cahokia, wrote to the county-lieutenant complaining that the writer's stock had been

1. "Hening's Statutes," X., 26, 32, 43, 161.
2. "Chicago Hist. Soc. Coll.," IV., 301; "Pub. Lands," I., 16.

killed by the French inhabitants. McCarty had allowed
his stock to run at large and they had destroyed unin-
closed crops, which crops, he contended, were not in their
proper place. Two months later, McCarty wrote from
Cahokia: "Col. Todd residence hear will spoil the people
intirely. I think it would be a happy thing could we get
Colo¹ Todd out of the country for he will possitively sett
the Inhabitants and us by the Ears. I have wrote him a
pritty sharp Letter on his signing a Death warrant against
my poor hog's for runing in the Oppen fields . . . . .
on some complaints by the Inhabitants the other day he
wished that there was not a Soldier in the country."[1]
McCarty's hogs were not his only trouble. A fellow-
officer wrote: "I received a line from Capt. McCarty [cap-
tain of troops at Cahokia] yesterday. He is well. He
writes to me that he has lost most of his French soldiers,
and that the inhabitants are so saucy that they threaten to
drive him and his soldiers away, telling him that he has
no business there—nobody sent for him. They are very
discontented. The civil law has ruined them."[2]

Col. Todd's position was difficult because of the discontent prevailing among both the French and the Americans
in Illinois. His salary was so small that he feared that he
must sell his property in Kentucky to support himself

1. Todd to Winston, June 15, 1779—"Chicago Hist. Soc. Coll.," IV.,
302; Todd to Judges at Kaskaskia, July 31, 1779—*Ibid.*, 304; McCarty to
Todd, from Cahokia, July 18, 1779—"Draper Coll., Clark MSS.," XLIX.,
72, original MS.; McCarty to Montgomery, from Cahokia, Sept. 19, 1779,
—*Ibid.*, XLIX., 71, original MS.

Richard McCarty had been a resident of Cahokia under British rule and
had warned the British against American encroachments. He was licensed
to trade by the county government upon the recommendation of the court of
the District of Cahokia, June 5, 1779—"Mich. Pioneer Coll.," IX., 368,
383; "Chicago Hist. Soc. Coll.," IV., 296-7-8.

2. Capt. John Williams to G. R. Clark, from Fort Clark, Kaskaskia,
Sept. 25, 1779—"Draper Coll., Clark MSS.," XLIX., 73, original MS.

THE COUNTY OF ILLINOIS. 21

while in public service. He regarded Kentucky as a much better place than Illinois for the ambitious man, the retired farmer, or the young merchant.[1] He had been scarcely more than three months in office when he wrote to the governor of Virginia: "I expected to have been prepared to present to your excellency some amendments upon the form of Government for Illinois, but the present will be attended with no great inconveniences till the Spring Session, when I beg your permission to attend and get a Discharge from an Office, which an unwholesome air, a distance from my connexions, a Language not familiar to me, and an impossibility of procuring many of the conveniences of Life suitable; all tend to render uncomfortable."[2] This letter was intercepted by the British and did not reach the governor.

Great difficulty was experienced in securing supplies for the soldiers. At times, both troops and people suffered from lack of clothing. The Spanish refused to allow the Americans to navigate the Mississippi, Virginia money entirely lost its credit, hard money was scarce, and peltry was difficult for the military commissaries to obtain. Col. Todd, in desperation, refused to allow the commander at Kaskaskia to pay the people peltry for provisions as had been promised, and calling the inhabitants in council, he told them that if they would not sell on the credit of the state they would be subject to military discipline.[3] The

1. Todd to Col. Will Fleming, senator from Botetourt, from Kaskaskia, Aug. 18, 1779—"Draper Coll., Clark MSS.," XXIII., 103, original MS.

2. Todd to Gov. of Va., from Kaskaskia, Aug. 18, 1779—"Chicago Hist. Soc. Coll.," IV., 319.

3. Capt. John Williams to Col. Wm. Preston, from Ft. Clark, Kaskaskia, Sept. 20, 1779—"Draper Coll.. Preston Papers," V., 9, original MS.
Montgomery to Clark, from Ft. Clark, Kaskaskia, Oct. 5, 1779—*Ibid.*, "Clark MSS.," XLIX., 78, original MS.

fall of 1779 saw the garrison at Vincennes without salt, and starving; while at Kaskaskia the money was worthless, troops were without clothes and deserting daily.[1] This great lack of supplies resulted in the impressment of supplies, in disagreement among the officers, and was a prominent factor in a resolution to withdraw the troops from their several situations and concentrate them at a single point on the Ohio River. The discontent of the French was extreme, and it was increased by the departure of Col. Todd for Virginia. The officers who were left in command ruled with a rod of iron and took cattle, flour, wood, and other necessaries, without payment.[2] Capt.

1. Shelby to Clark, from Vincennes, Oct. 10, 1779—*Ibid.*, XLIX., 79, original MS.; Montgomery to Clark, from Ft. Clark, Kaskaskia, Nov. 15, 1779—*Ibid.*, XLIX., 85, original MS.

2. Montgomery to Clark, from Kaskaskia, Feb. 1, 1780—"Draper Coll. Clark MSS.," L., 9, original MS.; Clark to Todd, from Louisville, March, 1780—"Cal. of Va. State Papers," I., 338–9; John McArthur from Ste. Genevieve, Mo., Oct. 22, 1883—"Draper Coll. Clark MSS.," VIII., 27.

I have been unable to determine just when Col. Todd left Illinois, whether he resigned as county-lieutenant, and whether he again returned. Boyd in his article in the "Am. Hist. Rev," IV., says that he left in 1780, resigned in the same year, and apparently did not return. Mason, in "Chicago Hist. Soc. Coll.," IV, 287, says that he seems to have left in 1779, seems not to have resigned, and not to have returned. Wickliffe, in Morehead, "Settlement of Ky.," 174, implies that he did not resign, and says that he several times revisited the county. No one of these writers gives any authority for his statement and I have found none. It is certain that Todd was at the Falls of Ohio on December 23, 1779; that he then wrote to the governor of Virginia expressing his intention of resigning; that the governor, Jefferson, strongly opposed his resigning—"Chicago Hist. Soc. Coll.," IV., 359; that he left some peltry in the joint care of his subordinates, Montgomery and Winston, in November, 1779; that goods were said to be consigned to him as county-lieutenant of Illinois in November, 1780; that he wrote "I still receive complaints from the Illinois," on April 15, 1781; that on April 29, 1781, Winston was referred to as "Deputy County-Lieutenant for the Illinois County;" and that Thimothé Demunbrunt signed as "Lt. Comd. par interim, &c." in February and again in March, 1782—"Chicago Hist. Soc. Coll.," IV., 315–16, 335, 343, 359; "Draper's Notes, Trip 1860," III., 40–4.

Dodge, of Kaskaskia, refused to honor a draft presented, apparently, by the government of Virginia, and when sued in the civil court, he declared that he had nothing but his body and that could not be levied upon; besides, he was an officer and as such was not amenable to civil law.[1]

In the very midst of starvation, the French, unaccustomed to English ways, were wishing to increase the expense of government. An unsigned official letter says, in speaking of affairs in Illinois: "I find that justices of the peace, appointed among them, expect to be paid, this not being the practice under our laws, there is no provision for it. Would it not be expedient to restrain these appointments to a very small number, and for these (if it be necessary) to require small contributions either from the litigants or the people at large, as you find would be most agreeable. In time, I suppose even this might be discontinued. The Clerks & Sheriffs perhaps may be paid, as with us, only converting Tobacco fees into their worth in peltry. As to the rules of decision & modes of proceding, I suppose ours can be only gradually introduced. It would be well to get their militia disciplined by calling them regularly together according to our usage; however, all this can only be recommended to your Discretion."[2] Some eight years later the exaction of exhorbitant fees was one of the chief reasons which caused the reform of the French court at Vincennes.[3]

---

1. Edward Murray to ―――――――, from Kaskaskia, Apr. 19, 1780— "Draper Coll., Clark MSS.," XLVI., 52, original MS. John Dodge had been an Indian trader between Detroit and Pittsburg. He was captured by the British, but escaped on Oct. 9, 1778, after thirty-three months detention. Washington recommended him to Congress as a man who would be useful because of his knowledge of the country—"Draper's Notes, Trip 1860," VI., 153–5.

2. Unsigned and unaddressed, from Williamsburg, Jan. 28, 1780—"Draper Coll., Clark MSS.," I., 5, original MS.

3. Hamtramck to Harmar, from Vincennes, Apr. 13, 1788—"Draper Coll., Harmar Papers," I., 386–7.

The plan for concentrating most of the Illinois troops at a single point was carried out in the spring of 1780. The chief objects sought were to procure supplies and to prevent the advance of the Spaniards. At first, it was thought advisable to locate the new fort on the north side of the Ohio near the Mississippi, and Col. Todd made some grants of land to such persons as were willing to settle in the vicinity and assist in raising provisions, but the fact that Virginia currency, although refused in Illinois, was accepted in Kentucky caused the fort to be built south of the Ohio, and it is probable that Todd's grants of land at the site first proposed lapsed.[1] As the troops had a great need for settlers to raise crops, Capt. Dodge suggested to the governor of Virginia that immigrants to Illinois should receive aid from Virginia. This would aid the troops and would stop emigration to the Spanish possessions west of the Mississippi.[2]

As the French could neither support the soldiers nor do without them, commissions in blank were sent to Maj. Bosseron, district commandant at Vincennes, with power to raise a company there, and to assure the company that pay would be allowed by the government. It was feared that the settlers at Vincennes would consider themselves abandoned upon the withdrawal of troops. It was proposed to leave enough troops among the French to satisfy them, but scarcely had the new fort been established when the people of Cahokia sent a special messenger to Clark at Fort Jefferson, the new fort, asking that troops be sent

[1]. Clark to Todd from Louisville, Mar., 1780 — "Cal. of Va. State Papers," I., 338–9; *see also* pp. 358, 360.
Unsigned and unaddressed official letter, from Williamsburg, Jan. 28, 1780 — "Draper Coll., Clark MSS.," L., 5, original MS.

[2]. Dodge to Gov. of Va., from Ft. Jefferson, Aug. 1, 1780 — "Cal. of Va. State Papers," I., 368.

THE COUNTY OF ILLINOIS. 25

to protect them. The Indians so surround the place, say the petitioners, that the fields can not be cultivated. If troops are sent the people can not feed them, but if they are not sent the people can not long feed themselves.[1] French creditors of the government were unpaid and some of them must have been in sore need.[2]

The act establishing the County of Illinois would terminate by limitation at the end of the May session of 1780, unless renewed. At that session, the act was renewed "for one year after the passing of this act, and from thence to the end of the next session of assembly."[3]

The condition of the people in the county during the latter half of 1780 was one of misery. Contemporary accounts have a melancholy interest. An attack by Indians upon Fort Jefferson being imminent, the few troops in the outlying districts were ordered to come to the aid of the garrison. The order reached Cahokia when its few defenders were sick and starving. Corn, without grease or salt, was their only food. Deaths were of frequent occurrence. The people of the village had petitioned Col. Montgomery to ease their burden by quartering some of the troops in other villages, but he refused the request of other officers for a council and threatened to abandon the country entirely. In such a condition of affairs, Capt. McCarty proceeded to obey the orders from Fort Jefferson. The only boats at the disposal of the garrison were unseaworthy, so five small boats were pressed for use. On the

---

1. Todd to Gov. Jefferson, from Richmond, June 2, 1780—"Cal. of Va. State Papers," I., 358; Address from the people of Cahokia to G. R. Clark, April 11, 1780—"Draper Coll., Clark MSS.," L., 27, original MS. in French.

2. Legras to Clark, from Vincennes, Aug. 1, 1780—"Draper Coll., Clark MSS.," L., 54, original MS. in French.

3. "Hening's Statutes," X., 303, 388–9.

way, several of the famished soldiers became so sick that they had to be left along the route. Even military discipline was bad in the country. Capt. McCarty, upon being arrested for having quarreled with Dodge, because the latter would not buy food for the starving troops, was left for months without trial because Col. Montgomery had left the country and a military court could not be convened.[1] In October, McCarty wrote: "In short, we are become the hated beasts of a whole people by pressing horses, boats, &c., &c., &c., killing cattle, &c., &c., for which no valuable consideration is given; even many not a certificate, which is here looked upon as next to nothing."[2]

Of the same tenor as McCarty's testimony to Illinois conditions is that of Winston. A remonstrance of the civil authorities against the extravagance of the military officers was treated as insolent and impertinent. The military power refused the civil department the use of the military prison, even when pay was offered, and made strenuous efforts to establish military rule. Col. Montgomery and Capt. Brashears had departed for New Orleans without settling the account for the peltry which Todd had committed to the joint care of Montgomery and Winston. Montgomery was openly accused of having taken a large amount of public property away with him. Capt. Dodge was a notorious disturber of the peace, and Capt. Bentley, a more recent arrival, was equally undesirable. In the closing paragraph of a long letter is the significant statement: "It Being so long a time since we

1. Extract from McCarty's journal, from Kaskaskia, Oct. 14, 1780—"Draper Coll., Clark MSS.," L., 66; McCarty to Col. Slaughter, Jan. 27, 1781—"Draper's Notes, Trip 1860," III., 1, 2; incomplete in "Cal. of Va. State Papers," I., 465; Montgomery to McCarty, between Aug. 27 and Aug. 30, 1780—"Draper Coll., Clark MSS.," L., 66, 68; *Ibid.*, L., 70, original MS.

2. McCarty to Todd, from Kaskaskia, Oct. 14, 1780—"Cal. of Va. State Papers," L., 380.

had any news from you, we conclude therefrom that the Government has given us up to do for Ourselves the Best we can, untill such time as it pleases Some other State or Power to take us under their Protection—a few lines from you would give Some of us great satisfaction, yett the Generality of the People are of Opinion that this Country will be given up to France . . . ."[1]

At the close of October, the troops, with the exception of a very few, were collected at Fort Jefferson. There the garrison was sick and starving,[2] clothes were much needed, desertion was rife, and the abandonment of the post seemed imminent.[3] Among the few troops that were not called to Fort Jefferson were those of Capt. Rogers, at Kaskaskia. This company "had to impress supplies, giving certificates for the value—thus would kill cattle when they wanted them, hogs, & take flour from the horse-mills—& thus lived very comfortably."[4]

Mutual recrimination was common among the officers. Todd, in a letter to Gov. Jefferson, in which he inclosed letters from the Illinois officers, said: "Winston is commandant at Kaskaskia; McCarty, a captain in the Illinois regiment, who has long since rendered himself disagreeable by endeavoring to enforce military law upon the civil department at Kohos.

1. Winston to Todd, from Kaskaskia, Oct. 24, 1780—"Cal. of Va. State Papers," I., 380-2.

2. Winston to Clark, from Kaskaskia, Oct. 24, 1780—"Draper Coll., Clark MSS.," L., 71, original MS.; "Draper's Notes, Trip 1860," II., 136-40; Helm to Slaughter, from Fort Jefferson, Oct. 29, 1780—"Cal. of Va. State Papers," I., 383; Williams to Clark, from Camp Jefferson, Oct. 28, 1780—*Ibid.*, I., 383.

3. Montgomery to Jefferson, from New Orleans, Jan. 8, 1781—"Cal. of Va. State Papers," I., 424-5.

4. "Draper Coll., Clark MSS.," VIII., 78.

"The peltry, mentioned by Winston as purloined or embezzled by Montgomery, was committed to their joint care by me in Nov^r, 1779; and from the circumstance of Montgomery's taking up with an infamous girl, leaving his wife, & flying down the river, I am inclined to believe the worst that can be said of him. Being so far out of the road of business, I can not do the State that justice I wish by sending down his case immediately to the Spanish commandants on the Mississippi."[1] From January 28, 1779, to October 18, 1780, Montgomery drew drafts upon Virginia to the amount of thirty-nine thousand three hundred twenty dollars.[2] Winston and McCarty accused Capt. Rogers, who succeeded Col. Montgomery in command at Kaskaskia, of shooting down the stock of the inhabitants without warrant. In a dignified defence, Capt. Rogers declared that he took only so much food as was absolutely required to save his starving sick, and that Mr. Bentley, who endeavored to secure supplies from the people, offering his personal credit, was persistently opposed by Winston and McCarty. "I can not conclude without informing you that 'tis my positive opinion the people of the Illinois & Post Vincennes have been in an absolute state of rebellion for these several months past, & ought to have no further indulgence shown them; and such is the nature of those people, the more they are indulged, the more turbulant they grow. I look upon it that Winston and McCarty have been principal instruments to bring them to the pitch they are now at."[3] Capt. Dodge, against whom complaints had become general, and Capt. McCarty,

1. Todd to Gov. Jefferson, from Lexington, Ky., Jan. 24, 1781 — "Cal. of Va. State Papers," I., 460.
2. "Draper's Notes, Trip 1860," II., 158.
3. Rogers to Gov. Jefferson, from Harrodsburg, Apr. 29, 1781 — "Draper's Notes, Trip 1860," III., 40–4; incomplete in "Cal. of Va. State Papers," II., 76–7. Rogers refers to Winston as "Deputy County Lieutenant for the Illinois County." Who was county-lieutenant?

whose quarrel has been narrated, were ordered to appear before a court of inquiry at Fort Jefferson.[1] Clark was very angry at Montgomery's conduct. He sent a message to New Orleans ordering him to return for trial; he warned all persons against trusting the offender on the credit of the State, and he requested the governor of Virginia to arrest the fugitive if he should come to Richmond.[2] How low public morals had sunk is shown by the fact that Montgomery had the effrontery to return to Fort Jefferson, where he arrived on May 1, 1781, and resumed his command. In February, 1783, he made his defense and asked for his pay.[3] In April, 1781, Todd wrote: "I still receive complaints from the Illinois. That Department suffers, I fear, through the avarice and prodigality of our officers; they all vent complaints against each other. I believe our French friends have the justest grounds of dissatisfaction."[4]

On June 2, 1781, Capt. McCarty was killed in a fight between the Illinois troops and some Indians on the one side and a party of Ouia Indians, who favored the British, on the other. The engagement took place near the Wabash. McCarty's papers were sent to the British, who laconically reported: "They give no information other than that himself and all the Inhabitants of the Illenoise were heartily tired of the Virginians."[5] There is slight

1. Slaughter to Gov. Jefferson, from Louisville, Jan. 14, 1781 — "Draper Coll., Clark MSS.," LI., 12, original MS.; Maj. Williams's orders, endorsed "pretended orders," from Fort Clark, Kaskaskia, Feb. 12, 1781.

2. Clark to Gov. of Va., from "Yough," Mar. 27, 1781 — "Cal. of Va. State Papers," I., 597.

3. Montgomery to Gov. of Va., from Falls of Ohio, Aug. 10, 1781 — "Cal. of Va. State Papers," II., 313; Montgomery to the Board of Commissioners for the Settlement of Western Accounts, from New Holland, Feb. 22, 1783 — *Ibid.*, III., 441-4.

4. Todd to Gov. Jefferson, from Lexington, Ky., Apr. 15, 1781 — "Cal of Va. State Papers," II., 44-5.

5. "Draper Coll., Clark MSS.," LX., 17, No. 2; Maj. de Peyster to Brig.-Gen. Powell, from Detroit, July 12, 1781 — "Mich. Pioneer Coll.," XIX., 646.

reason to doubt the truth of the statement. It is enforced by the fact that in 1781, a letter written in French to the governor of Virginia and said to be signed in the name of the inhabitants of Vincennes and to give the views of the people of Vincennes, Kaskaskia, Vermilion, Ouia, etc., declared that the French had decided to receive no troops except those sent by the king of France to aid in defeating the enemies of the country. The Indians who are friendly to the French, said the writer, would regard the coming of Virginia troops as a hostile act. A copy of the memoir sent by the French settlers to the French minister Luzerne was inclosed.[1]

On June 8, 1781, the garrison of Fort Jefferson, being without food, without credit, and for more than two years without pay, evacuated the place and withdrew to the Falls of Ohio, only to find themselves without credit in even the adjoining counties of Virginia. The troops were billeted in small parties.[2] Once again there comes a despairing plea from the feeble garrison at Vincennes, in the County of Illinois. The commander wrote: "Sir, I must inform you once more that I can not keep garrison any longer, without some speedy relief from you. My men have been 15 days upon half-allowance; there is plenty of provisions here but no credit—I can not press, being the weakest party— Some of the Gentlemen would help us, but their credit is as bad as ours, therefore, if you have not provisions send us Whisky which will answer as good an end."[3]

[1]. "Can. Archives," Series B., Vol. 182, 489; "Rept. on Can. Archives," 1888, 882.

[2]. Montgomery to Gov. Nelson, from Falls of Ohio, Aug. 10, 1781—"Cal. of Va. State Papers," II., 313; Same to same, same date—*Ibid.*, II., 315.

[3]. Capt. Bailey to Col. Slaughter, from "Port Vincennes," Aug. 6, 1781 —"Cal. of Va. State Papers," II., 338.

In the Virginia House of Delegates, a committee for courts of justice reported that the laws which would expire at the end of the session had been examined, together with certain other laws, and that a series of resolutions had been agreed upon by the committee. Among these resolutions was the following: "*Resolved, That it is the opinion of this committee*, That the act of assembly, passed in the year 1778, entitled 'an act, for establishing the county of Illinois, and for the more effectual protection and defence thereof;' which was continued and amended by a subsequent act, and will expire at the end of this present session of assembly, ought to be further continued." This report was presented and the resolutions agreed to by the House on November 22, 1781. Three days later, a bill in accordance with the resolution was presented. The consideration of the bill in a committee of the whole House was postponed from day to day until December 14, when it was considered and the question being upon engrossment and advancement to a third reading, it passed in the negative.[1] On January 5, 1782, the General Assembly adjourned, and the County of Illinois ceased to exist.[2] So far as instituting a civil goverment was concerned, the county was a failure. Its military history shows a mixture of American, British, French, and Spanish efforts at mastery.

The first important military operation in which the County of Illinois was concerned, after the well-known

1. "Jour. H. of Del.," Va., Oct. Sess., 1781, 13-39.

2. *Ibid.*, 72, 73, 74. Boyd states in "Am. Hist. Rev.," IV., 632, 635, that the county ceased to exist in 1781. This is erroneous. Mr. Boyd's article is the most scholarly treatment of the County of Illinois which has been published. Aside from the errors as to the time of the beginning and the ending of the county, and doubtful statements as to Todd's leaving Illinois and subsequently resigning, no errors of fact have been noted. A more complete, but unpublished, article on the subject is by Dr. Edith Lyle.

movements of Clark and Hamilton, was organized by the British at Detroit in compliance with a circular letter from Lord George Germain. The plan was to attack St. Louis, the French settlements near it on the east side of the Mississippi, Vincennes, Fort Nelson at the falls of the Ohio, and Kentucky. Large use was to be made of Indians, and British emissaries were busy among the tribes early in 1780. An expedition was to be led against Kentucky, while diversions should be made at outlying posts. It was thought that the reduction of St. Louis would present little difficulty, because it was known to be unfortified, and was reported to be garrisoned by but twenty men. In addition to this, it was regarded as an easy matter to use Indians against the place from the circumstance that many Indians frequented it. Less assurance was felt as to holding the place after it should have been captured, and to make this easier, it was proposed to appeal to the cupidity of the British fur traders. By the middle of February, a war-party had been sent out from Michilimackinac to arouse and act with the Sioux Indians, and early the next month another party was sent out to engage Indians to attack St. Louis and the Illinois towns. Seven hundred and fifty traders, servants, and Indians having been collected, on the 2d of May they started down the Mississippi, and at the lead mines, near the present Galena, seventeen Spanish and American prisoners were taken. In conjunction with this expedition, another, with a chosen band of Indians and French, was to advance by way of Chicago and the Illinois River; a third was to guard the prairies between the Wabash and the Illinois; and the chief of the Sioux was to attack St. Genevieve and Kaskaskia.[1]

[1]. Sinclair to Haldimand, from Michilimackinac, Feb. 17, 1780—"Mich. Pioneer Coll.," IX., 546; Same to same, May 29, 1780—*Ibid.*, IX.,

The expedition against St. Louis and the Illinois towns, as well as in its larger aspect, was not successful. It was impossible to keep it secret and as early as March, an attack was expected. Spanish and Americans joined in repulsing the intruders. Another potent element in the failure was the treachery of some of the traders who acted as leaders for the British, notably that of Ducharme and Calvé, who had a lucrative trade and regarded the prospect of increasing it by the proposed attack as doubtful. In the last week of May, 1780, the attack on St. Louis was made. Several persons were killed, but the place was not taken. Cahokia was beleaguered for three days, but it was so well defended by George Rogers Clark that on the third night the enemy withdrew, when Clark hastened to intercept the expedition against Kentucky, while the Illinois and Spanish troops pursued the retreating enemy and burned the towns of the Sauk and Fox Indians. The British were much chagrined at the result of the expedition, yet they resolved to continue their plan of using Indians and sending out several parties at once.[1]

An expedition which gains much interest from the character of its leader was that of Col. Augustin Mottin de la Balme. This man had been commissioned quartermaster of gendarmerie, by the authorities of Versailles, in 1766;

548-9; Same to De Peyster, Feb. 15, 1780— *Ibid.*, XIX., 500-1; Same to Lt.-Col. Bolton, June 14, 1780— *Ibid.*, XIX., 529; De Peyster to Lt.-Col. Bolton, from Detroit, June 8, 1780— *Ibid.*, XIX., 531-2; McKee to De Peyster, June 4, 1780— *Ibid.*, XIX., 530-1; Bird to De Peyster, from "a day's march from the Ohio," June 3, 1780— *Ibid.*, XIX., 527-9.

[1]. Sinclair to Bolton, from Michilimackinac, July 4, 1780—"Mich. Pioneer Coll.," XIX., 529-30; Same to Haldimand, July 8, 1780—*Ibid.*, IX., 558-9; Same to same, May 29, 1780—*Ibid.*, IX., 548-9; Same to De Peyster, July 30, 1780—*Ibid.*, IX., 586; "Draper Coll., Clark MSS.," XXVIII., No. 117, p. 6; Scharf to Lyman C. Draper, from Baltimore, Dec. 16, 1882 —*Ibid.*, p. 7; Capt. John Rogers' account—*Ibid.*, p. 3; Capt. John Murphy's account—*Ibid.*, VIII., 66-78; See also *Ibid.*, XXVI., 18.

had come to America and been recommended by Silas Deane and Benjamin Franklin to the president of Congress, John Hancock, as a man who would be of service in training cavalry; had been breveted lieutenant-colonel of cavalry, in May, 1777; made inspector of cavalry, with the rank of colonel, in July following; and had resigned in October of the same year. The next year, a public notice, in French with English and German translations, announced that carpenters, bakers, and some other classes of laborers could find shelter and employment at a workshop established by La Balme, twenty-eight miles from Philadelphia.[1] In the summer of 1780, La Balme went from Fort Pitt to the Illinois country.

A contemporary who writes from Vincennes speaks of La Balme as a French colonel. He was regarded by the Americans with much suspicion. Capt. Dalton, the American commander at Vincennes, whose character was later much questioned, allowed him to go among the Indians,[2] whereupon La Balme advised them to send word to the tribes which Clark was preparing to attack and to warn them of their danger. La Balme also ingratiated himself with the discontented French, asking why they did not drive "these vagabonds," the American soldiers, away, and saying that to refuse to furnish provisions was the most efficient method. "Everything he advances tends to advance the French interest and depreciate the American. The people here are easily misled; buoy'd up with the flattering hopes of being again subject to the king of France, he could easily prevail on them to drive every American out of the Place and this appears to me to be

1. "Rept. on Canadian Archives," 1888, p. 904; "Mag. of Am. Hist.," III., 366.

2. Bentley to Clark, from Vincennes, July 30, 1780—"Draper Coll., Clark MSS.," L., 51. A copy, incomplete and not exact, is in *Ibid.*, XXVI., 85.

his Plan." After thoroughly stirring up the people at Vincennes, the adventurer left, with an escort of thirty French and Indians, to visit Kaskaskia, Cahokia, and St. Louis. He and Col. Montgomery, then the superior officer in Illinois, did not meet, and he received not the slightest countenance from the Spanish commandant at St. Louis. By the French inhabitants, La Balme "was received . . . . just as the Jews would receive the Messiah — was conducted from the post here [at Kaskaskia] by a large detachment of the inhabitants as well as different tribes of Indians." The French in the towns near the Mississippi were so enthusiastic that La Balme had little difficulty in raising forty or fifty troops for an expedition against Detroit. Some of the American soldiers at Cahokia deserted to him, and when placed under arrest by the military authorities were rescued by a mob. On October 5, 1780, after telling the Indians to be quiet because they would see the French in Illinois in the spring, the French troops set out from Cahokia.[1]

The troops from Illinois were to be joined by a body from Vincennes, but without waiting for them La Balme pushed on to the Miami towns, where he hoped to capture a British Indian trader who was especially hated by the French. The trader was not found, but his store of goods to the amount of one hundred horse-loads was seized. The expected reinforcements not arriving, La Balme felt too weak to attack Detroit and started to return. He was attacked by the Indians on the river Aboite, eleven miles southwest of the present Fort Wayne, and he and some

[1]. Extracts from Capt. McCarty's Journal, at Kaskaskia — "Draper Coll., Clark MSS.," XXVI., 85-6; McCarty to Todd, from Kaskaskia, Oct. 14, 1780 — "Cal. of Va. State Papers," I., 380; Winston to Todd, from Kaskaskia, Oct. 24, 1780 — *Ibid*, I., 381-2; Auguste St. Jemme, son of an inhabitant of Kaskaskia, to Lyman C. Draper — "Draper's Notes, Trip 1851," I., 48-9 — "Draper Coll., Clark MSS.," XXVI., 82.

thirty of his men were killed and at least one hundred horses, richly laden with plunder, were taken by the Indians. It was reported that disaffected inhabitants of Detroit had concealed five hundred stands of arms with which to assist the forces of La Balme in taking the place. Among La Balme's papers, which fell into the hands of the British and are now in the Canadian archives, were addresses, in French, by M. Mottin de la Balme, French colonel, etc., to the French settled on the Mississippi, dated St. Louis, September 17, 1780; a declaration, in French, in the name of the inhabitants of the village of Cahokia, addressed to La Balme: "We unanimously request you to listen with a favorable ear to the declaration which we venture to present to you, touching all the bad treatment we have suffered patiently since the Virginian troops unfortunately arrived amongst us till now," dated Cahokia, September 21, 1780; a note from F. Trottier, a member of the court of Cahokia, elected under the Virginia government, to La Balme, saying that no meeting can be held until Sunday next, when he hopes the young men will show themselves worthy the high idea La Balme has of them, but that at present there are only twelve entirely determined to follow him wherever he goes, although others may follow their example, and asking La Balme to receive depositions against the Virginians, dated Cahokia, September 27, 1780; a petition, in French, addressed to the Chevalier de la Luzerne, minister plenipotentiary from France to the United States, by inhabitants of Post Vincennes, dated Vincennes, August 22, 1780; and a commission to Augustin Mottin de la Balme as quartermaster of gendarmèrie, dated Versailles, February 23, 1766.[1] The British promptly set about promoting the

[1] De Peyster to Powell, from Detroit, Nov. 13, 1780—"Mich. Pioneer Coll.," XIX., 581; Same to Haldimand, Nov. 16, 1780—*Ibid.*, X., 448-9;

Indian trader whom La Balme and the French had sought to kill, believing that he would be serviceable as a spy.[1]

In the autumn of 1780, a party of seventeen men from Cahokia went on an expedition against St. Josephs. The party was commanded by "a half Indian," and seems to have included but one American. The attack was so timed as to come when the Indians in the vicinity of St. Josephs were out hunting. The place was taken without difficulty, the traders of the place were captured and plundered, and the party, laden with booty, set out on the route to Chicago. A pursuing party was quickly organized and at the *Rivière du Chemin*, a small stream in Indiana, emptying into the southeastern part of Lake Michigan, the returning victors were summoned to surrender, on December 5, 1780. Upon their refusal, four were killed, two wounded, seven made prisoners, while three escaped.[2]

Linctot to Slaughter, "O'Post," Jan. 11, 1781 — "Cal. of Va. State Papers," I., 429; J. L. William to Lyman C. Draper, from Fort Wayne, Ind., Oct. 1, 1881 — "Draper Coll., Clark MSS.," XXVI., 92; McCarty to Slaughter, from Ill., Jan. 27, 1781 — "Cal. of Va. State Papers," I., 465; Col. Brodhead to Washington, from Fort Pitt, Mar. 10, 1781, "Olden Time," II., 391; Col. Levin Powell, from Harrodsburg, Jan. 21, 1781 — "Pa. Archives," VIII., 768; De Peyster to Haldimand, from Detroit, Nov. 13, 1780, Farmer "Hist. of Detroit and Michigan," 257; Letter from J. M. P. Legras, from Vincennes, Dec. 1, 1780 — "Draper Coll., Clark MSS.," L., 77, original corrected draft; "Rept. on Canadian Archives," 1888, 904–5; extract from "Scot's Magazine," May, 1781, in "Draper Coll., Clark MSS.," XXVI., 82. Whether La Balme had any countenance from either the French government or its representatives is an unsettled question. That France should regain her hold in America was desired by many Frenchmen, but on the other hand, the French government was pledged by its treaty of alliance to make no acquisitions of territory in America. The following references raise the question, but I know of none which settle it: Kingsford, "Canada," VI., 342–3; Sparks, "Washington," VI., 106 ff., 113; Stevens, "Facsimiles," XVII., No. 1609; "Secret Jour. of Cong.," II., 111–117, 125.

1. Haldimand to De Peyster, from Quebec, Jan. 6, 1781 — "Mich. Pioneer Coll.," IX., 641.

2. This amounts to but sixteen men. De Peyster says that the party was one of sixteen; McCarty says there were seventeen.

The one American, Brady, was among the prisoners. He told the British that the party was sent by the creoles to plunder St. Josephs, and that there was not a Virginian in all the Illinois country, including Vincennes.[1]

In the very midst of winter, on January 2, 1781, an expedition commanded by Eugenio Pierre, a Spanish captain of militia, set out from St. Louis against St. Josephs. According to a Spanish account, the party consisted of sixty-five militia men and sixty Indians, while an American account declares it to have contained thirty Spaniards, twenty men from Cahokia, and two hundred Indians.

The purpose of the expedition was to retaliate upon the British for the attack on St. Louis and for the defeat of La Balme. On the march, severe difficulties incident to the season were encountered. The post was easily taken, the Indians were conciliated by a liberal proportion of the booty, the Spanish flag was raised and the Illinois country with St. Josephs and its dependencies was claimed for the crown of Spain. The British flag was given to Commandant Cruzat, of St. Louis. These proceedings made some prominent Americans fear that Spain would advance claims to the region at the close of the Revolution.[2]

1. McCarty to Slaughter, from Ill., Jan. 27, 1781—"Cal. of Va. State Papers," I., 465; Sinclair to Mathews, from Michilimackinac, Feb. 23, 1781—"Mich. Pioneer Coll.," IX., 629; De Peyster to Powell, from Detroit, Jan. 8, 1781—*Ibid.*, XIX., 591-2; Same to Haldimand, same date—*Ibid.*, X., 450-1; Same to McKee, from Detroit, Feb. 1, 1781—De Peyster, "Miscellanies," p. xxvi.; Linctot to commanding officer at the Falls of Ohio, "Opost Vincennes," Jan. 13, 1781—"Cal. of Va. State Papers," I., 432; Draper on date of the expedition, "Draper Coll., Clark MSS.," XXVI., 88; De Peyster to Powell, from Detroit, Mar. 17, 1781—"Mich. Pioneer Coll.," XIX., 600; Sinclair to Powell, from Michilimackinac Id., May 1, 1781—*Ibid.*, XIX., 632; "Chicago Hist. Soc. Coll.," IV., 216.

2. Jay to Livingston, from Madrid, Apr. 28, 1782—"Secret Jour. of Cong.," IV., 64; or Wharton, "Dipl. Corr. of the Am. Rev.," V., 363-4; or Sparks, *Ibid.*, VIII., 76-8; McCarty to Slaughter, from Ill., Jan. 27,

THE COUNTY OF ILLINOIS. 39

In the summer of 1781, a party of seven men was sent out by the commandant at Michilimackinac with a letter to the inhabitants of Cahokia and Kaskaskia asking them to furnish troops to be paid by the king of England, and to assume the defensive against the Spaniards. The men reached St. Louis before visiting Cahokia or Kaskaskia, and were arrested by the Spanish commandant, who sent a copy of the letter to Major Williams, knowing no officer in Illinois superior to him. This created jealousy at Cahokia and Kaskaskia, each of several officers claiming superiority. Charles Gratiot, a man of some ability, who had removed from Cahokia to St. Louis because unable to endure the lawlessness at the former place, wrote that he did not know what course the Illinois people might have taken if Cruzat had not intercepted the British agents. Illinois was a country without a head where everyone expected to do as he pleased.[1]

In noting the operations of the medley of military forces in the County of Illinois, it is easy to conceive how the result might have been different, but the fact is that as the county ceased to exist, no nation had established a better title to the region than that of the Americans.

1781—"Draper's Notes, Trip 1860," III., 1-2; incomplete copy in "Cal. of Va.. State Papers," I., 465; Linctot to commanding officer at Falls of Ohio, from Vincennes, Jan. 13, 1781—"Cal. of Va. State Papers," I., 432; Franklin to Livingston, from Passy, Apr. 12, 1782—Sparks, "Dipl. Corr. of the Am. Rev.," III., 339. See also *Ibid.*, VIII., 150; Sparks, "Franklin's Works," IX., 206, Boston, 1856.

1. Linctot to ———, from St. Louis, July 31, 1781—"Draper Coll., Clark MSS.," LI., 75, original MS. in French; Gratiot to Clark, from St. Louis, Aug. 1, 1781—*Ibid.*, LI., 77, original MS. in French.

CHAPTER II.

The Period of Anarchy in Illinois[1]

ILLINOIS was practically in a state of anarchy during the time that it was a county of Virginia, and when that county ceased to be, anarchy became technically as well as practically its condition, and remained so until government under the Ordinance of 1787 was inaugurated in 1790.

Virginia's legacy from her ephemeral county was one of unpaid bills. Scarcely had the general assembly adjourned, in January, 1782, when Benjamin Harrison wrote: "We know of no power given to any person to draw bills on the State but to Col° Clarke and yet we find them drawn to an immense amount by Col° Montgomery, and Captn Robt. George and some others; we have but too much reason to suppose a collusion and fraud betwixt the drawers and those they are made payable to; most of them are for specie when they well knew we had none amongst us, and from the largeness of the sums, proves the transactions must have been in paper and the depreciation taken into account, when the bargains were made; indeed George confesses this to have been the case when he gave Philip Barbour a bill for two hundred and thirty two thousand, three hundred and twenty Dollars and uses the plea of ignorance." The transactions of Oliver Pollock, purchasing agent at New Orleans, should be carefully examined from the time he began to act with Mont-

[1]. This chapter was read, by request, before the Wisconsin Academy of Sciences, Arts, and Letters, on February 8, 1906.

gomery.¹ Thimothé Demunbrunt, as he signed his name, asked pay for his services as lieutenant, in order that he might not be a charge to his friends—a thing which would be shameful to one of noble descent. He wished to be able to support his family and to go with Clark on a proposed expedition. His petition was supported by a certificate from Col. Montgomery, testifying that Demunbrunt had been active in his military duty, had gone against the savages in the spring of 1780, had gone on the "Expedition up the Wabash," and had gone to the relief of Fort Jefferson when Montgomery could raise only twelve men.²

The military troubles continued. The commander at Vincennes reported his troops as destitute and unpaid. Richard Winston, of Kaskaskia, who had succeeded Todd as head of the civil government in Illinois, was arrested by military force and put in jail. The prisoner claimed that the proceedings were wholly irregular and that he was unacquainted with the nature of the charge against

1. In Council, Jan. 29, 1782 — "Draper Coll., Clark MSS.," XLVI., 69, original MS.

2. Demunbrunt to Clark, from Kaskaskia, Mar. 5, 1782—"Draper Coll., Clark MSS.," L., 70; LI., 25, original MS. Demunbrunt, whose name also appears as Demunbrun and De Munbrun, was prominent in early Illinois history. Records signed by him as Lieutenant Commandant *par interim* appear in "John Todd's Record-Book" under the dates June 14, 1779, Feb'y, 1782, and March 22, 1782. In 1783, 1784, and probably at other dates, he made grants of land in the Illinois country. He served under Clark. From the time Winston was appointed to the command of the County of Illinois, until the coming of St. Clair, Demunbrunt was "commandant of the village of Kaskaskia and its dependencies." He had important dealings with an embassy from the Cherokee Indians. He was allowed land under the Virginia grants. In his memorial to the General Assembly, he said: "Your memorialist, little acquainted with the mode of doing business in this State, never kept a regular account, depending altogether on the justice and generosity of the Legislature "—" Draper's Notes, Trip 1860," V., 15-18; "Chicago Hist. Soc. Coll.," IV., 315-16; "Pub. Lands," II., 146.

him.[1] The next year, he was accused of treason, the accuser declaring that Winston had proposed to turn Illinois over to Spain, but that his proposal had been despised by the Spanish commandant.[2] Upon Winston was also laid the chief blame for the discontent of the French, he being charged with having told Montgomery that the French were strangers to liberty and must be ruled with a rod of iron or the bayonet, and that if he wanted anything he must send his guards and take it by force; while, at the same time, he told the French that the military was a band of robbers and came to Illinois for plunder.[3] However, numerous and well-founded as the accusations might be, both accused and accuser laid their claims for salary before the Virginia Board of Commissioners for the Settlement of Western Accounts.[4] Even the notorious Col. Montgomery presented before this board his defence, which consisted of a recital of his meritorious deeds, others being omitted.[5]

Another visitor to the Board of Commissioners was Francis Carbonneaux, prothonotary and notary public for the Illinois country. Although he came to get some private affairs settled, his chief mission was to lay before the Board the confusion in Illinois, and the Board correctly surmised that if Virginia did not afford relief the messenger

[1]. Todd to Winston, June 15, 1779, in "Chicago Hist. Soc. Coll.," IV., 302; Legras to Clark, from Vincennes, Dec. 31, 1782—"Draper Coll., Clark MSS.," LII., 67, original MS.; "Chicago Hist. Soc. Coll.," IV., 289.

[2]. Letter from Capt. Dodge, from Kaskaskia, Mar. 6, 1783—"Draper Coll., Clark MSS.," LX., No. 3, p. 48.

[3]. Dodge to Clark, from Kaskaskia, Mar. 3, 1783—*Ibid.*, LII., 78.

[4]. Officers to Clark, from Ft. Nelson, Falls of Ohio, March 30, 1783 —*Ibid.*, LII., 80.

[5]. Montgomery to Board of Commissioners, from New Holland, Feb. 22, 1783—"Cal. of Va. State Papers," III., 441-4.

would proceed to Congress.[1] It was but natural that at this time, the people of Illinois should be in doubt as to whom to present their petition, because Virginia had offered to cede her western lands to Congress, although the terms of cession were not yet agreed upon. Carbonneaux complained that Illinois was wholly without law or government; that the magistrates, from indolence or sinister views, had for some time been lax in the execution of their duties, and were now altogether without authority; that crimes of the greatest enormity might be committed with impunity, and a man be murdered in his own house and no one regard it; that there was neither sheriff nor prison; and to crown the general confusion, that many persons had made large purchases of three and four hundred leagues, and were endeavoring to have themselves established lords of the soil, as some had done in Canada, and to have settlements made on these purchases, composed of a set of men wholly subservient to their views. The Spanish traded freely in Illinois, but strictly prohibited Illinois from trading in Spanish dominions. Complaint was also made that the Board of Commissioners had not settled the Illinois accounts in peltry according to the known rule and practice, namely: that fifty pounds of peltry should represent one hundred livres in money.

The petitioners prayed that a president of judicature be sent to them, with executive powers to a certain extent, and that subordinate civil officers be appointed, to reside in each village or station, with power to hear and decide all causes upon obligations not exceeding three hundred dollars, higher amounts to be determined by a court to be held at Kaskaskia and to be composed of the president and a majority of the magistrates. It was

[1]. Board of Commissioners to Gov. Benjamin Harrison, from Jefferson county, Feb. 17, 1783—"Chicago Hist. Soc. Coll.," IV., 350-1.

desired that the grant in which the Kaskaskia settlements lay should be considered as one district. It contained five villages, of which Kaskaskia and Cahokia were the largest. The grant extended to the headwaters of the Illinois River on the north. The land had been granted to the settlers by the Indians, and the Indians, having given their consent by solemn treaties, had never denied the sale. The tract referred to was probably the two purchases of the Illinois Company. Maps give but one of these and, in fact, the other was said to be so described as to comprise *a line only.* Naturally, this fact was not known at the time of purchase.

It was frankly acknowledged that Illinois had no man fitted for the office of president. It was hoped that Virginia would furnish one, and would send with him a company of regulars to act under his direction and enforce laws and authority. The president should be empowered to grant land in small tracts to immigrants. The privilege of trading in Spanish waters, especially on the Missouri, was much desired. It was said that Carbonneaux "appears to have been instructed as to the ground of his message by the better disposed part of the inhabitants of the country whose complaints he represents."[1]

At the time of Carbonneaux's petition, there was no legal way by which newcomers to Illinois could acquire public land. Virginia had prepared to open a land-office, soon after the conquest of the Illinois country, but she seems to have heeded the recommendation of Congress that no unappropriated land be sold during the war.[2] Some grants had been made by Todd, Demunbrunt, the Indians, and others with less show of right, but they were made without

1. Walker Daniel to Board of Commissioners, from New Holland, Feb. 3, 1783—"Cal. of Va. State Papers," III., 430-2.
2. "Jour. of Cong.," III., 383-5.

ANARCHY IN ILLINOIS. 45

governmental authority. The Indians had presented a tract of land to Clark, but the view consistently held was that individuals could not receive Indian land merely upon their own initiative.[1] One of the grants made at Vincennes, which seems to have been a typical one, was signed by Le Grand, "Colonel commandant and President of the Court," and was made by the authority granted to the magistrates of the court of Vincennes by John Todd, "Colonel and Grand civil Judge for the United States." The purpose of the grant, which comprised four hundred arpents "in circumference," was to induce immigration.[2] The grants made by the court of Vincennes became notorious from the fact that thousands of acres were granted by the court to its own members.[3]

On March 1, 1784, Virginia ceded her western lands to the United States, thus transferring to the general government the question of land titles. The country had been in a state of unconcealed anarchy for more than two years, all semblance of Virginia authority having ceased, and the cession is quite as much a tribute to Virginia's shrewdness as to her generosity. Never was so large a present made with less sacrifice. The cession was made with the following conditions, some of which were to have a direct and potent influence upon the settlement of the ceded region:

1. The territory should be formed into states of not less than one hundred nor more than one hundred and fifty square miles each;

2. Virginia's expenses in subduing and governing the territory should be reimbursed by the United States;

[1] "Jour. H. of Del.," Va., May Sess., 1780, 25, 69, 70.
[2] Law, "The Colonial Hist. of Vincennes," 1858, 117–8, gives a copy of the deed. For claims under such deeds see "Pub. Lands," I., 294–8.
[3] "Pub. Lands," I., 301.

3. Settlers should have their "possessions and titles confirmed;"

4. One hundred and fifty thousand acres, or less, should be granted to George Rogers Clark and his soldiers;

5. The Virginia military bounty lands should be located north of the Ohio River, unless there should prove to be enough land for the purpose south of that river;

6. The proceeds from the sale of the lands should be for the United States, severally.[1]

In the year of the Virginia cession, Congress passed the Ordinance for the Government of the Western Territory, but as it never went into effect, its importance is slight except as indicative of the trend of public feeling on the subjects which it involved. Should Jefferson's plan, proposed at this time, have been carried out, Illinois would have been parts of the states of Polypotamia, Illinois, Assenisipia, and Saratoga.[2]

Carbonneaux, the messenger from Illinois to Virginia, carried his petition to Congress. Congress paid the messenger, referred the petition to a committee, and upon the report of the committee voted to choose one or more commissioners to go to Illinois and investigate conditions there.[3] No record of the appointment of such commissioners has been found. Congress considered Carbonneaux's petition early in 1785. In November of the same year comes a record of the anarchy in Illinois. This was addressed to George Rogers Clark, who was the hope of the people of that neglected country. "The commandant at St. Louis is afraid of an attack from the Royalists at Michilimackinac, or he has given orders for all the people

1. "Jour. of Cong.," IV., 342-4.

2. *Ibid.*, IV., 379-80; Thwaites, "The Boundaries of Wisconsin," in "Wis. Hist. Soc. Coll.," XI., 452, gives a map of Jefferson's proposed states.

3. "Jour. of Cong.," IV., 473, 477.

in that place to be in readiness when called on, with their arms.

"The Indians are very troublesome on the rivers, and declare an open war with the Americans, which I am sure is nothing lessened by the advice of our neighbors, the French in this place, and the people from Michilimackinac, who openly say they will oppose all the Americans that come into this country. For my part, it is impossible to live here, if we have not regular justice very soon. They are worse than the Indians, and ought to be ruled with a rod of iron."[1]

During the year 1786, George Rogers Clark was the chief factor in Illinois affairs. He was regarded by the people as their advocate before Congress. In March, seven of the leading men of Vincennes, at the request of the French and American inhabitants, sent a petition to him asking him to persuade Congress to send troops to defend them from the Indians, and also saying: "We have unanimously agreed to present a petition to Congress for relief, apprehensive that the Deed we received from an office, established or rather continued by Col? Todd for lands, may possibly be a slender foundation; so that after we have passed through a scene of suffering in forming settlements in a remote and dangerous part may have the mortification to be totally deprived of our improvements."[2] In June, seventy-one American subscribers from Vincennes, "in the County of Illinois," asked Congress to settle their land-titles and give them a government. They held land from grants from an office established by Col. Todd, whose validity they questioned. The com-

[1]. John Edgar to Clark, from Kaskaskia, Nov. 7, 1785 — "Draper's Notes, Trip 1860," VI., 214-5.

[2]. Petition to Clark, from Vincennes, Mar. 16, 1786 — "Draper Coll., Clark MSS.," LIII., 23.

mandant and magistracy had resigned because of the disobedience of the people. There was no executive, no law, no government, and the Indians were very hostile.[1]

Clark was not unmindful of the needs of the people. He wrote to the president of Congress: "The inhabitants of the different towns in the Illinois are worthy the attention of Congress. They have it in their power to be of infinite service to us, and might act as a great barrier to the frontier, if under proper regulation; but having no law or government among them, they are in great confusion, and without the authority of Congress is extended to them, they must, in all probability, fall a sacrifice to the savages, who may take advantage of the disorder and want of proper authority in that country. I have recommended it to them, to re-assume their former customs, and appoint temporary officers until the pleasure of Congress is known, which I have flattered them would be in a short time. How far the recommendation will answer the desired purpose is not yet known."[2]

Clark's fears of the Indians were only too well grounded. During the summer, the American settlers were compelled to retire to a fort at Bellefontaine, and four of their number were killed. At the same time, about twenty Americans were killed about Vincennes. The French were still safe from Indian attacks and were very angry because the Americans complained of existing conditions.[3] The strife between the French and the Americans at Vincennes, over the proper relations of the whites to the Indians, became intense. The French contended that the Indians should

1. Petition to Congress, from Vincennes, June 1, 1786—*Ibid.*, LIII., 31.

2. Clark to Richard H. Lee, pres. of Cong., from Louisville, received June 8, 1786—"Draper's Notes, Trip 1860," VI., 208-9.

3. Moses Henry to Clark, from Vincennes, June 12, 1786—"Draper Coll., Clark MSS.," LIII., 32.

be allowed to come and go freely, while the Americans held that it was unsafe to grant such freedom. At last, upon the occasion of the killing of an Indian by the Americans, after they had been attacked by the Indians, the French citizens ordered all persons, who had not permission to settle from the government under which they last resided, to leave at once and at their own risk. The French told the Americans plainly that they were not wanted, and that they, the French, did not know whether the place belonged to the United States or to Great Britain.[1] This last assertion was probably true. The British Michilimackinac Company had a large trading-house at Cahokia for supplying the Indians, they held Detroit, and their machinations among the Indians were constant. The feeling of all intelligent Americans in Illinois must have been expressed by John Edgar when he wrote that the Illinois country was totally lost unless a government should soon be established.[2] Clark wrote a vigorous letter to the people at Vincennes, telling them that unless they stopped quarreling military rule would be established; that the government established under Virginia was still in force, having been confirmed by Congress upon the acceptance of the Virginia deed of cession, and that the court, if depleted, should be filled by election [3]

In one respect, even during this trying period, the western country gave promise of its future growth. There was a large crop. Flour and pork, quoted, strangely enough, together, sold at the Falls of Ohio at

[1]. Daniel Sullivan to Clark, from Vincennes, June 23, 1786—"Draper Coll., Clark MSS.," LIII., 35; John Small to Clark, same place and day—*Ibid.*, LIII., 36.
[2]. John Edgar to Clark, from Kaskaskia, Oct. 23, 1786—*Ibid.*, LIII., 56.
[3]. Clark to people of Vincennes—*Ibid.*, LIII., 52.

twelve shillings per hundred pounds, while Indian corn sold at nine pence per bushel.[1]

On August 24, 1786, Congress ordered its secretary to inform the inhabitants of Kaskaskia that a government was being prepared for them.[2] In 1787, conditions in the Illinois country became too serious to be ignored. The Indian troubles were grave and persistent, but graver still was the danger of the rebellion or secession of the Western Country or else of a war with Spain. The closure of the Mississippi by Spain made the West desperate. Discontent, anarchy, and petitions might drag a weary length, but when troops raised without authority were quartered at Vincennes, when these troops seized Spanish goods, and impressed the property of the inhabitants of Vincennes, and proposed to treat with the Indians, the time for action was at hand. In April, Gen. Josiah Harmar, then at Falls of Ohio, was ordered to move the greater part of his troops to Vincennes to restore order among the distracted people at that place. Intruders upon the public lands were to be removed, and the lawless and illegally levied troops were to be dispersed.[3]

Arrived at Vincennes, Gen. Harmar proceeded with vigor. The resolution of Congress against intruders on the public lands was published in English and in French. The inhabitants, especially the Americans whose hold on their lands was the more insecure, were dismayed, and French and Americans each prepared a petition to Con-

1. Letter from a man at Falls of Ohio to a friend in N. England, Dec. 4, 1786—"Secret Jour. of Cong.," IV., 321.

2. "Jour. of Cong.," IV., 688-9.

3. Harmar to Sec'y of War, from Fort. Harmar, May 14, 1787—"St. Clair Papers," II., 20-1; Maj. Wyllys to Harmar, from Fort Finney, Rapids of Ohio, Feb. 6, 1787—"Draper Coll., Harmar Papers," I., 281-2; Knox to Harmar, June 19, 1787—*Ibid.*, I., 303. See also *Ibid.*, I., 290; Sec'y of War to Harmar, Apr. 26, 1787—"St. Clair Papers," II., 22.

gress, and appointed Bartholomew Tardiveau, who was to go to Congress within a month, as their agent. Tardiveau was especially fitted for this task by his intimate acquaintance with the land grants of the region. Each party at Vincennes also prepared an address to Gen. Harmar, the Americans declaring that they were settled on French lands and feared that their lands would be taken from them without payment and asking aid from Congress, and the French expressing their joy at being freed from their former bad government. Many of Clark's militia had made tomahawk-rights, and this added to the confusion of titles.[1]

From August 9 to 16, Gen. Harmar, with an officer and thirty men, some Indian hunters, and Tardiveau, journeyed overland from Vincennes to Kaskaskia, where conditions were to be investigated. The August sun poured down its rays upon the parched prairies and dwindling streams. Water was bad and scarce, but buffalo, deer, bear, and smaller game were abundant.

Harmar found life in the settlements he visited as crude as the path he traveled. Kaskaskia was a French village of one hundred and ninety-one men, old and young, with an accompaniment of women and children of various mixtures of white and red blood. Cahokia, then the metropolis, had two hundred and thirty-nine Frenchmen, old and young, with an accompaniment similarly mixed. Between these settlements was Bellefontaine, a small stockade, inhabited altogether by Americans, who had settled without authority. The situation was a beautiful one; the land was fertile; there

1. Harmar to Sec'y of War, from Vincennes, Aug. 7, 1787—"St. Clair Papers," II., 27-9; Address of Am. settlers at Vincennes to Harmar, transmitted to the War Office, Aug. 7, 1787—"Draper Coll., Harmar Papers," I., 337-9; Address of French at Vincennes to Harmar, July 28, 1787—*Ibid.*, I., 331-3.

was no taxation, and the people had an abundance to live upon. They were much alarmed when told of their precarious state respecting a title to their lands, and they gave Tardiveau a petition to carry to Congress. On the route to Cahokia, another stockade, Grand Ruisseau, similarly inhabited by Americans, was passed. There were about thirty other American intruders in the fertile valleys near the Mississippi, and they, too, gave Tardiveau a petition to Congress.

The Kaskaskia, Peoria, Cahokia, and Mitcha tribes of Indians numbered only about forty or fifty members, of whom but ten or eleven individuals composed the Kaskaskia tribe; but this does not mean that danger from the Indians was not great, because other and more hostile tribes came in great numbers to hunt in the Illinois country. The significance of the diminished numbers of these particular tribes lies in the fact that they had the strongest claim to that part of Illinois which would be first needed for settlement. At Kaskaskia and Cahokia, the French were advised to obey their magistrates until Congress had a government ready for them, and Cahokia was advised to put its militia into better shape, and to put any turbulent or refractory persons under guard until a goverment could be instituted.[1]

Having finished his work in the settlements near the Mississippi, Harmar returned to Vincennes, where he held councils with the Indians, and on October 1, set out on his return to Fort Harmar. Although without authority to give permanent redress, he had persuaded the French at Vincennes to relinquish their charter and to throw themselves upon the generosity of Congress. "As it would have been impolitic, after the parade we had made, to

---

1. Harmar to Sec'y of War, from Fort Harmar, Nov. 24, 1787—"St. Clair Papers," II., 30-2.

entirely abandon the country," he left Maj. John F. Hamtramck, with ninety-five men, at Vincennes.[1] Harmar's visit was doubtless of some value, but he had not been gone five weeks when Hamtramck wrote to him: "Our civil administration has been, and is, in a great confusion. Many people are displeased with the Magistrates; how it will go at the election, which is to be the 2d of Dec^r, I know not. But it is to be hoped that Congress will soon establish some mode of government, for I never saw so injudicious administration. Application has repeatedly been made to me for redress. I have avoided to give answer, not knowing how far my powers extended. In my opinion, the Minister of War should have that matter determined, and sincerely beg you would push it. I confess to you, that I have been very much at a loss how to act on many occasions."[2]

Not earlier than the 24th of November, Tardiveau set out for Congress with his petitions from the Illinois country. Harmar was much pleased to have so able a messenger, and spoke of him as sensible, well-informed, and able to give a minute and particular description of the western country, particularly the Illinois. He had been preceded to Congress by Joseph Parker, of Kaskaskia. Harmar seems to have regarded Tardiveau as a sort of antidote to Parker, for he closes his recommendation of the former by saying: "There have been some imposters before Congress, particularly one Parker, a whining, canting Methodist, a kind of *would-be governor.* He is extremely unpopular at Kaskaskia, and despised by the inhabitants."[3]

1. Harmar to the Sec'y of War, from Fort Harmar, Nov. 24, 1787—"St. Clair Papers," II., 34.
2. Hamtramck to Harmar, from Vincennes, Nov. 3, 1787—"Draper Coll., Harmar Papers," I., 352.
3. Harmar to Sec'y of War, from Fort Harmar, Nov. 24, 1787—"St. Clair Papers," II., 35.

54   SETTLEMENT OF ILLINOIS.

This detracts from the value of Parker's representations, which had been made in a letter to St. Clair, the President of Congress. After explaining that when he left Kaskaskia, on June 5, 1787, the people did not have an intended petition ready, Parker complained of the lack of government in Illinois, the presence of British traders, the depopulation of the country by the inducements of the Spaniards, and the high rate at which it was proposed to sell lands. His complaints were true, although he may have failed to give them in their proper proportion.[1]

On July 13, 1787, the Ordinance of 1787 had been passed by Congress. The Illinois country was at that time ready for war against the Spanish, who persisted in closing the Mississippi. The troops, irregularly levied by George Rogers Clark at Vincennes, had seized some Spanish goods on the theory that if the Spanish would not allow the United States to navigate the lower Mississippi, the Spanish should not be allowed to navigate the upper Mississippi. John Rice Jones, later the first lawyer in Illinois, was Clark's commissary.[2]

The Ordinance of 1787 was the only oil then at hand for these troubled waters. The situation in Illinois was a complicated one, and probably the numerical weakness of the population alone saved the country from disastrous results. The few Americans in Illinois desired governmental protection from the Spanish, the Indians, the British, and any Americans who might seek to jump the claims of the first squatters; the few French desired protection from the Spanish, the Americans, the British, and soon from the Indians; the numerous Indians, permanent or transient, desired protection from the Spanish, the Americans, and in rare cases from an Americanized

1. "Draper's Notes, Trip 1860," VI., 170-3.
2. "Secret Jour. of Cong.," IV., 301-29.

Frenchman. Americans, French, Spanish, British, and Indians made an opportunity for many combinations.

For the French inhabitants, the somewhat paternal character of the government provided for by the Ordinance was a matter of no concern. The great rock of offense for them was the prohibition of slavery. An exodus to the Spanish side of the Mississippi resulted and St. Louis profited by what the older villages of Illinois lost.[1] In addition to a justifiable feeling of uncertainty as to whether they would be allowed to retain their slaves, the credulous French had their fears wrought upon by persons interested in the sale of Spanish lands. These persons took pains to inculcate the belief that all slaves would be released upon American occupancy. The Spanish officials were also active. The commandant at St. Louis wrote to the French at Kaskaskia, Cahokia, and Vincennes, respectively, inviting them to settle west of the Mississippi and offering free lands.[2] Mr. Tardiveau, the agent for the Illinois settlers to Congress, tried to induce Congress to repeal the anti-slavery clause of the Ordinance. He said that it threatened to be the ruin of Illinois. Designing persons had told the French that the moment Gen. St. Clair arrived all their slaves would be free. Failing in his efforts to secure a repeal, he wrote to Gen. St. Clair, asking him to secure from Congress a resolution giving the true intent of the act.[3] In this letter, Tardiveau advanced the doctrine, later so much used, that the evils of slavery would be mitigated by its diffusion.[4] The first panic of

1. St. Clair to the President, 1790—"St. Clair Papers," II., 175.

2. Hamtramck to Harmar, from Vincennes, Oct. 13, 1788—"Draper Coll., Harmar Papers," I., 479; extract in "St. Clair Papers," II., 105.

3. Tardiveau to St. Clair, from Danville, June 30, 1789—"St. Clair Papers," II., 117-19.

4. Extract from above letter.—*Ibid.*, II., 119-20, note.

the French only gradually subsided and the question of slavery was a persistent one.

One of the most industrious of those interested in the sale of Spanish lands was George Morgan, of New Jersey.[1] In 1788, he tried to secure land in Illinois also. He and his associates petitioned Congress to sell them a tract of land on the Mississippi. A congressional committee found upon investigation that the proposed purchase

1. George Morgan was much engaged in large land purchases. In 1763, some Shawanese and other Indians carried off the property of certain whites to the value of £85,916 10s., 8d. The offenders being tributary to the Six Nations, the latter granted to King George III., for the exclusive use of the sufferers, on November 3, 1768, at Fort Stanwix, the tract of some two million five hundred thousand acres, later known as the claim of the Indiana Company. The land lay southeast of the Ohio, and was claimed in part by both Virginia and Pennsylvania. For map see "States of America," by J. Russell, London, E. Dilly and G. G. and J. Robinson, 1799; Hutchins, "Topographical Desc. of Va.," etc., French ed., Paris, 1781; Winsor, "Westward Movement," 17. Morgan, who was a large shareholder in the company, was for years its agent. The claim was finally denied. Morgan was also the founder of New Madrid, in what is now Missouri, but he was unfortunate in assuming powers denied by the Spanish government. His experience in Illinois was likewise a failure—"Cal. of Va. State Papers" I., 273, 297, 320; VI., 1-36 (a history of the Indiana purchase); 261, 679, 301; "Jour. of Cong.," III., 359, 373; IV., 23; "Rept. on Canadian Archives," 1888, p. 939; "Draper Coll., Clark MSS.," LIII., 78; Gayerré, "Hist. of La.," index under Morgan refers to passages giving several quotations from sources; Kate Mason Rowland, "George Mason," I., 230, 324,-8, 289, 308, 333, 341-4; II., 21, 26, 239, 244, 262, 341-5, 406, 440-1. George Mason was manager for the commonwealth when, in 1791, the final effort was made by the Indiana Company to overthrow the Virginia settlement of its claim. Some original sources of importance are given in this work—"Plain Facts: being an Examination into the Rights of the Indian Nations of America, to their respective Countries, and a Vindication of the Grant, from the Six United Nations of Indians, to the Proprietors of Indiana, against the decision of Virginia, together with authentic documents, proving that the territory, westward of the Alleghany Mountain, never belonged to Virginia, etc., Philadelphia . . . : M.DCC.LXXXI." The work gives a resumé of the proceedings of the company to 1779, 164 pp. "View of the Title to Indiana, a tract of country on the River Ohio," 24 pp., printed about 1775.

comprised all of the French settlements in Illinois.[1] Thereupon was passed the Act of June 20, 1788. According to its provisions, the French inhabitants of Illinois were to be confirmed in their possessions and each family which was living in the district before the year 1783 was to be given a bounty of four hundred acres. These bounty-lands were to be laid off in three parallelograms, at Kaskaskia, Prairie du Rocher, and Cahokia, respectively. They were to be bounded on the east by the ridge of rocks—a natural formation trending from north to south, a short distance to the east of the French settlements. Morgan was to be sold a large described tract for not less than sixty-six and two-thirds cents per acre. Indian titles were to be extinguished if necessary.[2]

The Act of June 20, 1788, is an important landmark in the settlement of Illinois. The grant of bounty-lands was made for the purpose of giving the French settlers a means of support when the fur-trade and hunting should have become unprofitable from the advance of American settlement. This was a clear acknowledgment that the Indians were right in believing, as they did, that the American settlement would be fatal to Indian hunting-grounds. The Indians were soon bitterly hostile. Then, too, the claims of the settlers to land, founded upon French, British, or Virginia grants, were to be investigated. This investigation dragged on year after year, even for decades, and as it was the policy of the United States not to sell public land in Illinois until these claims were

1. "Jour. of Cong.," IV., 341-2, 823-5.

2. "Jour. of Cong.," IV., 823-5. The location of the ridge of rocks is clearly shown in Hutchins' "Topographical Desc of Va.," 1778, on a map opposite p. 41. French edition of 1781, facing p. 16; Winsor, "Nar. and Crit. Hist. of Am.," VI., 700; Collot, "Atlas of America," 1826.

settled, the country became a great squatters'[1] camp. The length of the investigation was doubtless due in part to the utter carelessness of the French in giving and in keeping their evidences of title.

By a congressional resolution of August 28, 1788, it was provided that the lands donated to Illinois settlers should be located east, instead of west, of the ridge of rocks. As this would throw the land too far from the settlements to be available, petitions followed for the restoration of the provisions of June 20, and in 1791 the original location was decreed. By a resolution of August 29, 1788, the governor of the Northwest Territory was ordered to carry out the provisions of the acts of June 20 and August 28, 1788, respectively.[2]

The beginning of operations, in accordance with the acts just cited, was delayed by the fact that the governor and judges, appointed under the Ordinance of 1787, and who alone could institute government under it, did not reach the Illinois country until 1790. In the meantime, anarchy continued. Contemporary accounts give a good idea of the attempts at government during the time, and the fact of their great interest, combined with the fact that most of them are yet unpublished, seems to warrant treatment of the subject at some length.

The court at Kaskaskia met more than a score of times during 1787 and 1788. Its record consists in large part of mere meetings and adjournments. All members of the court were French, while litigants and the single jury recorded were Americans. Jurors from Bellefontaine received forty-five livres each, and those from Prairie du

[1]. Throughout the period covered by this work, the term squatter denoted one who illegally settled on public land, without a title. Later laws permitted settling before securing a title, but in the early period, no squatting was legal.

[2]. "Jour. of Cong.," IV., 857-9.

Rocher, twenty-five livres each. This court seems to have been utterly worthless.[1] At Vincennes, matters were at least as bad. "It was the most unjust court that could have been invented. If anybody called for a court, the president had 20 livers in peltry; 14 magistrates, each 10 livers; for a room, 10 livers; other small expenses, 10 livers; total in peltry, 180 livers—which is 360 in money. So that a man who had twenty or thirty dollars due, was obliged to pay, if he wanted a court, 180 livers in peltry: This court also never granted an execution, but only took care to have the fees of the court paid. The government of this country has been in the Le Gras and Gamelin family for a long time, to the great dissatisfaction of the people, who presented me a Petition some days ago, wherein they complained of the injustice of their court—in consequence of which, I have dissolved the old court, ordered new magistrates to be elected, and established new regulations for them to go by."[2] Upon the dissolution of the court, Maj. Hamtramck issued the following:

"REGULATIONS FOR THE COURT OF POST VINCENNES.,

"In consequence of a Petition presented to me by the people of Post Vincennes, wherein they complain of the.

[1]. "John Todd's Record-Book," "Chicago Hist. Soc. Coll.," IV., 308-14.

[2]. Hamtramck to Harmar, from Vincennes, April 13, 1788—"Draper Coll., Harmar Papers," I., 386-7. At the time fees as above were being charged, prices current iu Vincennes were:

Corn, per bu....	$ 2.00	Whisky, per gal.	$ 8.00	A dunghill fowl.	$ 1.00
Flour, per cwt...	7.00	Butter, per lb...	1.00	Potatoes, per bu.	2.00
Pork, per lb.....	.30	Eggs, per doz...	1.00	Onions, per bu..	5.00
Beef, per lb....	.15	Loaf sugar, per lb...........	1.00	Cabbage, per head	.15
Bordeaux wine, per bottle.....	2.00	Brown sugar, per lb	.60	Turnips, per bu..	1.00
Spirits, per gal..	12.00	Coffee, per lb....	1.45	See *Ibid.*, 388-9.	

Beef was probably buffalo beef, as that was then the common meat for garrisons and settlers in the West.

great expence to which each individual is exposed in the recovery of his property by the present court, and as they express a wish to have another mode established for the administration of justice—I do, therefore, by these presents, dissolve the said court, and direct that five magistrates be elected by the suffrages of the people who, when chosen, will meet and settle their seniority.

"One magistrate will have power to try causes, not exceeding fifty livers in peltry. Two magistrates will determine all causes not exceeding one hundred livers in peltry,—from their decision any person aggrieved may (on paying the cost of the suit) appeal to the District Court, which will consist of three magistrates; the senior one will preside. They will meet the third Tuesday in every month and set two days, unless the business before them be completed within that time. All causes in this court shall be determined by a jury of twelve inhabitants. Any person summoned by the sheriff as a juryman who refuses or neglects to attend, shall be fined the price of a day's labour. In case of indisposition, he will, previous to the sitting of the court, inform the clerk, Mr. Antoine Gamelin, who will order such vacancies to be filled.

"The fees of the court shall be as follows: A magistrate, for every cause of fifty livers or upwards in peltry, shall receive one pistole in peltry, and in proportion for a lesser sum. The sheriff for serving a writ or a warrant shall receive three livers in peltry; for levying an execution, 5 per cent, including the fees of the clerk of the court.

"The clerk for issuing a writ shall receive three livers in peltry, and all other fees as heretofore. The jury being an office which will be reciprocal, are not to receive pay. All expenses of the court are to be paid by the person that is cast. This last part may appear to you to be an extraordinary charge—but my reason for mentioning it is, that formerly the court made the one who was most able pay the fees of the court, whether he lost or no.

"The magistrates, before they enter into the execution of their office, will take the following oath before the commandant: I, A., do swear that I will administer justice impartially, and to the best of my knowledge and understanding, so help me God.

"Given under my hand this 5th day of April, 1788.

(Signed) J. F. HAMTRAMCK,

Maj[r]. Comd'g."[1]

A little later, Hamtramck wrote: "Our new government has taken place; five magistrates have been elected by the suffrage of the people, but not one of the Ottoman families remains in. One Mr. Miliet, Mr. Henry, Mr. Bagargon, Capt. Johnson, and Capt. Dalton, have been elected. You will be surprised to see Dalton in office; but I found that he had too many friends to refuse him. I keep a watch-side eye over him, and find that he conducts himself with great propriety."[2]

The relief afforded by the new court was not complete, for soon came the report: "The people are very impatient to see Gen. St. Clair or some of the judges; in fact, they are very much wanted."[3] The term of the members of the court expired in April, 1789, and no new members were elected, because the early arrival of Gen. St. Clair was expected.[4] An interregnum occurred, and in November, 1789, Hamtramck wrote to Harmar: "It is high time

1. "Draper Coll., Harmar Papers," I., 389-92.

2. Hamtramck to Harmar, from Vincennes, May 21, 1788—"Draper Coll., Harmar Papers," I., 396. "Mr. Henry, of this place, who is very much connected with the Indians, particularly his wife," implies that Henry's wife was an Indian—*Ibid.*, 3-4.

3. Same to same, Aug. 31, 1788—*Ibid.*, I., 450.

4. Same to same, July 29, 1789—*Ibid.*, II., 70-1.

that government should take place in this country, and if it should happen that the Governor was not to come, nor any of the Judges, I would beg (for the sake of the people) that his Excellency would give me certain powers to create magistrates, a Sheriff and other officers, for the purpose of establishing Courts of Justice—for, at present, there are none, owing to the daily expectation of the arrival of the Governor. Those that had been appointed by the people last year, their authority has been refused in the courts of Kentucky, they declaring that by the resolve of Congress, neither the people of Post Vincennes, or the commanding officer, had a right to appoint magistrates; that the power was vested in the Governor only, and that it was an usurped authority. You see, Sir, how much to the prejudice of the people their present situation is, and how necessary it is that some steps should be taken to relieve them.

"The powers of the magistrates may be circumscribed as his Excellency may think proper, but the necessity of having such characters will appear when I assure you that at present no person here, can administer an oath which will be considered legal in the courts of Kentucky—and for the reasons above mentioned."[1]

At last, on June 19, 1790, the judges for the Northwest Territory arrived at Vincennes.[2]

The situation at Kaskaskia was even worse than that at Vincennes, because Vincennes had a garrison. To understand the complaints of the time, it is necessary to notice the relations with Spain. On the first day of 1788, Hamtramck wrote: "The Spanish commanding officers of the different posts on the Mississippi are encouraging settlers by giving them lands gratis. A village by the

---

1. Hamtramck to Harmar, from Vincennes, Nov. 11, 1789—"Draper Coll., Harmar Papers," II., 130–2.

2. Same to same, June 24, 1790—*Ibid.*, II., 254.

name of Zewapetas, which is about thirty miles above the mouth of the Ohio, and which was begun last summer, consists now of thirty or fifty families."[1] In the following October, Morgan made flattering offers to persons who would settle at New Madrid.[2] At the same time, the Mississippi was closed to Americans. Joseph St. Marie, of Vincennes, sent his clerk with a load of peltry to be traded to the Indians on the banks of the Mississippi. His goods were seized and confiscated by the Spanish commander at the Arkansas Post. The commander said that his orders were to seize all goods of Americans, found in the Mississippi below the mouth of the Ohio. Upon appeal to Gov. Miro, of Louisiana, the governor said that the court of Spain had given orders to send offending traders prisoners to the mines of Brazil.[3]

The combination of inducements to such as would become Spanish subjects and of severity to such as would not do so, secured Spain some settlers. Hamtramck said: "I am fearful that the Governor will not find many people in the Illinois, as they are daily going on the Spanish side. I believe that all our Americans of Post Vincennes will go to Morgan—a number of them are already gone to see him. I am told that Mr. Morgan has taken unwarrantable measures to invite the people of Illinois to come to him, saying that the Governor never would come in that country, and that their negroes were all free the moment the government should be established —for which all the remaining good inhabitants propose to go to him. I can not give you this for certain; I will

1. Same to ———, Jan. 1, 1788—*Ibid.*, I., 371.
2. Morgan's proclamation, Oct. 3, 1788—*Ibid.*, "Clark MSS.," LIII., 78, incomplete.
3. From Vincennes, Aug. 26, 1788—"Draper Coll., Harmar Papers," I., 455-61.

know better in a short time, and inform you."¹ "I have the honor to enclose you Mr. Morgan's letter *at his request*, and one for you. You will see in Mr. Morgan's that a post will be established opposite the Ohio; and if what Mr. Morgan says is true (which I doubt not), respecting the inhabitants of the Illinois, the Governor will have no occasion to go there. Will you be so good as to inform me if Congress have changed their resolution respecting the freedom of the negroes of this country; and if they are free from the day of the resolve, or if from the day it is published in a district."² A few weeks later, Harmar wrote to St. Clair: "The emigration continues, if possible, more rapid than ever; within these twenty days, not less than one hundred souls have passed [Fort Harmar, at Falls of Ohio] daily: the people are all taken up with Col. Morgan's New Madrid. . . . The generality of the inhabitants of Kaskaskias, and a number of those at Post Vincennes, I am informed, have quit those villages, and gone over to the Spanish side. The arrival of your Excellency amongst them, I believe is anxiously expected."³

The Indians were very hostile, and it is noteworthy that by the middle of 1789, the comparative immunity of the French from attack had ceased. Only negroes were safe, and they, probably, because they sold well.⁴ Civil government was at low ebb in the Kaskaskia region. By January, 1789, the court at Kaskaskia had dissolved.⁵

1. Hamtramck to Harmar, from Vincennes, Mar. 28, 1789—*Ibid.*, II., 17-18.
2. Hamtramck to Harmar, from Vincennes, Apr. 11, 1789—"Draper Coll., Harmar Papers," II., 27-28.
3. Harmar to St. Clair, from Fort Harmar, May 8, 1789—*Ibid.*, II., 51. Harmar to Knox, same date and of similar tenor—*Ibid.*, II., 53.
4. Hamtramck to Wyllys, from Vincennes, May 27, 1789—*Ibid.*, II., 39.
5. Hamtramck to Harmar, from Fort Knox, Vincennes, Jan. 19, 1789—*Ibid.*, II., 1.

The depopulation of Illinois led Hamtramck to write to Bartholomew Tardiveau, at the Falls of Ohio, asking whether it were true that the slaves of the French were to be free. Tardiveau responded that it was not true, and that he had written from New York, the preceding December, to Hamtramck and to Illinois concerning the matter, but that his letters had been intercepted. The true meaning of the resolve of Congress was published at Vincennes upon the receipt of Tardiveau's letter and was to be published in Illinois at the first opportunity. The narration of these facts was closed by the statement that if the governor or the judges did not come soon, most of the people would go to the Spanish side, "for they begin to think there are no such men as a Governor or Judges."[1]

In September, 1789, Hamtramck received the following petition from Kaskaskia:

"To John Francis Hamtramck, Esqr., Major of the 1st U. S. Regt. and commandant at Post Vincennes, &c. &c.

"The inhabitants of Kaskaskias, in the Illinois, beg leave to address you, as the next commanding officer in the service of the United States, to lay before you the deplorable situation we are reduced to, and the absolute necessity of our being speedily succoured to prevent as well our total ruin, as that of the place.

"The Indians are greatly more numerous than the white people, and are rather hostilely inclined; the name of an American among them is a disgrace, because we have no superior. Our horses, horned cattle, and corn are stolen and destroyed without the power of making any effectual resistance. Our houses are in ruin and decay; our lands are uncultivated; debtors absconded and absconding; our little commerce destroyed. We are apprehensive of a

1. Hamtramck to Harmar, from Vincennes, Aug. 14, 1798— "Draper Coll., Harmar Papers," II., 90-1.

dearth of corn, and our best prospects are misery and distress, or what is more than probable an untimely death by the hands of Savages.

"We are well convinced that all these misfortunes have befallen us for want of some superior, or commanding authority; for ever since the cession of this Territory to Congress, we have been neglected as an abandoned people, to encounter all the difficulties that are always attendant upon anarchy and confusion; neither did we know from authority until latterly, to what power we were subject. The greater part of our citizens have left the country on this account to reside in the Spanish dominions; others are now following, and we are fearful, nay, certain, that without your assistance, the small remainder will be obliged to follow their example.

"Thus situated, our last resource is to you, Sir, hoping and praying that you will so far use your authority to save an almost deserted country from destruction, and to order or procure the small number of twenty men with an officer, to be stationed among us for our defence; and that you will make order for the establishment of a civil court to take place immediately and to continue in force until the pleasure of his Excellency the Governor shall be known, and to whom we beg you would communicate our distress.

"We beg your answer by the return of the bearer, addressed to the Rev^d Mr. Le Dru, our Priest, who signs this in the name and at the request, of the inhabitants.

"Dated at Kaskaskia the fourteenth day of September, 1789.

"Ledru, curé Des Kaskaskias pour tous les habitans Français de l'endroit et outres voisins de la partie Americaine.   "JNO. EDGAR."[1]

[1] Inclosed in Hamtramck to Harmar, from Vincennes, Nov. 2, 1789— "Draper Coll., Harmar Papers," II., 124–7.

John Edgar offered to furnish provisions for the twenty soldiers asked for in the petition, and to take bills on Congress in payment.[1]

Hamtramck responded to the petition by saying that sickness prevailed among the troops at Vincennes to such an extent that twenty men could not be sent thence to Kaskaskia, but that the request would be sent to headquarters. As to the civil department, the people were advised to elect two or three magistrates in every village. These should prevent debtors from leaving, and should levy on the goods of such debtors as had already gone to the Spanish side. "Let your magistrates be respectable men by their moral character, as well as in point of property; let them attend with vigilance to all disputes that may arise amongst you, and in a particular manner to the Indian affairs."[2] This reply reached Edgar on the night of October 27, 1789. The next day, Edgar wrote to Hamtramck saying that it was probable that the recommendations in regard to establishing a civil government could not be carried out without a military force. The French were easily governed by a superior, but they knew nothing of government by an equal. Indians were constantly incited by the Spanish. They stole horses and escaped to the Spanish side. Edgar enclosed correspondence and depositions showing that on the night of the eighth of October, John Dodge and Michael Antanya, with a party of whites and Indians, came from the Spanish side to Kaskaskia, made an unsuccessful attempt to carry off some of Edgar's slaves, and threatened to burn the village. He adds "[In] the spring it is impossible I can

1. Offer dated Oct. 3, 1789. Inclosed in Hamtramck to Harmar, Nov. 2, 1789—"Draper Coll., Harmar Papers," II., 127–8.

2. Hamtramck's reply of Oct. 14, 1789, to petition of Sept. 14, preceding, inclosed as above—*Ibid.*, II., 128–30; "Draper Coll., Harmar Papers," II., 128–130.

stand my ground, surrounded as we are by savage enemies. I have waited five years in hopes of a government; I shall still wait until March, as I may be able to withstand them in the winter season, but if no succour nor government should then arrive, I shall be compelled to abandon the country, and I shall go to live at St. Louis. Inclination, interest and love for the country prompt me to reside here, but when in so doing it is ten to one but both my life and property will fall a sacrifice, you nor any impartial mind can blame me for the part I shall take."[1]

One day later, John Rice Jones wrote from Kaskaskia. The answer to the petition sent by Ducoigne and addressed to Ledru and Edgar, had been opened by the latter in the absence and by the consent of the former. Ledru had gone to be priest at St. Louis. At first he had refused the offer of the position, but when he received his tithes at Kaskaskia, he found that they would not support him, so he was compelled to move. He met no better treatment than de la Valiniere and Gibault before him, and no priest was likely to fare any better until a government was established. St. Pierre, priest at Cahokia, had gone to be priest at Ste. Genevieve, and it was said that Gibault was to be priest at L'Anse a la Graisse (New Madrid). Morgan had been coolly received at New Orleans, and his boasted settlement at New Madrid was almost broken up. The attempted seizure of Edgar's negroes could not be punished, because there was no one with authority to remonstrate with the Spanish, and private remonstrances were unheeded. The Spanish were making every effort to depopulate Illinois. They well knew that the people would follow their priests. Flattering offers had been made to Edgar by the Spanish, among them being free

[1]. Edgar to Hamtramck, from Kaskaskia, Oct. 28, 1789—"Draper Coll., Harmar Papers," II., 132–6.

ANARCHY IN ILLINOIS. 69

lands, no taxes, and free permission to work at the lead mines and salt springs. He had refused all offers, but if government was not established by the next March he would go to St. Louis, and if he went, Kaskaskia would be practically at an end. Twenty-four British trading-boats from Michilimackinac were on the Mississippi on the American side opposite the mouth of the Missouri. Their purpose was to attract Indian trade.[1]

Gov. St. Clair arrived at Kaskaskia on March 5, 1790.[2] With his coming anarchy technically ceased, but naturally the institution of an orderly government was a gradual process. In August, Tardiveau wrote to Hamtramck from Kaskaskia, saying that he hoped that Maj. Wyllys had given Hamtramck such a specimen of the difficulty of establishing a regular government and organizing the militia in Illinois as would induce the sending of a few regular troops from Vincennes. Even ten men would be a help. The Indians daily stole horses, and Tardiveau tried to raise a force to go and punish the offenders, but he was effectually opposed by a lawless band of ringleaders. A militia law and the Illinois civil power were useless to remedy the matter. There were plenty of provisions in Illinois to supply any soldiers that might be sent.[3] Tardiveau was then lieutenant-colonel of the first regiment of militia, and also judge of probate, having been appointed by the governor.[4] Harmar replied that it was utterly impracticable to comply with Tardiveau's request for soldiers.[5]

1. Jones to Hamtramck, from Kaskaskia, Oct. 29, 1789—"Draper Coll., Harmar Papers," II., 136-41.
2. *Ibid.*, II., 182; "St. Clair Papers," II., 164.
3. Tardiveau to Hamtramck, from Kaskaskia, Aug. 1, 1790—"Draper Coll., Harmar Papers," II., 302.
4. "St. Clair Papers," II., 165.
5. Harmar to Hamtramck, Sept. 3, 1790—"Draper Coll., Harmar Papers," II., 332.

On June 20, 1788, a congressional committee reported that there were about eighty families at Kaskaskia, twelve at Prairie du Rocher, four or five at Fort Chartres and St. Philips, and about fifty at Cahokia, making one hundred and forty-six or one hundred and forty-seven families in these villages.[1] In 1766-7, the same villages, with Vincennes, were supposed to have about two thousand inhabitants[2]; and about five years later, 1772, there were some fifteen hundred inhabitants in these villages, not including Vincennes.[3]

It is not surprising that the population of the Illinois country decreased from 1765 to 1790. During these years, British and Americans had attempted to impose upon the French settlers a form of government for which they had neither desire nor aptitude. The attempt to immediately transform a subject people was a signal failure, but neither the attempt nor the failure was unique.

1. "Jour. of Cong.," IV., 823,
2. Pittman, "European Settlements on the Miss.," 55.
3. Hutchins, "Topographical Desc. of Va." 36-8.

CHAPTER III.

I.

THE LAND AND INDIAN QUESTIONS, 1790 TO 1809

A PROCLAMATION issued by Estevan Miro, Governor and Intendant of the Provinces of Louisiana and Florida in 1789, offered to immigrants a liberal donation of land, graduated according to the number of laborers in the family; freedom of religion and from payment of tithes, although no public worship except Catholic would be allowed; freedom from taxation; and a free market at New Orleans for produce or manufactures. All settlers must swear allegiance to Spain.[1] This proclamation came at a time when the West was divided in opinion as to whether to make war upon Spain for her closure of the Mississippi or to secede from the United States and become a part of Spain.[2] It tended to continue the emigration from the Illinois country to Spanish territory, for public land was not yet for sale in Illinois.

To the professional rover, the inability to secure a title to land was the cause of small concern, but the more substantial and desirable the settler, the more concerned was he about the matter. Settlement and improvements were retarded. Before the affairs of the Ohio Company had progressed far enough to permit sales of land to settlers, the little company at Marietta saw, with deep chagrin, thousands of settlers float by on their way to Kentucky, where land could be bought.[3] Squatters in Illinois were constantly expecting that the public lands

1. "St. Clair Papers," II., 122-3.
2. "Secret Jour. of Cong.," IV., 301-29.
3. "St. Clair Papers," I., 150.

would soon be offered for sale. The natural result was petitions for the right of preëmption, because without such a right, the settler was in danger of losing whatever improvements he had made. In 1790, James Piggott and forty-five others petitioned for such a right. The petitioners stated that they had settled since 1783 and had suffered much from Indians. They could not cultivate their land except under guard. Seventeen families had no more tillable land than four could tend. The land on which they lived was the property of two individuals.[2]

Petitions from various classes of settlers, not provided for by the acts of June 20, August 28, and August 29, 1788, led Congress to pass the act of March 3, 1791. By this act, four hundred acres was to be given to each head of a family who, in 1783, was resident in the Illinois country or at Vincennes, and who had since moved from the one to the other. The same donation was to be made to all persons who had moved away, if they should return within five years. Such persons should also have confirmed to them the land they originally held. This was intended to bring back persons who had gone to the Spanish side of the Mississippi. Grants previously made by courts having no authority should be confirmed to persons who had made improvements, to an extent not exceeding four hundred acres to any one person. As these lands had in some cases been repeatedly sold, the parties making the improvements were frequently guiltless of any knowledge of fraud. The Cahokia commons were confirmed to that village. One hundred acres was to be granted to each militiaman enrolled on August 1, 1790, and who had received no other grant.[1] This act throws considerable light on the causes of discontent then prevailing among

2. "Pub. Lands," I., 20.
1. "Statutes at Large," I., 221–2.

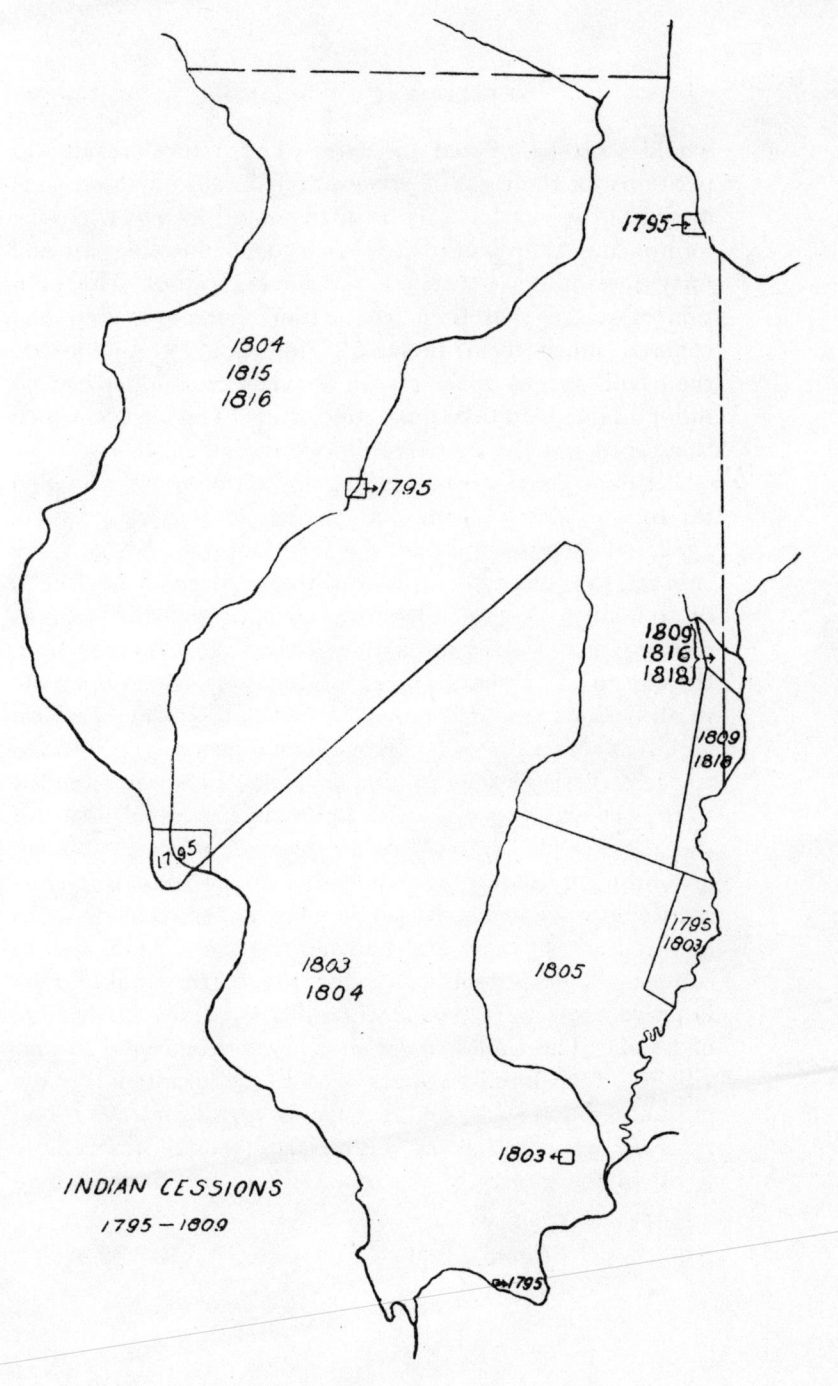

THE LAND AND INDIAN QUESTIONS. 73

the settlers and on the conditions to which immigrants came.

This same spring, about two hundred and fifty of the inhabitants of Vincennes had gone to settle at New Madrid.[1] It is not strange that the act of March 3, 1791, made provisions intended to induce the Americans who had emigrated to the Spanish possessions to return. The history of the threatened Spanish aggression upon the western part of the United States is known in essence to anyone who has made the slightest special study of the period at which it was at its height. Morgan's scheme for a purchase of land in Illinois was not carried out, and he turned his attention to peopling his settlement at New Madrid. Down the Mississippi to New Orleans seemed the natural route for Illinois commerce. Slavery flourished unmolested west of the Mississippi. In 1794, Baron de Carondolet gave orders to the governor of Natchez to incite the Chickasaw Indians to expel the Americans from Fort Massac. The governor refused to obey the order, because Fort Massac had been occupied by the Americans in pursuance of a request by the Spanish representative at the capital of the United States that the president would put a stop to the proposed expedition of the French against the Spanish. The claim was advanced by Carondolet that the Americans had no right to the land on which the fort stood, but that the land belonged to the Chickasaws, who were independent allies of Spain. Two other reasons given for not obeying the order were that it would preclude the successful issue of the Spanish intrigue for the separation of Kentucky from the United States, and would hinder negotiations, then pending, for a commercial treaty between Spain and the United States.[2]

1. Hamtramck to Harmar, from Vincennes, Apr. 14, 1791—"Draper Coll., Harmar Papers," II., 410.

2. "Draper MSS., Translation of Spanish Documents," 49-60.

Carondolet regarded the Indians as Spain's best defence against the Americans,[1] yet the whites prepared for defence, and in anticipation of the proposed French expedition of George Rogers Clark, a garrison of thirty men and an officer was placed at Ste. Genevieve, opposite Kaskaskia. Carondolet said: "This will suffice to prevent the smuggling carried on by the Americans of the settlement of Kaskaskias situated opposite, which increases daily."[2]

Early in 1796, a petition was sent from Kaskaskia to Congress. The petitioners desired that they might be permitted to locate their donation of four hundred acres per family on Long Prairie, a few miles above Kaskaskia, on the Kaskaskia River, and that the expense of surveying the land might be paid by the United States. The act granting the donation-land had provided for its location between the Kaskaskia and the Mississippi. This land the petitioners declared to be private land and some of it was of poor quality.[3] Confirmation of land claims directed to be made upon the Governor's visit in 1790 were delayed by the lack of a surveyor and the poverty of the inhabitants.[4] The petition was signed by John Edgar, William Morrison, William St. Clair, and John Demoulin[5] "for the inhabi-

---

1. Carondolet to Duke of Alcudia, from New Orleans, Sept. 27, 1793— "Draper MSS., Translation of Spanish Documents." 24, second pagination of typewritten matter.

2. Carondolet to ——, —*Ibid.*, 33, first pagination of matter in long hand.

3. "Pub. Lands," I., 69.

4. "St. Clair Papers," II., 398-9.

5. John Edgar, for years the wealthiest citizen of Illinois, was born in Ireland, came to Kaskaskia in 1784, and soon became a large landholder by purchasing French donation-rights. Wm. Morrison, a native of Bucks county, Pa., came from Philadelphia to Kaskaskia in 1790 and became a leading merchant and shipper. Wm. St. Clair, a son of James St. Clair, once captain in the Irish Brigade in the service of France, was the first clerk of the court of St. Clair county. John Dumoulin (or De Moulin) was a Swiss. In 1790, he was a judge of the Court of Common Pleas in the Cahokia district of St. Clair county.

THE LAND AND INDIAN QUESTIONS. 75

tants of the counties of St. Clair and Randolph"[1]—the Illinois counties. The petitioners ranked high in the mercantile and legal life of the Illinois settlements, but they must have been novices in the art of petitioning if they thought that a petition signed by four men from the Illinois country, with no sign of their being legally representative, would be regarded by Congress as an expression of the opinion of the Northwest Territory. The part of the petition relating to lands was granted, but the major part, which related to other subjects, was denied on the ground that the petitioners probably did not represent public sentiment.[2] During this same year Congress denied a number of petitions for the right of preëmption in the Northwest Territory, because such a right would encourage illegal settling. It was also during this year that the first sales of public land in the Northwest Territory were authorized. The land to be sold was in what is now Ohio. No tract of less than four thousand acres could be purchased.[3]

In 1800, two hundred and sixty-eight inhabitants of Illinois, chiefly French, petitioned Congress that Indian titles to land in the southern part of Illinois might be extinguished and the land offered for sale; that tracts of land at the distance of a day's journey from each other, lying between Vincennes and the Illinois settlements, might be ceded to such persons as would keep taverns, and

---

1. St. Clair county had been formed in 1790 and Randolph county in 1795. In 1796, they were the only counties lying wholly within the present State of Illinois. A strip of the eastern part of Illinois lay in Knox county. The line between St. Clair and Randolph was an east-and-west line, a little south of New Design, Randolph lying to the south—"St. Clair Papers," II., 165, 166, 345.

2. "Pub. Lands," I., 68–9; "Ind. Hist. Soc. Pub.," II., 447–52, 452–55.

3. "Pub. Lands," I., 68; Poore, "Desc. Catalogue of Govt. Publications," 43; "Laws of U. S. Relating to Pub. Lands," 420–5.

that one or two garrisons might be stationed in Illinois. The petitioners state that the Kaskaskia tribe of Indians numbered not more than fifteen members and that their title to land could be easily extinguished; that not enough land is open to settlement to admit a population sufficient to support ordinary county establishments; that roads are much needed, and that many of the inhabitants are crossing the Mississippi with their slaves. The petition was not considered.[1]

A new factor now appears in the forces affecting Illinois settlement. The Northwest Territory having advanced to the second grade of territorial government, in December, 1799, its delegate took his seat in Congress. The step was an important one for the struggling colony. Before this time such petitions as were prepared by inhabitants of the territory for the consideration of Congress had been subjected to all the vicissitudes of being addressed to some public officer or of being confided to some member of Congress who represented a different portion of the country. Up to this time the public lands could only be bought in tracts of four thousand acres. Largely through the influence of the delegate from the Northwest Territory, a bill was passed which authorized the sale of sections and half-sections. In consequence, emigration soon began to flow rapidly into Ohio. Land in Illinois was not yet offered for sale, but this bill is important because the policy of offering land in smaller tracts was to continue.[2]

The territorial delegate was also active in procuring the passage of a bill for the division of the Northwest Territory. While the bill was pending, a petition from Illinois, praying for the division and for the establishment of such

1. "Ind. Hist. Soc. Pub.," II., 455-61; "Annals of Cong.," 6th Cong., 735.
2. "Annals of Cong.," 6th Cong., 537-538; Poore, "Desc. Catalogue of Govt. Publications," 43; "Statutes at Large," II., 73-8.

THE LAND AND INDIAN QUESTIONS.

a government in the western part as was provided for by the Ordinance of 1787, was presented. The act for division was signed by the President on May 7, 1800; it formed Indiana Territory, with Vincennes as its capital.[1]

The propositions made by a convention of representatives elected by the citizens of Indiana to prepare petitions to Congress, near the close of 1802, illustrate the needs of the time. It was desired that the Indian title to land lying in Southern Illinois and Southwestern Indiana might be extinguished and the land sold in smaller tracts and at a lower price[2]; that a preëmption act might be passed; that a grant of seminary and school lands might be made; that land for taverns, twenty miles or less apart, might be granted along certain specified routes; that donation-lands might be chosen in separate tracts, instead of in three specified areas, in order to avoid "absolutely useless" prairies, and also lands claimed by ancient grants; and that the qualification of a freehold of fifty acres of land, prescribed for the electors of representatives to the territorial legislature, might be changed to manhood suffrage, because the freehold qualification was said to tend "to throw too great a weight in the scale of wealth." The petition was considered in committees, but it led to no legislation.[3]

1. "Statutes at Large," II., 58-9; "Annals of Cong.," 6th Cong., 507, 699, 701.

2. According to the Act of May 10, 1800, public land was to be sold in tracts, not smaller than one-half sections, and for a minimum price of two dollars per acre. One-twentieth of the purchase-money should be paid at the time of sale, the remainder of one-fourth of the price within forty days, one-fourth in two years, one-fourth in three years, and one-fourth in four years. On the last three payments, interest should be paid at six per cent from the date of sale, and on the same three payments a discount of eight per cent per year should be granted for prepayment. Land unpaid for reverted to the United States—"Statutes at Large," II., 73-8.

3. "Ind. Hist. Soc. Pub.," II., 461-70; "Annals of Cong.," 8th Cong., 1st Sess., 1023-4; 9th Cong., 1st Sess., 293-4, 466-8.

None of the above complaints was better founded than that concerning the restriction of the suffrage, and it is well to note subsequent proceedings in regard to it. No qualification less suitable to the time and place could well have been devised, and this is especially true of the Illinois portion of the territory, because there unsettled French claims were to delay the sales of public lands until 1814, and thus early settlers could neither buy land nor vote unless they owned it, unless indeed they purchased land claims from the needy and unbusiness-like French. An interesting petition of 1807 from the settlement on Richland Creek,[1] for the right of preëmption, throws light upon conditions then obtaining. The petitioner inclosed a map of the settlement, with the following explanation: "Those persons whose names are enclosed in said plot, within surveyed lines, have confirmed and located rights, amounting to 3,775 acres; . . . the residue of the said settlers, occupying about 6,000 acres of land, have, without any right, settled upon the public land." The map shows that there were eleven owners and twenty-two squatters.[2] As the law then stood, the twenty-two squatters, occupying more than three-fifths of the land, could not vote. The eleven land-owners must have secured their land either under the acts of 1788 or that of 1791, or by the purchase of French claims, a trade vigorously carried on. In 1808,[3] Congress so far extended the suffrage in Indiana as to make the ownership of a town lot worth one hundred dollars an alternative qualification to the possession of a

1. A western tributary of the lower part of the Kaskaskia.
2. "Pub. Lands," I., 591.
3. "Statutes at Large," II., 469; Poore, "Charters and Constitutions," 821, 832, 964, 973; McMaster, "Acquisition of the . . . Rights of Man in Am.," 111-22; "Proceedings and Debates of the Va. State Conv. of 1829-30," *passim;* Mowry, "The Dorr War," *passim.*

freehold of fifty acres. This was in advance of the law in some of the Eastern states.

After 1802, the land question can not be traced without reference to the Indian question in Illinois. That question became important as soon as American occupation was assured, and it remained important for fifty years after the Revolution. The desire of the American settlers for land was directly counter to the desire of the Indians to preserve their hunting-grounds. Before the close of the eighteenth century, the list of bloody deeds in Illinois had grown long.[1] The United States Government appreciated the gravity of the situation and early made efforts to purchase the land from the Indians. That part of the treaty of Greenville, of 1795, which affected Illinois, extinguished the Indian title to a tract six miles square, at the mouth of Chicago River; one six miles square, at Peoria; one twelve miles square, near the mouth of the Illinois River; the post of Fort Massac, and the land in the possession of the whites.[2] The treaty of Fort Wayne, in 1803, ceded four square miles or less, at the salt springs on Saline Creek, and some land west and southwest from Vincennes. This treaty, with another made in the following August, ceded three tracts of land, each one mile square, between Vincennes and Kaskaskia, to be sites for taverns.[3] The treaty of Vincennes, of August, 1803, ceded land in Illinois bounded by the Ohio, the Mississippi, the Illinois, and the western watershed of the Wabash, except three hundred and fifty

[1]. "Draper Coll., Ill. MSS.," 37, 39, 43, 54, 57, 58, 67, 102, 104, 107, 108, 113; "Pub. Lands," I., 20; "Wis. Hist. Soc. Coll.," VII., 300; "'Father Clark;' or, The Pioneer Preacher," 181 et seq.

[2]. "Indian Aff.," I., 562; "An. Rept. of the Bureau of Ethnology," 18, Pt. 2, 656-7, Plates CXXIV., CXXV.; see map of Indian cessions, 1795-1809.

[3]. "An. Rept. of the Bureau of Ethnology," 18, Pt. 2, 656-7; Plates CXXIV., CXXV.; "Indian Aff.," I., 688; see map of Indian cessions.

acres near Kaskaskia, and twelve hundred and eighty acres to be located. This last treaty was made with the depleted Kaskaskia tribe.[1] As the claims of various tribes overlapped, an Indian treaty rarely signifies that all controversy in regard to the land ceded is at an end. Frequently one or more treaties must yet be made with other tribes, and frequently a tribe refuses to abide by its agreement.

Previous to 1804, no land was sold in the Northwest Territory west of the mouth of the Kentucky River. An act of March 26 of that year provided for the opening of a land-office at Detroit to sell lands north of Ohio; one at Vincennes to sell lands in its vicinity ceded by the treaty of Fort Wayne; and one at Kaskaskia to sell so much of the land ceded by the treaty of Vincennes (August, 1803) as was not claimed by any other tribe than those represented in the cession. The register and the receiver of public moneys of these respective districts were to be commissioners to settle private land claims. Evidences of claims should be filed before January 1, 1805, and after the adjustment of claims the public lands should be sold at auction to the highest bidder. Two dollars per acre was to be the minimum price; no land should be sold in less than quarter-sections, except fractional portions caused by irregularities in topography or survey, and lands unsold after the auction might be sold at private sale. Although this act provided for the sale of public lands in Illinois after private claims should have been satisfied, and directed that such claims should be filed not later than January 1, 1805, Congress repeatedly extended the time for the filing of claims, and ten years after the passage of this act there were still unsatisfied claims.[2] Not until

1. "Indian Aff.," I., 687; "An. Rept. of the Bureau of Ethnology," 18, Pt. 2, 664-5, Plate CXXIV.; see map of Indian cessions.
2. "Statutes at Large," II., 277-83, 343-5, 446-8, 517, 590-1.

THE LAND AND INDIAN QUESTIONS. 81

1814 did sales of public land begin in Illinois. The delay retarded immigration of that class which would have made the most desirable citizens.

By the treaty of St. Louis, November 3, 1804, the Sauk and Foxes ceded that part of Illinois west of the Illinois and Fox rivers. Black Hawk, the principal chief of the Sauk, did not sign the treaty.[1] By the treaty of Vincennes, 1805, the Piankashaws ceded a tract lying between the lower Wabash and its western watershed.[2] No more Indian titles to land in Illinois were extinguished, and no public land was sold in Illinois until after that part of the country became a separate territory.

Early in 1806, there came to Congress from Illinois a petition which betrayed the anxiety of the French settlers, and of the Americans who had bought French claims, lest the peculiar shape of their holdings should be disturbed by the orderly system of goverment surveys. The petitioners asked that a line might be run from a point north of Cahokia to an unspecified river south of Kaskaskia, in such a manner as to include all settlements between the two points, and that the land so included be exempt from the mode of survey and terms of sale of other public lands of the United States. The petition was apparently not reported upon, but a detailed map of the region referred to shows that the holdings were left in their bewildering complexity.[3]

By the time Indiana Territory was divided some progress had been made in extinguishing Indian titles, and some

---

1. "Indian Aff.," I., 693-4; "An. Rept. of the Bureau of Ethnology," 18, Pt. 2, 666-7, Plate CXXIV.; see map of Indian cessions.

2. "Indian Aff.," I., 704-5; "An. Rept. of the Bureau of Ethnology," 18, Pt. 2, 672-3, Plate CXXIV.; see map of Indian cessions.

3. "Annals of Cong.," 9th Cong., 1st Sess., 339; see map in the "Hist. of Randolph, Monroe, and Perry Counties, Ill.," frontispiece.

also in investigating land claims of the French and their assignees; but the American immigrant had still the hard choice of buying a French claim with uncertain title or squatting on government land with the risk of losing whatever improvement he might make, and often the added risk of being killed by the suspicious, hostile, untrustworthy Indians. This was one class of hindrances to settlement. Another hindrance, next to be noticed, was the unstable governmental conditions following the anarchy already recited.

II.

Government Succeeding the Period of Anarchy, 1790 to 1809.

WHEN St. Clair County was formed, in 1790, it was made to include all the settlements of the Northwest Territory to the westward of Vincennes. On account of its geographical extent it was divided into three judicial districts, but it could not be made into three separate counties, because there were not enough men capable of holding office to furnish the necessary officials. The American settlers were few and a large proportion of them were unskilled in matters of government, while the French were totally unfit to govern. In 1795, St. Clair, when referring to conditions in 1790, wrote that since then the population of Illinois had decreased considerably.[1] Combining this decrease with the fact that there were in the settlements in what is now Missouri 1491 inhabitants in 1785, 2093 in 1788, and 6028, including 883 slaves, in 1799,[2] the conclu-

[1]. St. Clair to Judge Turner, from Marietta, May 2, 1795—"St. Clair Papers," II., 348-9.
[2]. Edwards, "Great West," 271, 274-5; figures from the official census.

GOVERNMENT SUCCEEDING PERIOD OF ANARCHY. 83

sion is inevitable that emigration across the Mississippi was the immediate cause of the decrease in Illinois.

In 1795, notwithstanding the decreased population, and perhaps in the hope of checking the decrease, St. Clair County was divided by proclamation of Governor St. Clair. The division was by an east and west line running a little south of the settlement of New Design.[1] St. Clair County lay to the north, Randolph County to the south of the line.[2]

The early laws of the Northwest Territory throw light upon the conditions existing upon the frontier. Minute provisions for establishing and maintaining ferries, with no mention of bridges, indicate the primitive methods of travel.[3] Millers were required to use a prescribed set of measures and to grind for a prescribed toll, the toll for the use of a horse-mill being higher than that for a water-mill, unless the owner of the grain furnished the horses.[4] Guide-posts were to be put up at the forks of every public road.[5] No stray stock should be taken up between the first of April and the first of November, unless the stray should have broken into the inclosure of the taker-up.[6] In those days stock was turned out and crops were fenced in. Prairies or cleared land were not to be fired except between December 1 and March 10, unless upon one's own land.[7] The following rates of county taxation were prescribed:

    Horses, per head _____ not more than $ .50

    Neat cattle _____ " " " .12½

    Bond servant _____ " " " 1.00

    Single man, 21 yrs. or older, with less than
        $200 worth of property, not more than 2.00
        nor less than _____ .50

    Retail merchants _____ 10.00[8]

1. See map of Illinois country.
2. "St. Clair Papers," I., 193; II., 345.
3. "Laws of N.-W. Ter.," 1800, I., 47-51.
4. *Ibid.*, 1800, I., 58-61.
5. *Ibid.*, 1800, I., 178.
6. *Ibid.*, 1800, I., 61-71.
7. *Ibid.*, 1800, I., 119-21.
8. *Ibid.*, 1800, I., 197.

A bounty, varying at different times between 1799 and 1810 from 50 cents to $2 per head, was given for killing wolves.[1] Imprisonment for debt, a law antedating by many years similar laws in several of the other parts of the United States, was practically abolished.[2] A frontier region does not have that social stratification which makes oppression of the debtor class easy. A county too poor to build a log jail without difficulty is not likely to be so senseless as to make a practice of confining and boarding its debtor class.

For the purpose of taxation land was to be listed in three classes according to value. No specification as to the value of the respective classes was prescribed. The tax was eighty-five, sixty, or twenty-five cents per one hundred acres, according as land was first, second, or third class. No unimproved land in Illinois was to be listed higher than second class.[3]

The laws above cited were enacted by the legislature of the Northwest Territory. In May, 1800, that territory was divided, the western part, including Illinois, becoming Indiana Territory. This made the Illinois country more distinctly frontier by again reducing it to the first grade of territorial government, Indiana Territory, as such, not being represented in Congress until December, 1805.[4] Among the reasons advanced for dividing the Northwest Territory was the fact that in five years there had been but one court for criminal cases in the three western counties.[5]

1. "Laws of N.-W. Ter., 1800," I., 226-7; "Laws of Ill. Ter., 1815-16;" *Ibid.*, "1816-17," 4; *Ibid.*, "17-19."

2. "Laws of N.-W. Ter., 1800," I., 157-61; McMaster, "Acquisition of the Pol., Social and Industrial Rights of Man in Am.," 64-66; 16th Cong., 2d Sess., "Rept. of Com. No. 63."

3. "Laws of N.-W. Ter., 1800," I., 184-5.

4. "Statutes at Large," II., 58-9; "Annals of Cong.," 6th Cong., 1007; *Ibid.*, 9th Cong., 1st Sess., 275. 5. "Misc.," I., 206-7.

GOVERNMENT SUCCEEDING PERIOD OF ANARCHY. 85

Illinois soon sought admission to the second grade of territorial government. In April, 1801, John Edgar wrote from Kaskaskia to St. Clair: "During a few weeks past, we have put into circulation petitions addressed to Governor Harrison, for a General Assembly, and we have had the satisfaction to find that about nine-tenths of the inhabitants of the counties of St. Clair and Randolph approve of the measure, a great proportion of whom have already put their signatures to the petition. . . . I have no doubt but that the undertaking will meet with early success, so as to admit of the House of Representatives meeting in the fall."[1] The movement for advancement to the second grade was not, however, destined to such early success, and when it did take place such a change had occurred that Illinois was much enraged.

The Illinois country early became restive under the government of Indiana Territory. Much the same causes for discontent existed as had caused Kentucky to wish to separate from Virginia, Tennessee from North Carolina, and the country west of the Alleghanies from the United States. In each case a frontier minority saw its wishes, if not its rights, infringed by a more eastern majority. In each case the eastern people were themselves too weak to furnish sufficient succor to the struggling West. The conflict was natural and inevitable. The grave charge against Governor Harrison, who had large powers of patronage, was local favoritism. So discontented was Illinois, that in 1803 it had petitioned for annexation to the territory of Louisiana when such territory should be formed.[2] Antagonism to the Indiana government became still more bitter when, in December, 1804, after an election which was so hurried that an outlying county did not get to vote,

1. "St. Clair Papers," II., 533-4.
2. "Annals of Cong.," 8th Cong., 1st Sess., 489, 1659-60.

the territory entered the second grade of territorial government.[2]

In the summer of 1805, discontent in Illinois was again expressed in a memorial to Congress. About three hundred and fifty inhabitants of the region petitioned for a division of Indiana Territory. From the Illinois settlements to the capital, Vincennes, was said to be one hundred and eighty miles, "through a dreary and inhospitable wilderness, uninhabited, and which during one part of the year, can scarcely afford water sufficient to sustain nature, and that of the most indifferent quality, besides presenting other hardships equally severe, while in another it is part under water, and in places to the extent of some miles, by which the road is rendered almost impassable, and the traveler is not only subjected to the greatest difficulties, but his life placed in the most imminent danger." It resulted that the attendance of Illinois inhabitants upon either the legislature or the supreme court was fraught with many inconveniences. Because of the extensive prairies between Illinois and Vincennes, "a communication between them and the settlements east of that river [the Wabash] can not in the common course of things, for centuries yet to come, be supported with the least benefit, or be of the least moment to either of them." Illinois objected to having been precipitated into the second grade of government. In the election for that purpose, said the memorialists, only Knox county voted in the affirmative, and Wayne county did not vote, because the writs of election arrived too late. Since entering the second grade the County of Wayne (Michigan) had been struck off. It was believed that if the prayer for separation should be granted, the rage for emigration to Louisiana would, in great measure, cease, the value of public lands in Illinois

2. "Ind. Hist. Soc. Pub.," II., 486-7.

would be increased, and their sale would also be more rapid, while an increased population would render Illinois flourishing and self-supporting rather than a claimant for governmental support.[1]

At the same time that Congress received the above memorial, it received a petition from a majority of the members of the respective houses of the Indiana legislature. This petition asked that the freehold qualification for electors be abolished; that Indiana Territory be not divided, and that the undivided territory be soon made a state. It was said that the people were too poor to support a divided government, and that as the general court met annually in each county it was slight hardship to the frontier to have the supreme court meet at Vincennes.[2] It was probably true at this time, as it certainly was in 1807, that the general court met as above stated. Appeal by bill of exceptions was, however, allowed. The supreme court had no original, exclusive jurisdiction.[3] Nothing daunted by this memorial from the legislature, Illinois, in a short time, prepared another memorial—this time with twenty signatures. This adds to the grievances recited in the previous memorial that the wealthy appeal cases against the Illinois poor to the supreme court at Vincennes; that landholders on the Wabash are interested in preventing the population of lands on the Mississippi; that preëmption is needed, and that it is hoped that the general government will not pass unnoticed the act of the last legislature authorizing the importation of slaves into the territory. It violates the Ordinance of 1787. The memorialists desired such importation, but it must be

[1]. "Ind. Hist. Soc. Pub.," II., 483-92; original among the House files at Washington.
[2]. "Ind. Hist. Soc. Pub.," II., 476-83.
[3]. "Laws of Ind. Ter.," 1807, pp. 12-13.

authorized by Congress to be legal. The population of Illinois was given as follows:

By the census of April 1, 1801 2,361
Inhabitants of Prairie du Chien and on the Illinois River, not included in above 550
"Emigration" since 1801, at least one-third increase 750
Settlements on the Ohio River 650
              4,311[1]

The truth of some of the complaints from Illinois is apparent. That a land company on the Wabash wished to hinder settlement on the Mississippi is probably true, for Matthew Lyon, of Kentucky, said in Congress, in the winter of 1805-6: "The price of lands is various. I know of two hundred thousand acres of land on the Wabash, which is offered for sale at twenty cents per acre."[2] It is to be presumed that the company making the offer could not give a secure title to the land.

In 1806, a congressional committee reported on the various memorials and petitions from Illinois, but the report led to no legislation and thus settled nothing, and in 1807 petitioning continued.[3] Illinois again petitioned for separation from the remainder of Indiana Territory, this petition bearing seventeen signatures. An inclosed census is lost, but a population of five thousand is spoken of. A new and significant paragraph occurs: "When your Memorialists contemplate the probable movements which may arise out of an European peace, now apparently about to take place, they cannot but feel the importance of union, of energy, of population on this shore of the

1. "Ind. Hist. Soc. Pub.," II., 498-506.
2. "Annals of Cong.," 9th Cong., 1st Session, 469.
3. *Ibid.*, 466-8; "Misc.," I., 450; "Ind. Hist. Soc. Pub.," II., 494-7.

Mississippi—they cannot but shudder at the horrors which may arise from a *disaffection in the West* . . ." A government was needed, and that of Indiana Territory was not acceptable to the people of Illinois. One hundred and two inhabitants of Illinois sent a counter-petition, in which they said that Illinois had paid no taxes and needed no separate government, also that the committee that prepared the above petition was not legally chosen. Most of the signers of the petition were Americans, while most of the signers of the counter-petition were French, forty-two of the latter being illiterate.[1] The report of a congressional committee on the petition was adverse,[2] as was also a report on three petitions for division that came from Illinois in the spring of 1808.[3] In the following December, the representative of Indiana Territory in Congress was appointed chairman of a committee to consider the expediency of dividing the territory, and to this committee petitions both for and against division were referred. This territorial delegate was in favor of division, and his committee presented a favorable report, in which the number of inhabitants of Indiana east of the Wabash was estimated to be seventeen thousand, and the number west of the Wabash to be eleven thousand—numbers thought to be sufficiently large to justify division, and an estimate which the census of 1810 proves to have been almost correct. In February, 1809, the bill providing for the division so ardently desired by Illinois was approved, the division to take place on the first of the next March. The western division was to be known as Illinois Territory and was to have for its eastern boundary a line due north from Vincennes to the Canadian line.[4] In the debate in

1. "Ind. Hist. Soc. Pub.," II., 505-10.
2. "H. J.," 8th and 9th Cong., 611.
3. "Annals of Cong.," 10th Cong., 1st Sess., 1976, 2067.
4. *Ibid.*, 10th Cong., 2d Sess., 971-3, 1093; "Stat. at Large," II., 514-16.

the House of Representatives, preceding the passage of the bill for division, the arguments in its favor were that the Wabash was a natural dividing line; that a wide extent of wilderness intervened between Vincennes and the western settlements; that the power of the executive was enervated by the dispersed condition of the settlements; that to render justice was almost impossible; that the United States would be more than compensated for the increased expense by the rise in value of the public lands. Opponents of the bill declared that the complaints made by Illinois were common to many parts of the country; that the number of officers would be needlessly increased by the proposed division; and that "a compliance with this petition would but serve to foster their factions, and produce more petitions." No significant geographical division of the vote on the bill is apparent.[1]

III

Obstacles to Immigration

1790 TO 1809.

IN addition to the inability to secure land titles on account of unsettled French claims, to the presence of Indians, and to the discontent with the government of Indiana Territory, almost every cause which made settlement on the frontier difficult was found in the Illinois country in its most pronounced form, because Illinois was the far corner of the frontier. The census reports of the United States give the following statistics of population:

1. "Annals of Cong.," 10th Cong., 2d Sess., 1093-4.

	1790.	1800.	1810.
Kentucky	73,677	220,955	406,511
Ohio		45,365	230,760
Indiana		2,517	24,520
Illinois		2,458	12,282

These figures show how conspicuously small was the immigration to Illinois. Enough has already been said to show some of the reasons for this sluggish settlement. When, in 1793, Governor St. Clair wrote to Alexander Hamilton, "In compassion to a poor devil banished to another planet, tell me what is doing in yours, if you can snatch a moment from the weighty cares of your office,"[1] he doubtless felt that the language was not too strong, and voiced a feeling of loneliness that was common to the settlers. Nor was there a lack of land in the East to make westward movement imperative. Massachusetts was much opposed to her people emigrating to Ohio, because she wished them to settle on her own eastern frontier (Maine), and Vermont and New York had vacant lands.[2]

One who settled in Illinois at this period came through danger to danger, for Indians lurked in the woods and malaria waited in the lowlands. The journey made by the immigrants was tedious and difficult, and was often rendered dangerous by precipitous and rough hills and swollen streams, if the journey was overland, or by snags, shoals and rapids, if by water. A large proportion of the settlers came from Maryland, Virginia, or the Carolinas. Those from Virginia and Maryland were induced to emigrate by the glowing descriptions of the Illinois country given by the soldiers of George Rogers Clark, and these soldiers sometimes led the first contingent. A typical Virginia settlement in Illinois was that called New

1. "St. Clair Papers," II., 318.
2. Cutler, "Life of Manasseh Cutler," II., 382.

Design, located in what is now Monroe county, between Kaskaskia and Cahokia. Founded about 1786 by a native of Berkeley county, the settlement received important additions in 1793, and four years later a party of more than one hundred and fifty arrived from near the headwaters of the south branch of the Potomac, this last contingent led by a Baptist minister, who had organized a church on a previous visit.[1] In general, persons Scotch-Irish by birth were opposed to slavery, as were also the members of the Quaker church. This caused a considerable emigration from the Carolinas, Another motive for people from all sections was that expressed by settlers of Illinois, in 1806, when they said that they came west in order to secure "such an establishment in land as they despaired of ever being able to procure in the old settlements."[2] We have seen how long deferred was the fulfillment of their hope of getting a title to the coveted land. Although the East was not crowded, it is true that land there was more expensive than that of the same quality in the West. In 1806, three dollars per acre was the maximum price in even the settled parts of Indiana Territory, while fifty dollars per acre had been paid for choice Kentucky land.[3]

The greater number of immigrants came by water, but a family too poor to travel thus, or whose starting-point was not near a navigable stream, could come overland. Illinois was favored by having a number of large rivers leading toward it; the Ohio, Kentucky, Cumberland, Tennessee, and their tributaries were much used by emigrants.

1. "'Father Clark,' or the Pioneer Preacher," 202; Moses, "Illinois," I., 228.
2. "Pub. Lands," I., 256.
3. "Annals of Cong.," 9th Cong., 1st Sess., 469. The land bought in Kentucky was probably near Eddyville, which the purchaser founded.

OBSTACLES TO IMMIGRATION. 93

The chief route by land was the Wilderness Road, over which thousands of the inhabitants of Kentucky had come. Its existence helps to explain the wonderful growth of Kentucky—in 1774 the first cabin, in 1790 a population of 73,000. It crossed the mountains at Cumberland Gap, wound its way by the most convenient course to Crab Orchard, and was early extended to the Falls of the Ohio and later to Vincennes and St. Louis. The legislature of Kentucky provided, in 1795, that the road from Cumberland Gap to Crab Orchard should be made perfectly commodious and passable for wagons carrying a weight of one ton, and appropriated two thousand pounds for the work. Two years later five hundred dollars were appropriated for the repair of the road, and the highway was made a turnpike with prescribed toll, although it did not become such a road as the word turnpike suggests.[1]

A traveler of 1807 described the river craft of the period. The smallest kind in use was a simple log canoe. This was followed by the pirogue, which was a larger kind of canoe and sufficiently strong and capacious to carry from twelve to fifteen barrels of salt. Skiffs were built of all sizes, from five hundred to twenty thousand pounds burden, and batteaux were the same as the larger skiffs, being indifferently known by either name. Kentucky boats were strong frames of an oblong form, varying in size from twenty to fifty feet in length and from ten to fourteen in breadth, were sided and roofed, and guided by huge oars. New Orleans boats resembled Kentucky boats, but were larger and stronger and had arched roofs. The largest could carry four hundred and fifty barrels of flour. Keel boats were generally built from forty to eighty feet in length and from seven to nine feet in width. The largest

1. Littell, "Laws of Ky.," I., 275-7, 687; Speed, "The Wilderness Road," *passim.*

required one man to steer and two to row in descending the Ohio, and would carry about one hundred barrels of salt; but to ascend the stream, at least six or eight men were required to make any considerable progress. A barge would carry from four thousand to sixty thousand pounds, and required four men, besides the helmsman, to descend the river, while to return with a load from eight to twelve men were required.[1]

Shipments of produce from Illinois were usually made in flat-bottomed boats of fifteen tons burden. Such a boat cost about one hundred dollars, the crew of five men was paid one hundred dollars each, the support of the crew was reckoned at one hundred dollars, and insurance at one hundred dollars, thus making a freightage cost of eight hundred dollars for fifteen tons. The boat was either set adrift or sold for the price of firewood at New Orleans. It was estimated that the use of boats of four hundred and fifty tons burden would save four dollars per barrel on shipping flour to New Orleans, where flour had often sold at less than three dollars per barrel, but such boats were not yet used in the West.[2] Canoes cost an emigrant from one to three dollars; pirogues, five to twenty dollars; small skiffs, five to ten dollars; large skiffs or batteaux, twenty to fifty dollars; Kentucky and New Orleans boats, one dollar to one and one-half dollars per foot; keel boats, two dollars and a half to three dollars per foot; and barges, four to five dollars per foot.[3]

Horses, cattle, and household goods were carried on boats. Travel by either land or water was beset with difficulties. The river, without pilot or dredge, had dan-

1. Schultz, "Travels on an Inland Voyage," I., 129–32.
2. "Annals of Cong.," 9th Cong., 1st Sess., 1049. Speech by Matthew Lyon of Kentucky.
3. Schultz, "Travels on an Inland Voyage," I., 132.

OBSTACLES TO IMMIGRATION.

gers peculiar to itself. Sometimes, when traveling overland, a broken wheel or axle, or a horse lost or stolen by Indians, caused protracted and vexatious delays. It is well to notice, also, that to travel a given distance into the wilderness was more than twice as difficult as to travel one-half that distance, because of the constantly increasing separation between the traveler and what had previously been his base of supplies.[1]

Sometimes immigrants debarked at Fort Massac and completed their journey by land. Two roads led from Fort Massac, one called the lower road and the other the upper road, the former, practicable only in the dry season and then only for travel on foot or on horseback, was some eighty miles long, while the latter was one hundred and fifty miles long. Roads of a like character connected Kaskaskia and Cahokia.[2]

A party of more than one hundred and fifty, which came from Virginia to the New Design settlement in 1797, set out from the south branch of the Potomac. They came from Redstone (now Brownsville), on the Monongahela, to Fort Massac, on flat-boats, and then by land, in twenty-one days, to New Design. The summer was wet and hot, a malignant fever broke out among the newcomers, and one-half of them died before winter. The old settlers were not affected by the fever, but they were too few to properly care for so many immigrants.[3]

Commerce in Illinois was in its infancy. Some cattle,

---

1. For vivid accounts of journeys between the East and Ohio, giving an excellent idea of the difficulties of transit, in the period 1795-1809, see Cutler, "Life and Times of Ephraim Cutler," 17-22, 38-41, 90-103; also, many passages in Cutler, "Life, Journals and Corr. of Rev. Manasseh Cutler." A similar journey made in 1790 is described in "St. Clair Papers," II., 164.

2. Collot, "Journey in N. A.," I., 192-3, 239.

3. "'Father Clark,' or The Pioneer Preacher," 193.

corn, pork, and various other commodities were sent at irregular intervals to New Orleans.[1] The fur trade was carried on much as under the French régime. Salt was made at the salt springs on Saline Creek, the labor being performed chiefly by Kentucky and Tennessee slaves under the supervision of contractors who leased the works from the United States. The contractors agreed to sell no salt at the works for more than fifty cents per bushel, but by means of silent partners to whom the entire supply was sold, the price was sometimes raised as high as two dollars per bushel.[2] The commerce of the West suffered from a lack of vessels going from New Orleans to Atlantic ports, and as a result corn sold in New Orleans at fifty cents per bushel in 1805, while in some of the Atlantic ports it sold for more than two dollars. At the same time the West had a good crop, and Kentucky alone could have spared five hundred thousand bushels of corn, if it could have been shipped.[3]

To secure laborers was difficult. A petition of 1796 said that farm laborers could not be secured for less than one dollar per day, exclusive of washing, lodging, and boarding; that every kind of tradesman was paid from one dollar and a half to two dollars per day, and that at these prices laborers were scarce. Labor was cheaper on the Spanish side of the Mississippi, because of the larger proportion of slaves.[4] These wages were doubtless high in comparison with those paid in the East, just as the one dollar per day and board paid at the Galena lead mines in

---

1. Schultz, "Travels on an Inland Voyage," II., 38.

2. Cuming, "Sketches of a Tour," 245; Schultz, "Travels on an Inland Voyage," I., 199; Moses, "Illinois," I., 265.

3. "Annals of Cong.," 9th Cong., 1st Sess., 1049. Speech by Matthew Lyon of Kentucky.

4. "Pub. Lands," I., 69; "Ind. Hist. Soc. Pub.," II., 448.

1788 was more than double the wages then paid in New England,[1] but an Illinois price list of 1795 shows that the wages of 1796 were by no means comparable to those of today in purchasing power. Making shoes was two dollars per pair; potatoes were one dollar per bushel; brandy, one dollar per quart; corn, one dollar per bushel.[2]

Among the early difficulties in the way of settlement, one of the most persistent was the presence of prairies. This is by no means far-fetched, although it sounds so to modern ears. In 1786, Monroe wrote to Jefferson concerning the Northwest Territory: "A great part of the territory is miserably poor, especially that near Lakes Michigan and Erie, and that upon the Mississippi and the Illinois consists of extensive plains which have not had, from appearances, and will not have, a single bush on them for ages. The districts, therefore, within which these fall will never contain a sufficient number of inhabitants to entitle them to membership in the confederacy."[3] Some of the most fertile of the Illinois prairies were not settled until far into the nineteenth century. The false prophets of the early days will be judged less harshly if we recall that wood was then a necessity, that no railroads and few roads existed, that wells now in use in prairie regions are much deeper than the early settlers could dig, and that the vast quantities of coal under the surface of Illinois were undiscovered.

As causes for the fact that more than a quarter of a century after the Revolution, Illinois had a population estimated at only eleven thousand, may be suggested the

1. Ethelbert Stewart, "A Few Notes for an Industrial Hist. of Ill.," in "Pub. No. 8 of the Ill. Hist. Lib.," 120.

2. "Draper Coll., Ill. MSS.," 73, 74. Original accounts of Wm. Biggs, high sheriff of the county of St. Clair in the N.-W. Ter.

3. Hamilton, "Writings of James Monroe," I., 117.

presence of hostile Indians; the inability of settlers to secure a title to their land; the unsettled condition of the slavery question; the great distance from the older portions of the United States and from any market; the fact that Kentucky, Ohio, and Indiana had vast quantities of unoccupied land more accessible to emigrants than was Illinois; the danger and the cost of moving; privation incident to a scanty population, such as lack of roads, schools, churches and mills; the existence of large prairies in Illinois. To remove or mitigate these difficulties was still the problem of Illinois settlers. On some of them a beginning had been made before 1809, but none were yet removed.

CHAPTER IV.

ILLINOIS DURING ITS TERRITORIAL PERIOD
1809 TO 1818.

I.

THE LAND AND INDIAN QUESTIONS.

PROBABLY nothing affected settlement in Illinois from 1809 to 1818 more profoundly than did changes in the land question, for during this period Congress passed important acts relative to land sales, and this was also the period of the first sales of public lands in the territory. It seems strange that such sales should have been so long delayed, yet the settlement of French claims, although begun by the Governor of the Northwest Territory at an early day, and continued by commissioners authorized by Congress and appointed in 1804, was incomplete when Illinois became a separate territory, and the United States government adhered to its policy of selling no land in the territory until the claims were finally adjudicated. When a list of decisions reported by the commissioners to Congress late in 1809 was confirmed in the following May,[1] and the next year a long list of rejected claims arising chiefly from the work of professional falsifiers, was reported,[2] it seemed probable that the work was nearing completion, but a final settlement was still delayed, and the long-suffering Illinois squatters were bitterly disappointed when, in February, 1812, in accordance with a resolution presented by the Committee on Public Lands, Congress made provision for the appointment of a committee to revise the confirmations made by the Governor years before.[3] The

---
1. "Statutes at Large," II., 607.   2. "Pub. Lands," II., 123.
3. "Statutes at Large," II., 677; "Pub. Lands," II., 254-5, 257-8, 210-41.

first legislature of Illinois met in the succeeding November, and adopted a memorial to Congress in which it was pointed out that the establishment of a land-office in the territory, several years before, had led to the opinion that the public land would soon be sold, and that because of this opinion those who constituted the majority of the inhabitants of the territory had been induced to settle, hoping that they would have an opportunity to purchase land before they should have made such improvements as would tempt the competition of avaricious speculators. The fulfillment of this hope having been long deferred, many squatters had now made valuable improvements which they were in danger of losing, either at the public sales of land or through the designs of the few speculators who had bought from the needy and unbusinesslike French most of the unlocated claims. For the relief of the squatters a law was desired that would permit actual settlers to enter the land on which their improvements stood, and requiring persons holding unlocated claims to locate them on unimproved lands lying in the region designated by Congress for that purpose. It was also hoped that as Congress had given one hundred acres of land to each regular soldier, as much would be granted to each member of the Illinois militia, since the militiaman had not only fought as bravely as the regular, but had also furnished his own supplies. If such a donation was not made it was hoped that a right of preëmption would be given to the militia, or failing even this, that they might be given the right, legally, to collect from anyone entering their land, the value of their improvements.[1] In proof of the fact stated in the memorial, that speculators had bought many French claims, it may be noted that William Mor-

---

1. "Territorial Records of Ill.," ("Pub. of Ill. State Hist. Lib.," No. III., 109-10).

rison had ninety-two of the claims granted at Kaskaskia, his affirmed claims comprising more than eighteen thousand acres, exclusive of a large number of claims measured in French units, while John Edgar received a satisfactory report on claims aggregating more than forty thousand acres, in addition to a number of claims previously affirmed to him.[1]

A few days after preparing the above memorial, the legislature prepared an address to Congress, in which reference was made to the arrangement made between Congress and Ohio by the Act of April 30, 1802, granting to Ohio two salt springs on condition that the state should agree not to tax such public lands as should be sold within her borders, until after five years from the date of sale. Illinois wished in similar fashion to gain control of the salt springs on Saline creek. The Illinois delegate in Congress was instructed that if the bargain could not be made, he should attempt to secure an appropriation for opening a road from Shawneetown to the Saline and thence to Kaskaskia. It was also desired that the Secretary of the Treasury should authorize the designation of the college township reserved by the Ordinance of 1787 and by the Act of 1804, and because "labor in this Territory is abundant, and laborers at this time extremely scarce," it was hoped that slaves from Kentucky or elsewhere might be employed at the salines for a period of not more than three years, after which they should return to their masters.[2] Each prayer of this address was granted. The enabling act and the Illinois constitution ceded the salt springs to the state and agreed that public lands sold in

---

1. "Pub. Lands," II., 157-81, 210-41.

2. "Territorial Records of Ill.," ("Pub. of the Ill. State Hist. Lib.," No. III., 118-20); "Statutes at Large," II., 175; "Annals of Cong." (ed. 1853), 12th Cong., III., 883, 1011, 1015.

Illinois should be exempt from taxation for five years from date of sale; the Illinois Constitution provided for the employment of slaves at the salt works; an act provided for the location of the college township; and in 1816 the making of the desired road was authorized, although at the beginning of 1818 the route had been merely surveyed and mapped.[1]

The memorial which preceded the address was also in large measure successful. An act of February, 1813, granted to the squatters in Illinois the right of preëmpting a quarter section, each, of the lands they occupied, and of entering the land upon the payment of one-twentieth of the purchase money, as was then required in private sales.[2] This act was of prime importance. For more than thirty years settlers in Illinois had improved their lands at the risk of losing them. Since the appointment, in 1804, of commissioners to settle the French land claims, the settlers had been expecting the public lands, including those they occupied, to be offered for sale; thus it was inevitable that anxiety concerning the right of preëmption should increase as the settlement of claims neared completion, and contemporaries record that the inability to secure land titles seriously retarded settlement;[3] now, however, the granting of the right of preëmption, before any public lands in Illinois were offered for sale, ended the long suspense of the settlers. Years before this, Kentucky, now selling its public lands at twenty cents per acre, had passed liberal preëmption laws, and they were repeatedly renewed,[4] facts which increased the anxiety of Illinois.

1. "State Papers," 15th Cong., 1st Sess., III., No. 61, p. 6; Poore, "Charters and Constitutions," Pt. I., 436, 438, 445; "Statutes at Large," III., 318.

2. "Statutes at Large," II., 797.

3. Reynolds, "Illinois—My Own Times," 156.

4. Littell, "Laws of Ky.," I., 430; "Acts of 1811" (Ky.), 213-15; "Acts of 1816" (Ky.), 107; "Acts of 1817" (Ky.), 326.

TERRITORIAL PERIOD.

Year after year the settlement of land claims dragged on, thus delaying the sales of land.[1] In an official report of December, 1813, it is stated that: "In the Territory of Illinois, two land-offices are directed by law to be opened; one at Kaskaskia, the other at Shawneetown, so soon as the private claims and donations are all located, and the lands surveyed, which are in great forwardness."[2] A tract of land was set apart in April, 1814, to satisfy the claims recommended by the commissioners for confirmation.[3] A report of November, 1815, said that the commissioners hoped to open the land-office at Kaskaskia on May 15, 1816; and finally, in a report on the public lands sold from October 1, 1815, to September 30, 1816, we find that about thirty-four thousand acres have been sold at Shawneetown and somewhat less than thirteen thousand acres at Kaskaskia, the price at the latter place being precisely the two dollars per acre which was then the minimum, while that at Shawneetown was slightly higher,[4] presumably due to the sale of town lots, which had been authorized in 1810, although no sales took place earlier than 1814.[5]

The long delay in opening the land-offices in Illinois was fatal to an early settlement of the region, because the old states had public lands which they offered for sale at low rates, thus depriving Illinois of a fair chance as a competitor. In 1779 Kentucky granted to each family which had settled before January 1, 1778, the right of preëmption—four hundred acres if no improvement had been made and one thousand acres if a hut had been built. The preëmptor, by a law of 1786, was to pay 13s.

1. "Pub. Lands," III., 2.
2. *Ibid.*, II., 873-4.
3. "Statutes at Large," III., 125.
4. "State Papers," II., 14th Cong., 2d Sess., folio. Other volumes of the same number and session are quarto.
5. "Statutes at Large," II., 591; III., 113; "Pub. Lands," II., 873-4.

4d. per one hundred acres.¹ In 1781 the sheriffs of Lincoln, Fayette, and Jefferson counties, Virginia, were authorized to survey not more than four hundred acres for each poor family in Kentucky, for which twenty shillings per one hundred acres should be paid within two and one-half years.² In 1791 more than three and one-half millions of acres were sold in New York at eight pence per acre, while many thousands of acres in addition were sold for less than four shillings per acre—many for less than two shillings.³ Pennsylvania offered homestead claims, in 1792, at seven pounds ten shillings per hundred acres.⁴

In December, 1796, Kentucky sheriffs were ordered to sell no more land for taxes until directed by the legislature to do so.⁵ In 1800, and again in 1812, Kentucky offered land at twenty cents per acre, and in 1820 at fifteen cents per acre,⁶ while during the interval preëmption acts were repeatedly passed.⁷ Land in Tennessee sold at from twelve and one-half to twenty-five cents per acre in 1814, and in 1819 at fifty cents.⁸

In 1816 various classes of claimants were given increased facilities and an extension of time for locating their claims in Illinois. The business of satisfying claims was to linger

1. Littell, "Laws of Ky.," I., 395–7, 456.
2. *Ibid.*, I., 430.
3. O'Callaghan, "Doc. Hist. of N. Y.," III., 1069–83, quarto; 649–57, folio.
4. Agnew, "Settlement and Land Titles of N.-W. Pa.," 118–19. See also "Jour. of H. of R." (Pa.), 1792-1794, first page of second appendix to record of 1st Sess. of 3d House; *ibid.*, first page of second appendix to record of 1st Sess. of 4th House; Sergeant, "View of the Land Laws of Pa., with Notices of Its Early Hist. and Legislation," *passim*.
5. Littell, "Laws of Ky.," I., 516.
6. *Ibid.*, II., 420–2; "Acts of 1811" (Ky.), 213–15; "Acts of 1817" (Ky.), 554; "Acts of 1819" (Ky.), 832.
7. "Acts of 1816" (Ky.), 107; "Acts of 1817" (Ky.), 326.
8. Phelan, "Hist. of Tenn.," 303. Quoted from Jones, "The Chickasaw Country Lately Ceded to the U. S." (1819).

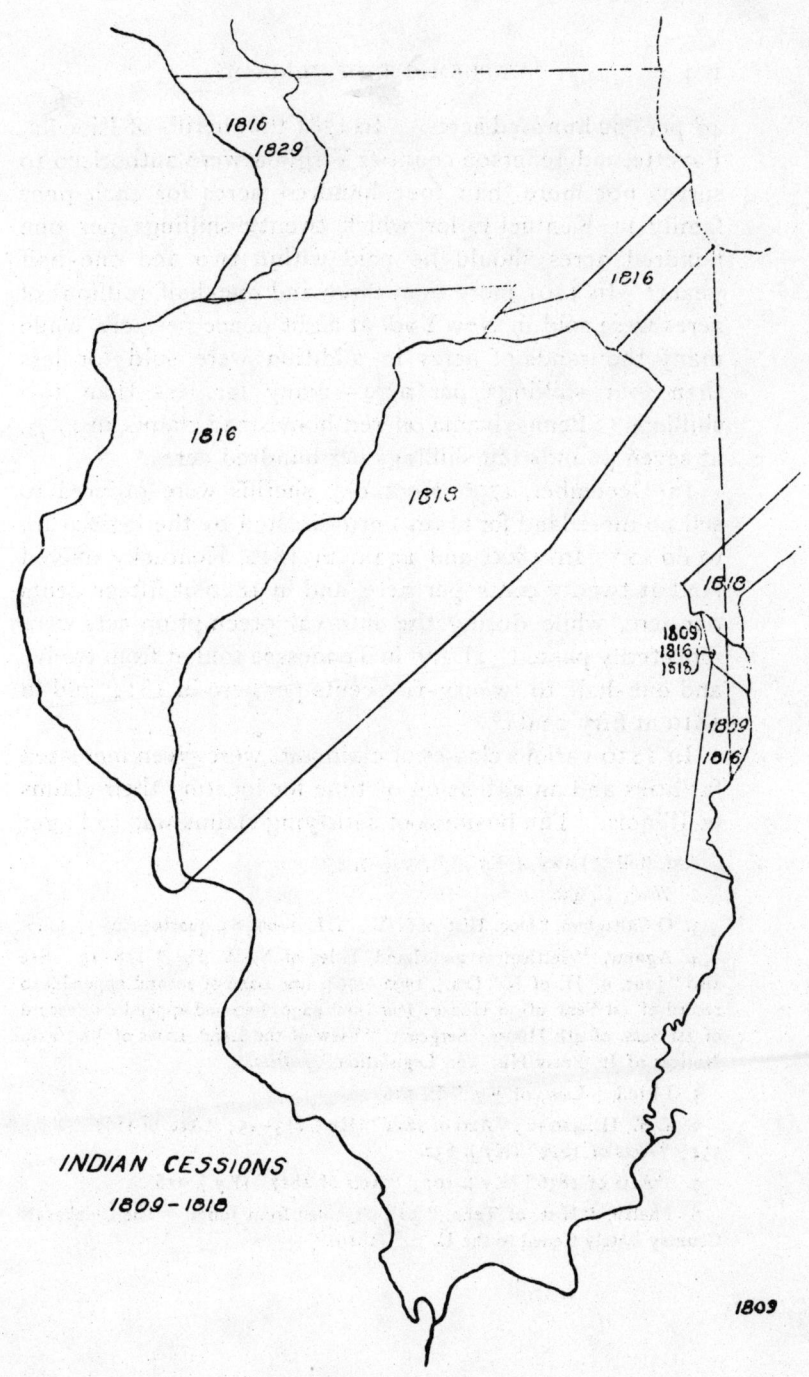

TERRITORIAL PERIOD.

for years, but with the opening of the land-offices it ceased to be a potent factor in retarding settlement.¹

One writer says of Illinois: "The public lands have rarely sold for more than five dollars per acre, *at auction*. Those sold at Edwardsville in October, 1816, averaged four dollars. Private sales at the land-office are fixed by law, at two dollars per acre. The old French locations command various prices, from one to fifty dollars. Titles derived from the United States government are always valid, and those from individuals rarely false." At this time emigrants were going in large numbers to Missouri, and the Illinois river country, not yet relieved of its Indian title, was being explored.⁷

Reports concerning the sales of public lands give the quantity of land sold in Illinois toward the close of the territorial period, the figures for 1817 and 1818 being as follows:

	Acres in 1817.	Acres in 1818.	Total balance due: Jan. 1, 1818.	Sept. 30, 1818.
Shawneetown,	72,384	216,315	$291,429	$ 637,468
Kaskaskia,	90,493	121,052	209,295	406,288
Edwardsville,⁵	149,165	121,923	301,701	451,499⁴
	312,042	459,290	$802,425	$1,495,255

The percentage of debt showed a marked increase in the first nine months of 1818. There were received in three-quarters of 1817 and 1818, respectively:

1. "Statutes at Large," III., 307; "Pub. Lands," II., 741; III., 1-5, 384-5.
2. Brown, "Western Gazetteer, or Emigrants' Directory" (1817), 33.
3. White, "Descendants of John Walker," 458-9, 461.
4. "State Papers," No. 52, 15th Cong., 2d Sess., IV. Hundredths of acres and cents are omitted from the tables. The figures for Shawneetown cover the periods from Jan. 1 to Sept. 30; those for the other offices, from Jan. 1 to Aug. 31.
5. A land-office was established at Edwardsville by an act of Apr. 29, 1816.

	1817.	1818.
At Shawneetown	$32,837	$112,759
At Kaskaskia	41,218	68,975
At Edwardsville	41,426	78,788

During this same period the receipts at Steubenville, Marietta, and Wooster, Ohio, decreased,[1] showing that Illinois was beginning to surpass Ohio as an objective point for emigrants wishing to enter land.

The Indian question was interwoven with the land question during the territorial period. In 1809 the Indians relinquished their claim to some small tracts of land lying near the point where the Wabash ceases to be a state boundary line.[2] No more cessions were made until after the war of 1812. Although the population of Illinois increased, during the territorial period, from some eleven thousand to about forty thousand, the increase before the war was slight, and thus it came about that during the war the few whites were kept busy defending themselves from the large and hostile Indian population. So well does the manner of defence in Illinois illustrate the frontier character of the region that a sketch of the same may be given. When, in 1811, the Indians became hostile and murdered a few whites, the condition of the settlers was precarious in the extreme. Today the term city would be almost a favor to a place containing no more inhabitants than were then to be found in the white settlements in Illinois. Moreover, few as were the whites, they were dispersed in a long half-oval extending from a point on the Mississippi near the present Alton southward to the Ohio, and thence up that river and the Wabash to a point considerably north of Vincennes. This fringe of settlement was but a few miles

---

1. "Pub. Lands," III., 405.

2. "Indian Aff.," I., 761-2; 18th An. Rept. of the Bureau of Ethnology," Pt. 2, 678; Nos. 73, 74, Plate CXXIV. See map of Indian cessions.

wide in some places, while so sparse was the population near the mouth of the Ohio that the communication between northern and southern Indians was unchecked. Carlyle was regarded as the extreme eastern boundary of settlements to the westward; a fort on Muddy River, near where the old Fort Massac trace crossed the stream, was considered as one of the most exposed situations; and Fort La Motte, on a creek of the same name above Vincennes, was a far northern point. The exposed outside was some hundreds of miles long, and the interior and north were occupied by ten times as many hostile savages as there were whites in the country, the savages being given counsel and ammunition by the British garrisons on the north.[1] Under conditions then existing, aid from the United States could be expected only in the event of dire necessity. Stout frontiersmen were almost ready to seek refuge in flight, but no general exodus took place, although in February, 1812, Governor Edwards wrote to the Secretary of War: "The alarms and apprehensions of the people are becoming so universal, that really I should not be surprised if we should, in three months, lose more than one-half of our present population. In places, in my opinion, entirely out of danger, many are removing. In other parts, large settlements are about to be totally deserted. Even in my own neighborhood, several families have removed, and others are preparing to do so in a week or two. A few days past, a gentleman of respectability arrived here from Kentucky, and he informed me that he saw on the road, in one day, upwards of twenty wagons conveying families out of this Territory. Every effort to check the prevalence of such terror seems to be ineffectual, and although much of it is unreasonably indulged, yet it is very certain the Territory will very shortly be in considerable

[1]. Reynolds, "Illinois—My Own Times," 81-4.

danger. Its physical force is very inconsiderable, and is growing weaker, while it presents numerous points of attack."[1]

To the first feeling of fear succeeded a determination to hold the ground. Before the middle of 1812, Governor Edwards had established Fort Russell, a few miles northwest of the present Edwardsville, bringing to this place, which was to be his headquarters, the cannon which Louis XIV. had had placed in Fort Chartres;[2] and two volunteer companies had been raised, and had "ranged to a great distance—principally between the Illinois and the Kaskaskia rivers, and sometimes between the Kaskaskia and the Wabash—always keeping their line of march never less than one and sometimes three days' journey outside of all the settlements"[3]—which incidentally shows what great unoccupied regions still existed even in the southern part of Illinois. As the rangers furnished their own supplies, the two companies went out alternately for periods of fifteen days. Sometimes the company on duty divided, one part marching in one direction and the other in the opposite, in order to produce the greatest possible effect upon the Indians. Settlers on the frontier—and that comprised a large proportion of the population—"forted themselves," as it was then expressed. Where a few families lived near each other, one of the most substantial houses was fortified, and here the community staid at night, and in case of imminent danger in the daytime as well. Isolated outlying families left their homes and retired to the nearest fort. Such places of refuge were numerous and many were the attacks which they successfully withstood.

1. Edwards, "Hist. of Ill. and Life of Ninian Edwards," 301.
2. Reynolds, "Illinois—My Own Times," 82.
3. Edwards, "Hist. of Ill. and Life of Ninian Edwards," 329.

TERRITORIAL PERIOD. 109

Rangers and frontier forts were used with much effect, but the great dispersion of settlement and the large numbers of Indians combined to make it wholly impossible to make such means of defence entirely adequate. In August, 1812, the Governor wrote to the Secretary of War: "The principal settlements of this Territory being on the Mississippi, are at least one hundred and fifty miles from those of Indiana, and immense prairies intervene between them. There can, therefore, be no concert of operations for the protection of their frontiers and ours. . . . No troops of any kind have yet arrived in this Territory, and I think you may count on hearing of a bloody stroke upon us very soon. I have been extremely reluctant to send my family away, but, unless I hear shortly of more assistance than a few rangers, I shall bury my papers in the ground, send my family off, and stand my ground as long as possible."[1] The "bloody stroke" predicted by the Governor fell on the garrison at Fort Dearborn, where Chicago now stands. Some regular troops were subsequently sent to the territory, but the war did not lose its frontier character. One of the most characteristic features was that troops sometimes set out on a campaign of considerable length, in an uninhabited region, without any baggage train and practically without pack horses, the men carrying their provisions on their horses, and the horses living on wild grass.[2] Unflagging energy was shown by the settlers, several effective campaigns being carried on, and by the close of 1814 the war was closed in Illinois.[3]

Extinction of Indian titles to land was retarded by the war and also by the policy of the United States, which was expressed by Secretary of War Crawford, in 1816, as fol-

1. Edwards, "Hist. of Ill. and Life of Ninian Edwards," 335.
2. Reynolds, "Illinois—My Own Times," 86-7.
3. *Ibid.*, 102.

lows: "The determination to purchase land only when demanded for settlement will form the settled policy of the Government. Experience has sufficiently proven that our population will spread over any cession, however extensive, before it can be brought into market, and before there is any regular and steady demand for settlement, thereby increasing the difficulty of protection, embarrassing the Government by broils with the natives, and rendering the execution of the laws regulating intercourse with the Indian tribes utterly impracticable."[1] Some progress, however, was made in extinguishing Indian titles during the territorial period after the close of the war. In 1816, several tribes confirmed the cession of 1804 of land lying south of an east and west line passing through the southern point of Lake Michigan, and ceded a route for an Illinois-Michigan canal.[2] At Edwardsville, on September 25, 1818, the Peoria, Kaskaskia, Michigamia, Cahokia, and Tamarois ceded a tract comprising most of southern and much of central Illinois.[3] The significance of this cession would have been immense had it not been that it was made by weak tribes, while the powerful Kickapoo still claimed and held all that part of the ceded tract lying north of the parallel of 39°—a little to the north of the mouth of the Illinois river. This Kickapoo claim included the fertile and already famous Sangamon country, in which the state capital was eventually to be located, and squatters were pressing hard upon the Indian

1. "Indian Aff.," II., 99.

2. "Indian Aff.," II., 95–6; "18th An. Rept. of the Bureau of Ethnology," Pt. 2, 680–3, No. 77, Plate CXXV., and No. 78, Plate CXXIV. See map of Indian cessions.

3. "Indian Aff.," II., 167; "18th An. Rept. of the Bureau of Ethnology," Pt. 2, 692–3; No. 96a, Plate CXXIV. See also No. 48 on the same plate, and No. 77, Plate CXXV. See map of Indian cessions.

frontier, yet the Indians still held the land when Illinois became a state.

During the territorial period, Illinois gained the long-sought right of preëmption; the French claims ceased to retard settlement; some progress was made in the extinction of Indian titles, and the sale of public land was begun. The new state was to find the Indian question a pressing one, and some changes in the land system were yet desired, but the crucial point was passed.

II.
Territorial Government of Illinois 1809 to 1818.

The act for the division of Indiana Territory provided that Illinois, during the first stage of its territorial existence, should have a government similar to that of the Northwest Territory under the Ordinance of 1787. In 1809 there were in Illinois two distinct and hostile parties, which had been formed on questions arising in Indiana Territory before division. It was with sound judgment, therefore, that the President, going outside of Illinois, appointed as Governor, Ninian Edwards of Kentucky, a native of Maryland, who successfully resisted all efforts to involve him in party quarrels.[1]

Laws for the government of the territory were to be chosen by the Governor and the judges from the laws of the states. The judges were Jesse B. Thomas and William Sprigg, natives of Maryland, and Alexander Stuart, a native of Virginia. It is worthy of note that of the twelve laws chosen before the meeting of the first territorial

1. "Territorial Records of Ill.," ("Pub. of the Ill. Hist. Lib.," No. III., 3, 6, 7).

legislature, five were from Kentucky, three from Georgia, two from Virginia, one from South Carolina, and one from Pennsylvania.[1] A people practically southern in origin was being governed by officials from the south under southern laws.

Illinois entered the second grade of territorial government in 1812, electing its first legislature in October.[2] In the preceding May, Congress had passed an act making radical and most important extensions in the suffrage in Illinois, over that which had been prescribed by the Ordinance of 1787. The new provision was: "Every free white male person who shall have attained the age of twenty-one years, and who shall have paid a county or territorial tax, and who shall have resided one year in said Territory previous to any general election, and be at the time of any such election a resident thereof, shall be entitled to vote for members of the Legislative Council and House of Representatives of the said Territory." Each county was to elect one member of the Legislative Council, to serve for four years. The territorial delegate to Congress was also made elective by the citizens.[3] One has but to consider what a complete revolution this act brought about to appreciate its great significance. Previously the Legislative Council had been appointive by the President of the United States, from nominees of the territorial House of Representatives, the nominees being twice the number

1. "Territorial Records of Ill." ("Pub. of the Ill. Hist. Lib.," No. III., 10–19). Of the thirty-eight laws selected by the Governor and judges in the Northwest Territory, three were from the codes of southern states; of the fifteen so selected in Indiana Territory, thirteen were from southern codes— "Ind. Hist. Soc. Pamphlets," No. I., 16; contained in Vol. 2 of "Publications." Illinois was thus most southern of the three.

2. "Territorial Records of Ill." ("Pub. of the Ill. Hist. Lib.," No. III., 23, 26–7).

3. "Statutes at Large," II., 741–2.

necessary; the delegate to Congress had not been chosen by popular vote; and a freehold qualification for the elective franchise had obtained. Early petitions show how much the people complained of a landed aristocracy,[1] and letters written by Governor Edwards early in 1812 show how well founded was the complaint. No preëmption act had yet been passed, and of the more than twelve thousand inhabitants of Illinois some two hundred and twenty possessed a freehold of fifty acres, thus giving the balance of power, if the territory should enter the second grade under the old provision, to one hundred and eleven persons. Nearly one-third of the entire population lived either near the Ohio or between it and the Kaskaskia, and among them there were not more than three or four freeholders, and not one who possessed two hundred acres—the necessary qualification for a representative. With no public lands yet offered for sale, with no right of preëmption, with a freehold qualification for the suffrage, this law enfranchising squatters was of prime importance.[2]

The first legislature had few French members, and was apparently southern in nativity.[3] After more than three

1. "Ind. Hist. Soc. Pub.," II., 461–70.
2. Edwards, "Hist. of Ill. and Life of Ninian Edwards," 296, 306.
3. "Territorial Records of Ill." ("Pub. of Ill. Hist. Lib.," No. III., 62, 86).

Legislative Council.	Nativity.	County.	Territorial Judges.	
Pierre Menard,	Canada,	Randolph.	Jesse B. Thomas,	Maryland.
Wm. Biggs,	Md.	St. Clair.	Alexander Stuart,	Virginia.
Sam'l Judy,	Swiss or Md.	Madison.	William Sprigg,	Maryland.
Thos. Ferguson,		Johnson.	Territorial Secretaries.	
Benjamin Talbott,		Gallatin.	Nathaniel Pope,	Kentucky.
House of Reps.			Joseph Philips,	Tennessee.
Dr. George Fisher, Va.,		Randolph.	Delegates in Congress.	Term.
Rev. Joshua Oglesby,		St. Clair.	Shadrach Bond, Md, Dec. 3, 1812–14.	
Jacob Short,		St. Clair.	Benj. Stephenson, Ky, Nov 14 1814–16.	
Rev. Wm. Jones	N. C.	Madison.	Nathan'l Pope, Ky, Dec. 2, 1816–18.	
Philip Trammell,		Gallatin.		
Alex. Wilson,	Va.,	Gallatin.	Governor.	
John Grammar,		Johnson.	Ninian Edwards, Md., 1809–1818.	

Officers other than members are added to the above in order to emphasize the southern origin of Illinois territorial officials. New England was not yet a factor in Illinois politics.

years and a half of legislation by the Governor and judges, the inhabitants at last had an elective legislature. The journals of the two houses indicate that the belief that had been expressed in petitions to Congress some years before that such a body would provide an efficient government, was well founded. The laws passed were eminently practical for the frontier conditions under which they were to operate.[1] A man contemplating settlement in Illinois could now be sure that he would be governed by Illinois men whom he had a share in electing.

The rude character of the facilities for transportation is indicated by the fact that the earlier laws of the territory deal with ferries only rarely and with bridges not at all, while as time progresses and population increases, ferries multiply and bridges begin to be constructed. By 1817-18 the desire for banks and for internal improvements, which was to be disastrous to the state at a later period, began to show itself. As examples, the Bank of Cairo and the Illinois Navigation Company will suffice. Nine men purchased the low peninsula lying near the junction of the Ohio and the Mississippi, and were incorporated by "An Act to Incorporate the City and Bank of Cairo." A site for a city comprising at least two thousand lots, with streets eighty feet wide, was to be laid out. The lots were to be sold at one hundred and fifty dollars each and were to be not less than one hundred and twenty by sixty-six feet in size. Of the purchase money, two-thirds should go into the stock of the Bank of Cairo, and one-third to a fund to build dykes to keep the city from being flooded.[2] Considering the time and the location, the scheme was utterly impracticable "An Act to Incor-

[1] "Territorial Records of Illinois" ("Pub. of the Ill. Hist. Lib.," No. III., 62-170).

[2] "Laws of Ill. Ter., 1817-18," pp. 72-82; *Ibid.*, 1815-16, p. 44.

porate the Stockholders of the Illinois Navigation Company" authorized the formation of a company with a capital of one hundred thousand dollars, for the purpose of cutting a canal through the peninsula between the Ohio and the Mississippi. Within twelve years a canal sufficiently large for the passage of a vessel of twenty tons burden should be completed. The company was given the right of eminent domain.[1] Here again the character of the project was unsuited to existing conditions. Population was increasing rapidly at the time these laws were passed, but they required for their success an increase much more rapid. They were, however, pleasing to the settlers and the prospective settlers of the day.

On January 16, 1818, Mr. Pope, of Illinois, was appointed chairman of a select committee to consider a petition from the Illinois legislature praying for a state government. One week later the committee reported a bill to enable Illinois to form such a government, and to admit the state into the union. When the enabling act came up for discussion, Mr. Pope offered the amendment which changed the northern boundary of Illinois from a line due west from the southern extremity of Lake Michigan, as provided by the Ordinance of 1787, to a line running from that lake to the Mississippi on the parallel of 42° 30´. "The object of this amendment, Mr. Pope said, was to gain, for the proposed state, a coast on Lake Michigan. This would offer additional security to the perpetuity of the union, inasmuch as the state would thereby be connected with the states of Indiana, Ohio, Pennsylvania, and New York, through the lakes. The facility of opening a canal between Lake Michigan and the Illinois River, said Mr. Pope, is acknowledged by every one who has visited the place. Giving to the proposed state the port of Chicago

1. "Laws of Ill. Ter., 1817-18," pp. 57-64.

(embraced in the proposed limits), will draw its attention to the opening of the communication between the Illinois River and that place, and the improvement of that harbor. It was believed, he said, upon good authority, that the line of separation between Indiana and Illinois would strike Lake Michigan south of Chicago, and not pass west of it, as had been supposed by some geographers . . . ." Although an avowed violation of the Ordinance of 1787, the amendment was adopted without division or recorded debate. Mr. Pope also secured an amendment to the effect that the state's proportion of the proceeds of the sales of public lands, instead of being applied to the making of roads and canals in the state, should be used in making roads leading to the state, and for the encouragement of learning, two-fifths being applied to the former purpose. Pope pointed out that people would build roads as they needed them, much more readily than they would supply schools, and that waste school lands in a new country would produce slight revenue. Subsequent history of the state justified both statements. The enabling act met with little opposition and was signed by President Monroe on April 18, 1818.[1]

One of the provisions of the enabling act was that, in order to become a state, Illinois must have as many as forty thousand inhabitants. In anticipation of such a provision, the territorial legislature had passed a law in January, 1818, providing that a census of the territory should be taken between April 1 and June 1. A supplemental act provided that as a great increase in population might be expected between June 1 and December, census takers should continue to take the census in their districts

1. "Annals of Cong.," 15th Cong., 1st Sess., 1677, 1738; "H. J.," 15th Cong., 1st Sess., 151, 174; Benton, "Abridgment of Debates in Cong.," VI., 173; "Wis. Hist. Soc. Coll.," XI., 494-501.

of all who should remove into them between June 1 and December 1. The law as framed gave an opportunity to count not only immigrants, but to re-count all who moved from one county to another (such moving being common), and to count in each successive county persons passing through the state. There is no reasonable doubt that at the time the census was taken, the territory had fewer than forty thousand inhabitants. Dana gives a census of 1818, in which the number is given as thirty-four thousand six hundred and sixty-six, and adds: "Another enumeration having been taken a few months after, the amount of population returned was forty thousand one hundred and fifty-six, which exceeded the number entitling the territory to become a state."[1]

In August, 1818, the Constitution of Illinois was completed. Its provisions most likely to influence settlement were those concerning the elective franchise and slavery. It provided that "In all elections, all white male inhabitants above the age of twenty-one years, having resided in the state six months next preceding the election, shall enjoy the right of an elector; but no person shall be entitled to vote except in the county or district in which he shall actually reside at the time of the election." Slaves could not hereafter be brought into the state, but existing slavery was not abolished, and existing indentures—and some were for ninety-nine years—should be carried out, although future indentures should not run for a longer term than one year. Male children of slaves or indentured servants should be free at the age of twenty-one, and females at eighteen. Slaves from other states could be employed only at the Saline Creek salt works, and there only until 1825.[2]

---

1. "Statutes at Large," III., 428; "Laws of Ill. Ter.," 1817–18, pp. 42–5; Dana, "Sketches of Western Country," 1819, 153; "Niles' Register," XIV., 359 (July 18, 1818); Babcock, "Memoir of John Mason Peck," 99.

2. Poore, "Charters and Constitutions," Pt. I., 442, 445. Of the members

During the congressional debate on the acceptance of the Illinois Constitution, objection to admitting the state was made on the ground that the number of inhabitants was doubtful, and that slavery was not distinctly prohibited, Tallmadge, of New York, who later wished to restrict slavery in Missouri, being the chief objector. The state was admitted, however, and on December 4, 1818, the representatives and senators from Illinois took their seats in Congress.[1]

Between 1809 and 1818, Illinois passed from a non-representative territorial government to a liberal state government. The energy of the settlers had done much to hasten the change, and the change, in turn, did much to hasten settlement.

IV.

Transportation and Settlement, 1809 to 1818.

AT the close of the War of 1812, an unparalleled emigration to the frontiers of the United States began. Contemporary accounts speak of its great volume. "Through New York and down the Alleghany River is now the track of many emigrants from the east to the west. Two hundred and sixty waggons have passed a certain house on this route in nine days, besides many persons on horseback and on foot. The editor of the Gennessee

---

of the Constitutional Convention of Illinois whose nativity has been learned, ten were natives of the South, two were natives of Illinois born of southern parents, two were Irishmen from the South, and five were natives of the North. New England was represented by one man, John Messinger, a son-in-law of Matthew Lyon.

[1]. "Annals of Cong.," 15th Cong., 2d Sess., 38, 305-11; "Statutes at Large," III., 536.

Farmer observes, that he himself met on the road to Hamilton a cavalcade of upwards of twenty waggons, containing one company of one hundred and sixteen persons, on their way to *Indiana*, and all from one town in the district of Maine. So great is the emigration to *Illinois* and *Missouri* also, that it is apprehended that many must suffer for want of provisions the ensuing winter."[1] "Nothing more strongly proves the superiority of the western territory than the vast emigration to it from the eastern and southern states; during the eighteen months previous to April, 1816, fifteen thousand waggons passed over the bridge at Cayuga, containing emigrants to the western country."[2] "Old America seems to be breaking up, and moving westward. . . . The number of emigrants who passed this way [St. Clairsville, Ohio], was greater last year than in any preceding; and the present spring they are still more numerous than the last. Fourteen waggons yesterday, and thirteen today, have gone through this town. Myriads take their course down the Ohio. The waggons swarm with children. I heard today of three together, which contain forty-two of these young citizens."[3] From Hamilton, New York: "It is estimated, that there are now in this village and its vicinity, three hundred families, besides single travellers, amounting in all to fifteen hundred souls, waiting for a rise of water to embark for 'the promised land.'"[4] "The numerous companies of emigrants that flock to this country, might appear, to those who have not witnessed them, almost incredible. But there is scarce a day, except when the river is impeded with ice, but what there is a greater or less number of

1. "Niles' Register," XIII., 1817, 224.
2. Kingdom, "America and the British Colonies," 1816, 17.
3. Birkbeck, "Journey from Va. to Ill.," 1817, 25, 29.
4. Wright, "Letters from the West, or, A Caution to Emigrants," 1818, 1.

boats to be seen floating down its gentle current, to some place of destination. No less than five hundred families stopped at Cincinnati at one time, and many of them having come a great distance, and being of the poorer class of people, before they could provide for themselves, were in a suffering condition; but to the honor of the citizens of Cincinnati, they raised a donation and relieved their distress."[1] Of the remote districts, Missouri and Michigan were receiving crowds of immigrants.[2]

The changes in government and in the land question in Illinois were typical of changes in other frontier regions, but although worthy of note as helping to make a more attractive place for settlement, they are by no means sufficient to account for the great migration to the westward. Why that migration took place and how it was accomplished are interesting and important questions.

Emigration from New England resulted largely from financial and industrial disorganization caused by the close of the war, and a year of such continued cold weather as to produce a famine. This movement was interesting, dramatic, and large in volume, but its influence upon Illinois was slight, because the tide was stayed to the eastward of that state.[3] Migration from the South was also large, and it was from this source that most of the immi-

1. Harding, "Tour through the Western Country," 1818-19, 5.

2. "Am. Mag. and Review," III., 1818, 152; I., 1817, 473.

3. Goodrich, "Recollections of a Life Time," II., 78 ff.; Birkbeck, "Journey from Va. to Ill.," 1817, 25; "Va. Patriot," Sept. 7, 21, 1816; Varney, "A Brief Hist. of Me.," 239; Abbott, "Hist. of Me.," 424; Willlamson, "Hist. of Me.," II., 664-6; Sanborn, "Hist. of N. H.," 265; Whiton, "Hist. of N. H.," 188; Barstow, "Hist. of N. H.," 392; Thompson, "Hist. of the State of Vt.," 1833, 222; same, 1853, Pt. I., 20; Hoskins, "Hist. of the State of Vt.," 232; Wilbur, "Early Hist. of Vt.," III., 162-3; Heaton, "Story of Vt.," 136; Beckley, "Hist. of Vt.," 171-2; "Gov. and Council, Vt.," VI., 429-31.

grants to Illinois came. In 1816 there was a severe drought in eastern North Carolina, and many planters cut their immature corn for their cattle, while great numbers sold their property and joined the emigrants.[1] Kentucky, still a favorite place for settlement, was in the midst of a land boom which reached such proportions as to cause a large volume of emigration to Illinois, Missouri, and the southwest. The buyer of Kentucky land was often a neighbor who wished to enlarge his farm and work on a larger scale, or some well-to-do immigrant who preferred the location to a more remote region. Land sold on credit and at fictitious prices, the seller in turn buying land for which he frequently could make only the first payment. Retribution did not come, however, until after 1820, and for some years it seemed as if Kentucky was to become a source of population, for it was to Illinois and Missouri, and to a lesser degree to Alabama, what New England was to Ohio.[2] Probably chief among the reasons for migration from the South was the increase of slavery, with the resulting changes in industrial and social conditions. Early in the century the growing importance of the cotton crop began to hasten a stratification of opinion which was determined by physiographic areas. The western parts of Virginia, North Carolina, and South Carolina, the northern part of Georgia, and the eastern parts of Kentucky and Tennessee, respectively, being hilly and less fertile than the coastal plain, became the center of the southern anti-slavery sentiment. On the plain settled the wealthy planters, and later the poorer Germans and Quakers settled in the uplands. Only when cotton-raising became very profitable was slavery to intrude upon the latter location.[3]

1. "Va. Patriot," Sept. 11, 1816.
2 White, "Descendants of John Walker," 425, 453, 461.
3. Bassett, "Anti-Slavery Leaders of N. C." (J. H. U. Studies, XVI., 267-71).

During the war the production of cotton in the United States had been almost constant in amount and less than in preceding years, but 1815 saw an increase of over forty-two per cent and 1816 an increase of twenty-four per cent,[1] while in the latter year South Carolina, after an interval of thirteen years, resumed its slavery legislation by passing the first of a series of acts which show that the slavery problem was becoming increasingly difficult. Similar legislation took place in Tennessee, and to a lesser degree in Kentucky.[2] Increased production of cotton was accompanied by an increase in price, middling upland cotton selling at New York at 15 cents per pound in 1814, at 21 cents in 1815, at 29½ cents in 1816, at 26½ cents in 1817, and at 34 cents in 1818, while South Carolina sea-island cotton sold at Charleston in 1816 at 55 cents a pound.[3] An increase in cotton production meant an increase of the plantation system with its slaves, this meant an increased demand for large farms, and also a strengthening of the antagonism between pro-slavery and anti-slavery parties. Even in 1812, a man who wished to sell, lease, or rent his manufacturing establishment in the northwestern part of Virginia, Frederick county, lamented in his advertisement that "some good men of strict moral or religious principles should object against forming settled abodes in

---

1. De Bow, "Industrial Resources of the U. S.," I., 122-3. Millions of pounds of cotton raised in the U. S.:

1808, 75.	1812, 75.	1816, 124.	1820, 160.	In Ga.	{ 1811, 20.
1809, 82.	1813, 75.	1817, 130.	1821, 180.		{ 1821, 45.
1810, 85.	1814, 70.	1818, 125.	1822, 210.		{ 1811, 3.
1811, 80.	1815, 100.	1819, 167.		In Tenn.	{ 1821, 20.

2. "Statutes at Large," S. C., VII., 451-66; "Laws of Tenn., revision of 1831," I., 314-30; "Acts of 1818," Ky., 623, 787; "Acts of 1815," Ky., Feb. 8, 1815.

3. J. L. Watkins, in "U. S. Dept. of Agric., Div. of Statistics, Misc. Ser., Bulletin No. 9," p. 8.

Virginia" or other slave states.[1] Census reports show that the proportion of negroes to whites increased in the western counties of North Carolina during the decade 1810 to 1820 over the proportion in 1800 to 1810. Conditions above described naturally led to the emigration of at least four classes of people: those who were anti-slavery, those who did not wish to change from small farming to the plantation system, the poor whites who found themselves increasingly disgraced and who at the same time found that their land was in demand, the slave-holder who wished a large tract of virgin soil. It is very important to note that these forces were merely beginning to operate in the time from 1814 to 1818, and that they did not reach their maximum of influence until after 1830, yet as the population of Illinois increased less than twenty-eight thousand from 1810 to 1818, it is altogether probable that a considerable proportion were influenced by the causes suggested. It is also true that some pioneers moved merely from habit, without any well-defined cause.

Although it is true that the first steamboat that passed down the Ohio and Mississippi made its trip in the winter of 1811–12, and by 1816 an enterprising captain had made a successful experiment of running a steamboat with coal for fuel, also that the speed of steamboats in eastern waters was a matter for enthusiastic comment, yet it is also true that immigrants to Illinois did not usually arrive by steamer.[2] The development of steamboat navigation in western waters was slow, the first steamboat reaching St. Louis on August 2, 1817.[3] Peter Cartwright wrote of his trip from the West to the General Conference in Baltimore, in 1816: "We had no steamboats, railroad cars, or comfortable

1. "National Intelligencer," Washington, D. C., Apr. 18, 1812.
2. "Rambler in N. A.," I., 104–11; "Am. Register," II., 1817, 202–3.
3. "Memoir of John Mason Peck," 81.

stages in those days. We had to travel from the extreme West on horseback. It generally took us near a month to go; a month was spent at General Conference, and nearly a month in returning to our fields of labor."[1]

Some instances of the manner and cost of emigration may be given. A man with his wife and brother having arrived at Philadelphia from England, *en route* to Birkbeck's settlement[2] in Illinois, the party was directed to Pittsburg, which they reached after a wearisome journey of over three hundred miles across the mountains. At Pittsburg they bought a little boat for six or seven dollars, and came down the Ohio to Shawneetown, whence they proceeded on foot.[3] In the summer of 1818, a party of eighty-eight came over the same route in much the same manner, using flat-boats on the river.[4] In 1817, John Mason Peck, with his wife and three children, went from Litchfield, Connecticut, to Shawneetown, Illinois, in a one-horse wagon. The journey was begun on July 25 and Shawneetown was reached on the sixth of November. "Nearly one month was occupied in passing from Philadelphia through the State of Pennsylvania over the Alleghany Mountains, till on the 10th of September he passed into Ohio. Three weeks he journeyed in that State, and on the 23d of October recrossed the Ohio River into the State of Kentucky . . . , and on the 6th of November

[1] "Autobiography of Peter Cartwright," 156.

[2] Morris Birkbeck and George Flower, from England, founded in 1817, in Edwards County, Illinois, what was the most famous of the English settlements in Illinois. Birkbeck was an educated man and his writings are among the important sources for the early history of Illinois. He was at one time Secretary of State of Illinois. George Flower became the historian of the settlement.

[3] Birkbeck, "Letters from Ill.," 56.

[4] Flower, "Hist. of the Eng. Settlement in Edwards Co., Ill.," "Chicago Hist. Soc. Coll.," I., 95-99.

again crossed the Ohio River, into the then Territory of Illinois, at Shawneetown."[1] Here the family was delayed by floods which rendered the roads impassable. Leaving the horse and wagon at Shawneetown to be brought on by a friend, they proceeded to St. Louis in a keel-boat, paying twenty-five dollars fare, and arrived at their destination on the first of December.[2]

Shawneetown was a sort of center from which emigrants radiated to their destinations. It owed much to its location, being on the main route from the southern states to St. Louis and what was then called the Missouri, and being also the port for the salt works on Saline Creek. It was the seat of a land-office. The town thus had a business which was out of all proportion to the number of its permanent inhabitants. In 1817 it consisted of but about thirty log houses, a log bank, and a land-office. When a certain traveler came to the place from the South, in 1818, he found the number of wagons, horses, and passengers waiting to cross the Ohio, on the ferry, so great that he had to wait "a great part of the morning" for his turn.[3]

During the latter part of the territorial period freight charges from Philadelphia to Pittsburg, by land, were from seven to ten dollars per hundredweight;[4] from Pittsburg to Shawneetown, one dollar; from Louisville to Shawneetown, thirty-seven cents; and from New Orleans to Shawneetown, four dollars and a half.[5] The use of arks

1. "Memoir of John Mason Peck," 71, 74.

2. *Ibid.*, 74-81. The disparity in dates in the latter part of the quotation suggests that "23d of October" should probably read "3d of October."

3. Fearon, "Sketches of America," 258; William Tell Harris, "Remarks Made During a Tour through the U. S. of America in the Years 1817, 1818, 1819."

4. Birkbeck, "Journey from Va. to Ill.," 1817, 128.

5. Fearon, "Sketches of Am.," 1817, 260. In Fearon's work 2*s*. 3*d*. is equal to 50 cents, p. 5.

was common. These were flat-bottomed boats of a tonnage of from twenty-five to thirty tons, covered, square at the ends, of a uniform size of fifty feet in length and fourteen in breadth, usually sold for seventy-five dollars, and would carry three or four families. A common practice was to re-sell them at a somewhat reduced price to someone going further down the river. Two dollars was the charge for piloting an ark over the falls of the Ohio.[1]

There is much truth in the remarks made by a German traveler in 1818-19. He said: "The State of Illinois is from one thousand to twelve hundred miles distant from the sea ports. The journey thither is often as costly and tedious, for a man with a family, as the sea passage. Any father of a family, unless he is well-to-do, can certainly count on being impoverished upon his arrival in Illinois. At Williamsport, on the Susquehanna, I found a Swiss, who, with his wife and ten children, had spent one thousand French crown-dollars for their journey. In the village of Williamsport, an old German schoolmaster, who seems to have been formerly a merchant in Nassau, told me that the passage of himself and family had cost thirteen hundred dollars. For an adult the fare is seventy-five dollars—one dollar is equal to one thaler, ten groschen, Prussian—for children under twelve years, half so much, for children of two years, one-fourth so much, and only babes in arms go free."[2]

It can now be understood why people emigrated to the West, and also why many went overland. A family too poor to go by water could go in a buggy or wagon, and if poorer still they might walk, as many actually did. The immigration to Illinois, which was but a small fraction of

1. Kingdom, "Am. and the British Colonies," 2.
2. Hecke, "Reise durch die Vereinigten Staaten von Nord-Amerika," 1818-19, I., 34.

the great westward movement, was still largely southern in origin, Ohio, Michigan, Indiana, and even New York still staying, in large measure, the tide from New England. In New England it was the "Ohio fever" and not the Illinois fever which carried away the people, and the designation is geographically correct. The men prominent in Illinois politics at the close of the territorial period, and at the beginning of the state period, were natives of southern states, a fact hardly conceivable if New England had been largely represented in Illinois. Then, too, the natural routes from the South led to, or near to, Illinois, the great road from the South crossing the Ohio River at Shawneetown, and the Kentucky and Cumberland rivers being natural water routes. Another fact to be noticed is that much of the emigration was of relatives and friends to join those who had gone before, and as Virginia, Maryland, Kentucky, Tennessee, the Carolinas, and even Georgia, had furnished a large number of early settlers to Illinois, this was a powerful inducement to continued emigration from the same sources. Similarly Ohio and Michigan had early received settlers from the East.

Immigration to Illinois was not large in comparison to that to neighboring states or territories. Indians still held the greater part of Illinois, and the inconveniences incident to frontier life were more pronounced as the distance from the East increased. Pro-slavery men, and anti-slavery men as well, were still in doubt as to the ultimate fate of slavery in Illinois. This had a deterrent effect upon immigration.

IV.
Life of the Settlers.

ACCORDING to the marshal's return the manufactures in Illinois, in 1810, were as follows:

	Value.
Spinning-wheels	$ 630
Looms, 460; cloth produced, 90,039 yards	54,028
Tanneries, 9; leather dressed	7,750
Distilleries, 10,200 gallons	7,500
Flour, 6,440 barrels	32,200
Maple sugar, 15,600 ℔s	1,980[1]—$104,088

This list incidentally indicates the average price of several manufactured articles. For the first six months of 1814, the internal revenue assessed in Illinois was:

Licenses for stills and boilers	$490.14
Carriages	62.00
Licenses to retailers	835.00
Stamps	5.60—$1392.74

Of this amount ($1392.74), $1047.37 had been paid by October 10, 1814.[2] For the period from April 18, 1815, to February 22, 1816, the following were the internal duties:

Hats, caps, and bonnets	$ 66.50½
Saddles and bridles	65.25
Boots and bootees	7.26
Leather	184.35½—$323.37

This was the smallest sum listed in any part of the United States, except Michigan Territory.[3] For 1818:

1. Warden, "Acct. of the U. S. of N. A.," 1819, III., 62.
2. "State Papers," 13th Cong., 3d Sess.
3. "State Papers," 14th Cong., 2d Sess., II., folio. Another volume with the same number is a quarto.

LIFE OF THE SETTLERS.

Licenses for stills	$ 214.91	
Duty on spirits { at 20c. per gal.	549.23	
{ at 25c. per gal.	701.26	
On eighteen carriages	36.75	
Licenses to retailers	1248.80	
On stamped paper and banknotes	4.50	
Manufactured goods	220.14	—$2975.59

Of this amount, $1966.41 was paid, only Indiana and Missouri territories paying a smaller proportion of their assessment.[1] The small proportion paid in these three territories may have been due to the poverty of their inhabitants.

Most of the manufactured articles were consumed within the territory. Both cotton and flax were raised and made into cloth; maple sugar was sometimes sold and exported, but a large proportion of the supply was used as a substitute for sugar, another substitute much used being wild honey. A certain Smith's Prairie was celebrated for the numerous plum and crabapple orchards that grew around its borders. The large red and yellow plums grew there in such abundance that people would come from long distances and haul them away by the wagon-loads, and would preserve them with honey or maple sugar, which was the only sweetening they had in pioneer times.[2]

Previous to the War of 1812, little commerce was carried on, although a few trips had been made to New Orleans with keel-boats or pirogues, and some goods were occasionally brought over the Alleghany Mountains by means of wagons. The round trip to New Orleans and back then required six months; the trip down was easy and required a comparatively short time, but the return trip

---

1. *Ibid.*, 14th Cong., 2d Sess., I.
2. Ross, "Early Pioneers and Pioneer Events," 65.

was slow. It was entirely a barter trade, money being almost unknown. Furs, wild honey, and other commodities of Illinois as well as lead from the Missouri mines, were carried down and exchanged for groceries, cloth, and other articles of a large value and small bulk. As a natural consequence of having to be transported up stream, goods of that nature were extremely dear, the common price of tea being sixteen dollars a pound, of coffee fifty cents, and of calico fifty cents per yard.[1] To go up the Mississippi from St. Louis to Prairie du Chien, in 1815, required from twelve days to a month, while the return trip was made in from six to ten days.[2]

In the great American Bottom of the Mississippi, extending from the mouth of the Kaskaskia almost to the mouth of the Illinois, cattle raising was a leading industry, the cattle being driven to the Philadelphia or Baltimore markets.[3] Towards the close of the period land could easily be secured by government entry. The fertility of the land was such as must have been new to those immigrants who came from the poorer parts of the older states. Land was subject to a tax of a little more that two cents per acre, the tax being about equally divided between the territory and the county.[4] Public lands were not to be taxed by the state, after 1818, until five years from the date of their sale. Governor Edwards, who was a large landowner, offered to pay three dollars per acre for plowing.[5] Prairies were not yet settled to any considerable extent, but it is worthy of note that a traveler of 1818–19

1. Kingston, "Early Western Days," in "Wis. Hist. Soc. Coll.," VII., 313.
2. Shaw, "Personal Narrative," in "Wis. Hist. Soc. Coll.," II., 225.
3. Fearon, "Sketches of Am.," 1817, 258; Brown, "Western Gazetteer; or, Emigrant's Directory," 1817, 20.
4. Birkbeck, "Journey from Va. to Ill.," 1817, 137.
5. Burnham, in "Pub. of the Ill. State Hist. Lib.," No. VIII., 181.

suggested what was eventually to be the solution of the question of prairie settlement. He wrote: "It will probably be some time before these vast prairies can be settled, owing to the inconvenience attending the want of timber. I know of no way, unless the plan is adopted of ditching and hedging, and the building of brick houses, and substituting the stone coal for fuel. It seems as if the bountiful hand of nature, where it has withheld one gift has always furnished another; for instance, where there is a scarcity of wood, there are coal mines."[1] The remedy suggested was the one adopted, except that brick houses did not become common.

Really good roads were entirely lacking. Most of the settlements were connected by roads that were practicable at most seasons for packers and travelers on horseback, but in times of flood the suspension of travel by land was practically complete. A post-road had been established between Vincennes and Cahokia in 1805, and in 1810 a route was established from Vincennes, by way of Kaskaskia, Prairie du Rocher, and Cahokia, to St. Louis. At this time and place, however, a post-route does not necessarily imply anything more than a bridle-path. Mail was received at irregular intervals, although the trips were regularly made in good weather. The post-office nearest Chicago was Fort Wayne, Indiana, whence a soldier on foot carried the mail once a month.[2] A report for the first six months of 1814 shows, in Illinois, nine post-offices, three hundred and eighty-eight miles of post-roads, about $143 received for postage, and $1002 paid for transportation of mail—a bal-

1. Harding, "Tour through the Western Country," 8. This passage is practically plagiarized in Ogden, "Letters from the West," and in Thwaites, "Early Western Travels," XIX., 56.

7. Palmer, "U. S. and Canada," 1818, 417; "Statutes at Large," II., 584; "Incidents and Events in the Life of Gurdon Saltonstall Hubbard," 38.

ance of some $859 against the United States.[1] At this time even Cleveland, Chillicothe, and Marietta received mail but twice per week.[2]

Books were very scarce,[3] and no newspapers had been published in Illinois before its separate territorial organization. Between 1809 and 1818 there were founded the *Illinois Herald* and the *Western Intelligencer*, at Kaskaskia, the latter becoming the *Illinois Intelligencer* on May 27, 1818; and the *Shawnee Chief*, at Shawneetown.[4] In 1816 the citizens of Shawneetown gave notice through the papers of Kaskaskia, Frankfort, Kentucky, and Nashville, Tennessee, that they would apply to the Legislature of Illinois for the establishment of a bank.[5] This may indicate that the papers of the places named had a considerable circulation in Illinois.

The character of the immigrants left much to be desired. A good observer wrote: "After residing awhile in White County, Tennessee, I migrated in May, 1817, to the southern part of the then Territory of Illinois, and settled in Madison County, twenty-five miles east of St. Louis, which town then contained about five thousand inhabitants. The surrounding country, however, was quite sparsely settled, and destitute of any energy or enterprise among the people; their labors and attention being chiefly confined to the hunting of game, which then abounded, and tilling a small patch of corn for bread, relying on game for the

1. "State Papers," 13th Cong., 3d Sess.

2. *Ibid.*, 13th Cong., 2d Sess., II.

3. "Autobiography of Peter Cartwright," 178; Birkbeck, "Journey from Va. to Ill.," 1817, 128.

4. James and Loveless, "Newspapers in Ill. Prior to 1860," "Pub. of the Ill. State Hist. Lib.," No. I., 41, 42, 64, 73, 74; Palmer, "U. S. and Canada," 1818, 416.

5. Burnham, "An Early Ill. Newspaper," "Pub. of the Ill. State Hist. Lib.," No. VIII., 182.

remaining supplies of the table. The inhabitants were of the most generous and hospitable character, and were principally from the southern states; harmony and the utmost good feeling prevailed throughout the country."[1] Naturally this description was not of universal application, but the source of the population and the reasons for removing from the old homes make it probable that it was widely appropriate.

If it was difficult for an emigrant to reach Illinois, and if, after reaching it, he was inconvenienced by the poor facilities for commerce, the bad roads, the infrequency of mails, the scarcity of schools and churches, he at least found it easy to obtain a living, and to some of the immigrants of the territorial period it was worth something not to starve, even though living was reduced to its lowest terms. The poorest immigrant had access to land on the borders of settlement, because the laws against squatting were not enforced. This same class could procure game in abundance, while maple sugar, wild honey, persimmons, crabapples, nuts, pawpaws, wild grapes, wild plums, fish, mushrooms, "greens," berries of several kinds, and other palatable natural products known to the Illinois frontiersman, were to be had in most, if not all, of the localities then settled. Hogs fattened on the mast. Log houses could be built without nails. The problem of clothing was probably more difficult at first than that of food, but although clothing could not be picked up in the woods, the materials for making it could be grown in the fields. Spinning, and the processes necessarily preceding and following it, involved a certain amount of labor. Taxes were not high, nor were tax laws rigidly enforced. It is thus easy to understand the reasoning that may have led a large proportion of the immigrants during this period to leave their old homes.

1. Col. Daniel M. Parkison, "Pioneer Life in Wis.," in "Wis. Hist. Soc. Coll.," II., 326-7, cf. "Memoir of John Mason Peck," 76, 87.

CHAPTER V.

THE FIRST YEARS OF STATEHOOD, 1818 TO 1830.

THE INDIAN AND LAND QUESTIONS.

ONE of the most important cessions of land in Illinois ever made by the Indians was that made by the Kickapoo in 1819, of the vast region lying north of the parallel of 39°—a little north of the mouth of the Illinois River, and southeast of the Illinois River.[1] Settlement had been crowding hard upon this region and many squatters anxiously awaited the survey and sale of the land, especially of that in the famous Sangamon country. In northern Illinois settlement was still retarded by the presence of Indians. In 1825, the Menominee, Kaskaskia, Sauk and Fox, Potawatomi, and Chippewa tribes claimed over 5,314,000 acres of land in Illinois,[2] and there was a licensed Indian trader at Sangamo, one at the saline near the present Danville, and two on Fever River.[3] Two years later there were three such traders at Fever River, and two at Chicago,[4] and in 1827-28 there was one at Fever River with a capital of about $2000.[5] In February, 1829, there were Indian agents at Chicago, Fort Armstrong, Kaskaskia, and Peoria, as well as others near the borders of

---

1. "Indian Aff.," II., 196-7; "18th An. Rept. of the Bureau of Ethnology," Pt. 2, 696-9, Plate CXXV.; Dana, "Sketches of Western Country," 1819, 147. See map of Indian cessions.

2. "State Papers," No. 64, 18th Cong., 2d Sess., IV.

3. *Ibid.*, No. 118, 19th Cong., 1st Sess., VI.

4. *Ibid.*, No. 96, 20th Cong., 1st Sess., III.; "Ex. Doc.," No. 140, 20th Cong., 1st Sess., IV.

5. "Senate Doc.," No. 47, 20th Cong., 2d Sess., I.

Illinois.[1] At this time, the Ottawa, Chippewa, Potawatomi, Kaskaskia, and Winnebago claimed land in the state, although only about 6000 of the more than 25,000 members of these tribes resided in the state. The eight members of the Kaskaskia tribe held a small reservation near the Kaskaskia River. Of the twenty-two hundred members of the Kickapoo tribe, which had relinquished all claim to land east of the Mississippi, about two hundred still lived on the Mackinaw River, but they were expected to move in a few weeks.[2] By a treaty of July 29, 1829, the Chippewa, Ottawa, and Potawatomi ceded their claims in northern Illinois.[3] There still remained the Winnebago tribe, and not until 1833 was Illinois to be free from Indian claims.[4]

A war with the Winnebago tribe was imminent in 1827. Settlers in the northern part of the state either fled to the southward or collected at such points as Galena or Prairie du Chien. "This was a period of great suffering at Galena. The weather was inclement and two or three thousand persons driven suddenly in, with scant provisions, without ammunition or weapons encamped in the open air, or cloth tents which were but little better, were placed in a very disagreeable and critical position."[5] The prompt action of Governor Lewis Cass, of Michigan, averted what would in all probability have been a bloody war, if prompt action had not been taken.[6]

1. *Ibid.*, No. 72, 20th Cong., 2d Sess., I.

2. "Senate Doc.," No. 72, 20th Cong., 2d Sess., I.; see also *ibid.*, No. 27.

3. "State Papers," No. 24, 21st Cong., 1st Sess., II.; "18th An. Rept. of the Bureau of Ethnology," Pt. 2, 722-5, Plate CXXV.

4. *Ibid.*, Pt. 2, 736-7, 738-9, 750-1, Plates CXXIV. and CXXV.

5. Tenney, "Early Times in Wis.," in "Wis. Hist. Soc. Coll.," I., 96.

6. McLaughlin, "Lewis Cass," 125; Young, "Life of Gen. Lewis Cass," 93.

To September 30, 1819, the record of land sales in Illinois was as follows:

	Acres Unsold.	Acres Sold.	Price.
Shawneetown	4,561,920	562,296	$1,153,897
Kaskaskia	2,188,800	407,027	1,781,773
Edwardsville	2,625,960	394,730	795,531 [1]

The balances unpaid by purchasers of public lands steadily increased from 1813 to 1819 until on September 30, 1819, there was due from purchasers of land in the area of the old Northwest Territory nearly ten million dollars.[2] An increase would have resulted merely from an increased sale of public lands under the credit system, but it is also true that the difficulty of collecting the unpaid balances became so great that the government at last abolished the credit system, by the act of April 24, 1820. The act provided that after July 1, 1820, no credit whatever should be given to the purchasers of public lands; that land might be sold in either sections, half-sections, quarter-sections, or eighth-sections; that the minimum price should be reduced from two dollars to one dollar and twenty-five cents per acre; and that reverted lands should be offered at auction before being offered at private sale.[3] At least two of the provisions of this act had long been desired by Illinois in common with other frontier regions: the reduction of the minimum price and the sale in smaller tracts. Under the new law a man with one hundred dollars could buy eighty acres of land, while previously the same man would have had to pay eighty of his one hundred dollars as the first payment on one hundred and sixty acres, the smallest tract then sold. The great danger had been that the second, third, and fourth payments could not be made. In Illinois,

1. "State Papers," Senate, No. 87, 16th Cong., 1st Sess., II.
2. *Ibid.*, No. 57, 16th Cong., 1st Sess., V.
3. "Statutes at Large," III., 566–7.

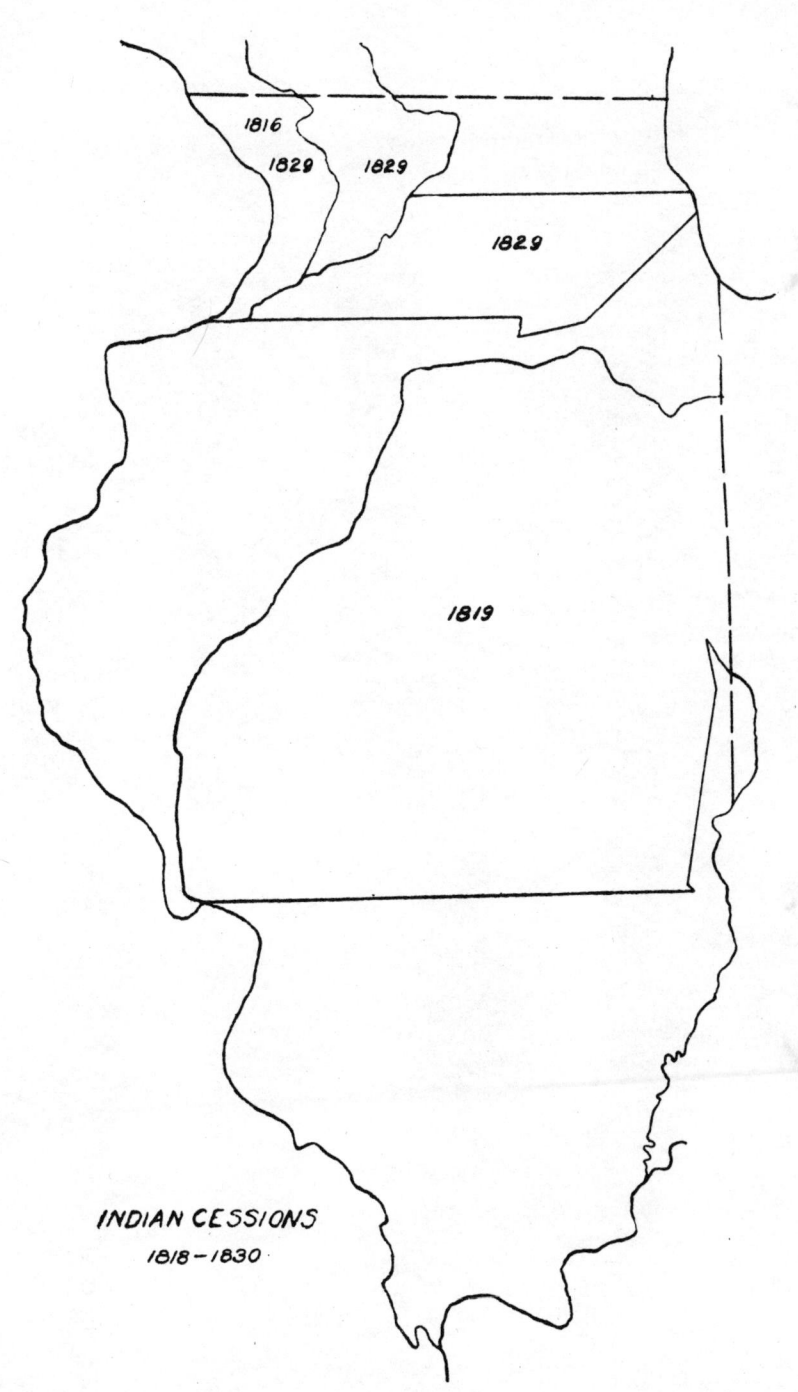

FIRST YEARS OF STATEHOOD.

before July 1, 1820, there had been sold 1,593,247.53 acres of the public land at an average price of about $2.02 per acre. Some of this reverted from non-payment.[1]

During the third quarter of 1820, all sales in Illinois were at the minimum price and a considerable proportion were of the minimum area. At the same time some of the land in Ohio, and a very few tracts in Indiana, sold at a higher price, one tract in Ohio, but only one, selling for more than seven dollars per acre.[2] To October 1, 1821, the land-offices in Illinois reported:

	Acres Sold.	Surveyed, but Unsold.
Shawneetown	592,464	2,401,936
Kaskaskia	419,898	1,615,942
Palestine	714	2,880,720
Edwardsville	437,993	2,696,727
Vandalia	7,923	2,545,677

All land in the districts of Shawneetown and Kaskaskia had been surveyed, but the remaining districts were still indefinite on the north.[3] At this time, Illinois money passed in the state at par, and the Bank of Illinois was among those whose notes were received in payment for public lands.[4]

As more and more land was opened to settlement, a new difficulty arose and became increasingly troublesome. All public land was to be entered at the same minimum price, and as a natural result, the poorest land was not taken

1. Donaldson, "Public Domain," 200 ff.
2. "State Papers," No. 35, 16th Cong., 2d Sess., II.
3. "Pub. Lands," III., 533. It is interesting to note that for the five years ending in 1822, the Pulteney estate of 380,000 acres of land in Steuben and Alleghany counties, New York, had sold an average of 10,000 acres per year, at an average price of $3.37 per acre—"Columbian Centinel," Boston, Oct. 2, 1822.
4. "Illinois Intelligencer," Oct. 30, 1821.

up and settlement became widely dispersed on the best tracts of land. In December, 1824, the Illinois legislature sent a memorial to Congress portraying the evils of sparse settlement, and asking that land that had been offered for sale for five years or more might be sold at fifty cents per acre. Better roads, better markets, and better institutions were expected to result from such sales.[1] Two years later, another memorial was sent. This asked that land be offered for sale at prices graduated according to the quality of the land, suggested that the poorest land might well be donated to settlers, and declared that settlement was retarded by the high minimum price of land.[2] Governor Ninian Edwards pointed out that in 1790, Hamilton had recommended that public lands be sold at twenty cents per acre, which "was the price at which Kentucky, long afterward, sold her lands."[3] In 1828, the Committee on Public Lands recommended that public lands unsold at public sale be first offered at one dollar per acre, and if still unsold, that the price be reduced twenty-five cents per acre each two years until sold or reduced to twenty-five cents per acre; that eighty-acre homestead claims be given to such persons as would cultivate and occupy them for five years; and that lands unsold at twenty-five cents per acre be ceded to the states in which they lay, upon payment of the cost of survey and twenty-five cents per acre. At this time, there was in Illinois 1,403,482 acres surveyed and sold; 19,684,186 acres surveyed and unsold, of the 39,000,000 acres estimated to be in the State.[4] Still another memorial from the legislature was sent to Congress in 1829. It

1. "Pub. Lands," IV., 148; "Repts. and S. Doc.," No. 25, 18th Cong., 2d Sess., II.
2. "Pub. Lands," IV., 871; "S. Doc.," No. 17, 19th Cong., 2d Sess., II.
3. "H. J.," Ill., 1826-27, p. 54.
4. "Repts. of Com.," No. 125, 20th Cong., 1st Sess., II.

pointed out, in strong terms, the inconvenience arising from the high price at which public land was offered for sale. Unsold public land could neither be taxed nor legally settled. It was stated that of the forty millions of acres in Illinois, little over one and one-half millions had been sold at public sales. A granting of the right of preëmption, which implies the presence in the state of squatters, is suggested.[1]

The implication of the presence of squatters was well founded. When Peter Cartwright, in 1823, visited a settlement in the Sangamon country, he found it a community of squatters, on land which had been surveyed, but was not yet offered for sale. Money was hoarded up to enter land when Congress should order sales. Cartwright paid a squatter two hundred dollars for his improvement and his claim, bought some stock, and rented out the place, to which he was to remove from Kentucky the following year.[2] This squatting on surveyed land, and even on unsurveyed land, was a regular procedure. It added much to the difficulty of governing the state—hence the memorials to Congress, and hence the great significance to Illinois of an act of May 29, 1830, which gave to all settlers who had cultivated land in 1829 the right to preëmpt not more than one hundred and sixty acres.[3] This law was of general application. Even now the Illinois legislature sent another petition concerning preëmption to Congress, because one of the provisions of the act of May, 1830, was that the plat of survey should have been filed

---

[1] "Senate Doc.," No. 58, 20th Cong., 2d Sess., I. For the long and futile effort made in Congress to secure a law graduating the price of public lands, see Meigs, "Life of Thomas Hart Benton," ch. xi., with the foot references thereto.

[2] Strickland, "Autobiography of Peter Cartwright," 246, 254.

[3] "Statutes at Large," IV., 420-1.

in the land-office, and this provision debarred about one thousand Illinois squatters from the benefit of the act. A modification in their favor was desired.[1]

The land claims of the ancient settlers, as they are called in government documents, continued to occupy the attention of Congress, in a desultory way, throughout the period, but their influence upon settlement had practically ceased with the opening of the public land-offices.[2]

Among the obstacles to settlement was the holding of land by non-residents. Such lands were subject to a triple tax in case of delinquency, and when sold for taxes and costs frequently did not bring enough for that purpose, in which event they reverted to the state and the state paid the costs. Redemption, although possible, was rare.[3] In 1823, about nine thousand quarter-sections of land in the Military Tract, lying between the Illinois and the Mississippi, were advertised for sale, because of the non-payment of taxes by non-resident landholders.[4] At this time, two of the prominent men of the state who wished to dispose of a large amount of state paper, advertised that they would pay such delinquent taxes at twenty-five per cent discount.[5] In 1826, thirty-eight pages of the *Illinois Intelligencer* were filled with a description, in double column, of lands owned by non-residents, the lands being for sale for taxes. In 1829, a similar list filled thirty-two pages.[6] Much discontent was manifested in the state on account of the laws

1. "Pub. Lands," VI., 249.

2. "Statutes at Large," III., 786; "Repts. of Com.," No. 58, 17th Cong., 1st Sess., I.; "Pub. Lands," III., 406, 412-3, 421, 462-3; VI., 23-5; "S. Doc.," No. 10, 21st Cong., 1st Sess., I.

3. "Illinois Intelligencer," Vandalia, Ill., Apr. 24, 1821.

4. "Niles' Register," XXV., 117.

5. "Washington (D. C.) Republican," Sept. 27, 1823.

6. "Illinois Intelligencer," Oct. 3, 1829.

concerning the public lands, and Governor Edwards' message to the legislature, in 1830, elaborated a theory that all public lands belonged of right to the states in which they lay.[1]

Illinois early understood that an Illinois-Michigan canal would help to people her northern lands. This led to many efforts to secure such a waterway. In 1819 a favorable topographical report concerning the route for the proposed canal was made,[2] and in 1822 the state was authorized to construct the canal, but no tangible aid was given.[3] In 1825 the legislature petitioned Congress for a grant of the townships through which the canal would pass. A committee report of March, 1826, which was almost identical with another presented in February, 1825, pointed out that the cost of transporting a ton of merchandise from Philadelphia, New York, or Baltimore was about ninety dollars, and required from twenty to twenty-two days. The probable cost by the proposed canal, the Lakes, and the Erie Canal, from St. Louis to New York was from sixty-three to sixty-five dollars per ton, and the time from twelve to fifteen days. The canal would bind Illinois and Missouri to the North.[4] Congress received a memorial from the legislature on the same subject in January, 1827, requesting the grant of "two entire townships, along the whole course of the canal," and declaring that markets at New Orleans fluctuated because of speculators, and that grain and goods sent from the West to the Atlantic ports by way of New Orleans was exposed to the

1. "Senate Jour.," Ill., 1830-31, 8-51. The message was delivered on Dec. 7, 1830, and Edwards' successor was inaugurated the following day.
2. "State Papers," No. 17, 16th Cong., 1st Sess., II.
3. "Statutes at Large," III., 659-60; "Niles' Register," XXII., 59.
4. "Pub. Lands," IV., 437-8; "Repts. of Com.," No. 147, 19th Cong., 1st Sess., II.; *ibid.*, No. 53, 18th Cong., 2d Sess., I.; "S. Doc.," No. 49, 19th Cong., 1st Sess., II.

dangers of both the southern climate and the sea.[1] A few weeks later the desired grant was made, the state being given one-half of five sections in width on each side of the canal, the United States reserving the alternate sections.[2] The canal commissioners promptly platted the orginal town of Chicago and sold lots at from twenty to eighty dollars each, but no immediate settlement followed the land sale, and Chicago remained for some years longer an Indian town. The prospect of having a canal doubtless had some influence upon settlement, but at the close of 1830 the actual construction of the canal was still a thing of the future. By the close of 1828, Congress had donated to Illinois, for various purposes, chiefly for schools and internal improvements, 1,346,000 acres.[3]

The salt springs had been vested in the state of Illinois with the provision that no part of the reservations should be sold. Large reservations were made at the Saline River salt works and at the Vermilion saline near Danville, the object being to reserve a supply of wood for the making of salt. Upon the discovery of coal near the springs the state was permitted to sell not more than thirty thousand acres of the Saline River reservation.[4]

Illinois as a landowner sometimes mingled church and state. The original proprietors of Alton having donated one hundred lots, one-half for the support of the gospel, and one-half for the support of a public school, the state vested the donated lots in the trustees of the town, upon its incorporation in 1821. A similar donation made by the proprietors of Mt. Carmel was confirmed in the same

1. *Ibid.*, No. 46, 19th Cong., 2d Sess., II.; "State Papers," No. 81, 19th Cong., 2d Sess., V.
2. "Pub. Lands," VI., 27; "Statutes at Large," IV., 234.
3. "S. Doc.," No. 11, 21st Cong., 1st Sess., I.
4. "Pub. Lands," IV., 888, 921; V., 33, 35, 620; "Statutes at Large," IV., 305.

manner.[1] The Cumberland Presbyterians having built a church on a school section, the state provided that for ninety-nine years the building should be used as a schoolhouse also, the school being under the joint direction of the trustees of the township and the church society.[2]

The receipts for public lands in 1828 and 1829, respectively, were:

	1828.	1829.
Kaskaskia	$ 4,639.82	$ 10,503.99
Shawneetown	7,250.28	16,058.79
Edwardsville	23,536.49	38,001.35
Vandalia	4,489.71	24,258.13
Palestine	25,671.62	59,026.81
Springfield	56,507.63	108,175.47
	$122,095.55	$256,024.54[3]

The receipts for 1828 were for 96,092.91 acres; of 1829, for 196,324.92 acres.[4] From October 1, 1829, to September 30, 1830, sales, receipts, and prices were:

	Acres.		Average Price per Acre.
Illinois	291,401.28	$364,369.87	$1.2504
Indiana	413,253.63	521,715.13	1.2624
Alabama	233,369.27	291,715.20	1.25
Missouri	182,929.63	228,748.12	1.2505
Michigan	106,201.28	132,751.68	1.25
Ohio	160,182.14	201,923.50	1.2606
Mississippi	103,795.61	130,475.87	1.257 [5]

The northward movement of population in Illinois is well

1. "Laws of Ill.," 1820-21, 39-45; 1824-25, 72.
2. *Ibid.*, 1820-21, 153-4.
3. The total receipts from sales of 1829 is erroneously given as $256,124.54 in the original.
4. "Pub. Lands," VI., 158-9.
5. *Ibid.*, VI., 219; "H. Ex. Doc.," No. 19, 21st Cong., 2d Sess., I.

indicated by the figures for 1828 and 1829. The Indian barrier was being pushed back, and the Sangamon country, with its land-office at Springfield, was a favorite place for settlement. The rapid increase in the amount of land sold is also striking. As the third decade of the century closed Indiana was the favorite place for frontier settlement. The sales of public lands in Ohio were diminishing. A prophetic glance would have seen that as the ever-shifting frontier passed westward Illinois was to overtake and then to far surpass Indiana in number of settlers.

The period from 1818 to 1830 saw the Indian title to a great fertile tract of land in Illinois extinguished, the price of all public lands lowered and the land offered for sale in smaller tracts, the right of preëmption granted to squatters who had settled before 1830, considerable grants of land made to the state for internal improvements, the great salt spring reservations reduced. These changes did much to make Illinois a more attractive place for settlement. When a committee of workingmen in Wheeling, Virginia, made a report, in October, 1830, on a method of escaping from the ills of workingmen, they presented an elaborate plan for buying land and forming a colony in Illinois.[1] The experience of the squatter who settled with four or five sows for breeders and in four years or less drove forty-two fat hogs to market and sold them for $135, with which he bought eighty acres of land and paid his debts, was not a rare one.[2]

As 1830 closed there were still problems connected with the land to solve. The Indian question persisted, non-resident landholders were troublesome, and the state

[1] "Rept. of a Meeting of Workingmen in the City of Wheeling, Va., on Forming a Settlement in the State of Ill.," Oct. 4, 1830, 1-12.

[2] "Information for Emigrants," London, 1848, 33, first pagination. The hogs were sold in 1829.

FIRST YEARS OF STATEHOOD.   145

would still seek grants for internal improvements, but none of these was to be long a serious impediment to settlement.

THE GOVERNMENT AND ITS REPRESENTATIVES, 1818 TO 1830.

In some respects the character of the state government of Illinois shows the character of the settlers. The nativity of the governors and the congressmen of the state indicates that the South was the origin of a majority of the population. Before the end of 1830 there had been no northern-born representative of the state in the national House of Representatives; the first northern-born senator was chosen in the last month of 1825, and the first northern governor in 1830.[1] Pierre Menard, a French Canadian, the first

1. Senators from Illinois:

	Nativity.	
Ninian Edwards	Maryland	Dec. 4, 1818—Mar. 4, 1824
Jesse B. Thomas	Maryland	Dec. 4, 1818—Mar. 3, 1829
John McLean	North Carolina	Dec. 20, 1824—Mar. 3, 1825
		Dec. 7, 1829—Oct. 14, 1830
Elias K. Kane	New York	Dec. 5, 1825—Dec. 11, 1835
David J. Baker	Connecticut	Dec. 6, 1830—Jan. 4, 1831

Representatives from Illinois:

John McLean	North Carolina	Dec. 4, 1818—Mar. 3, 1819
Daniel P. Cook	Kentucky	Dec. 6, 1819—Mar. 3, 1827
Joseph Duncan	Kentucky	Dec. 3, 1827—Nov. 1834

Governors of Illinois:

1809—1818	Ninian Edwards	Maryland
1818—1822	Shadrach Bond	Maryland
1822—1826	Edward Coles	Virginia
1826—1830	Ninian Edwards	Maryland
1830—1834	John Reynolds	Pennsylvania

The governors from 1834—1842 were from Kentucky, 1842—1861 from the North, 1861—1873 from Kentucky. During the period 1846—1853, Illinois had a Democratic governor (Augustus C. French), from New Hampshire, this being the only instance of an Illinois governor from New England.

lieutenant-governor, came to Illinois in 1790, and can not fairly be cited as a type of the French descendants of the first white settlers of Illinois.[1] As a matter of fact, the French element was not a political factor of importance. Nor is it true that all southerners were pro-slavery, for the most noted anti-slavery governor of Illinois, and her governor during the Civil War, were from the South, while her first northern senator was pro-slavery. The great influx of immigrants from New England and the rest of the North did not come until after 1830. It was retarded, after the opening of the Erie Canal (1825), by the Winnebago and Black Hawk wars, and did not reach its height until the latter war had closed and the Indian claims to land in northern Illinois had been extinguished. Immigration from the northern states increased proportionally, however, after 1820.

Illinois men in Congress give a number of indications of the feeling of the people on questions having a more or less intimate relation to settlement. Constant and insistent demands for more land-offices, more post-roads, more pensions, donations of land for poor settlers, grants of land for internal improvements, the right of preëmption for squatters, and the reduction of the price of public lands show that the frontier was in favor of a liberal governmental expenditure.[2] Congressmen from Illinois, without exception, favored the tariff bills of 1824 and 1828.[3] In 1828, the only senator from Illinois who voted on the

[1]. Sulte, "Histoire des Canadiens-Français," VIII., 53.

[2]. "Annals of Cong.," 15th Cong., 2d Sess., 436, 704; "H. J.," 15th Cong., 2d Sess., 100, 136-7, 273, 308; "S. J.," 15th Cong., 2d Sess., 239, 240, 278-85, 322; 16th Cong., 1st Sess., 107, 201-2, 245; "Annals of Cong.," 16th Cong., 1st Sess., I., 450-2, 482-5; II., 1331-3; "S. J.," 21st Cong., 2d Sess., 38, 48, 51.

[3]. "S. J.," 18th Cong., 1st Sess., 401; "H. J.," 18th Cong., 1st Sess., 428; "Cong. Debates," 20th Cong., 1st Sess., IV. 786, 2471.

FIRST YEARS OF STATEHOOD. 147

question, voted for the bill abolishing imprisonment for debt on processes issuing from a United States court.[1] Since Illinois early abolished such imprisonment, it is interesting to note that three hundred and thirty-eight persons were committed to the Essex county jail in New Jersey, for debt, in the year ending April 1, 1823, of whom one hundred and forty-one were in close confinement. The aggregate of debt was fifty-five thousand dollars.[2]

Within the state one of the phenomena which has characterized frontier regions appeared about the year 1821. A desperate gang of immigrants had robbed and plundered until, after a most notable robbery, "a public meeting was held, and among other things, a company was formed, consisting of ten law-abiding men of well-known courage, who bound themselves together, under the name of the Regulators of the Valley, to rid the country of horse thieves and robbers. . . . A regular constitution was drawn up and subscribed to." After the leader of the desperadoes had been killed the remainder fled.[3] A frontier condition is indicated also by the fact that when Sangamon county was formed, on January 30, 1821, a special law provided that housekeepers in the county should perform the duties and receive the privileges of freeholders. The same provision was made for Morgan county two years later. As land sales in the Sangamon country, in which these counties lay, did not begin until

3. "Cong. Debates," 20th Cong., 1st Sess., IV., 90.
4. "Ohio Republican," April 19, 1823.
1. Eames, "Historic Morgan and Classic Jacksonville," 22. A letter from the son of Mr. Eames, now deceased, says that search has failed to recover the constitution of the Regulators of the Valley. Regulators were also useful in preventing speculators from entering the claims of squatters, even when the squatter was too poor to enter his own claim — Henderson, "Early Hist. of the Sangamon Country, 21. For another instance, see Blaney, "Excursion through the U. S.," 233-6; also, Reynolds, "My Own Times," 1879, 113.

November, 1823, these laws probably resulted from the formation of counties whose entire population consisted of squatters.[1] The persistence of wolf bounties bears testimony to continued wild surroundings.[2] In 1829 alien Irish, and presumably all other aliens, could vote at all elections. An election law of this year provided that voting should be by the voter's approaching the bar, in the election room, and naming in an audible voice the persons for whom he voted, or, if the voter preferred, by delivering to the judges a ballot which should be read aloud by them, the alternative being for the benefit of illiterate voters. Voting had previously been by ballot.[3]

Although frontier conditions obtained, there were evidences of their gradual amelioration. A law of 1823 provided that counterfeiting, which, in the territorial period, had been punishable by death, should be punished by a fine of not more than one thousand dollars, whipping with not fewer than one hundred nor more than two hundred lashes, imprisonment for not more than twelve months, and being rendered forever infamous.[4] The state established a system of common schools to be supported, in part, by the state, in 1825; but in 1829 the sections of the act which provided that two per cent of all money received into the state treasury, and five-sixths of the interest of the school fund, should be for the support of public schools, were repealed,[5] taxation for such a purpose not being then in accord with public sentiment. A

[1] "Laws of Ill.," 1820-21, pp. 45-6; 1822-23, p. 109; Henderson, "Early Hist. of the Sangamon Country," 21.
[2] "Laws of Ill.," 1822-23, p. 86 ff.; 1824-25, p. 116.
[3] "Miners' Journal," Galena, Dec. 22, 1829; "Revised Laws of Ill.," 1829, 57; "H. J.," (Ill.), 1828-29, p. 57.
[4] "Laws of Ill.," 1822-23, pp. 149-51.
[5] Ibid., 1824-25, pp. 121-8; "Revised Laws of Ill.," 1829, 149.

FIRST YEARS OF STATEHOOD. 149

mechanic's lien law, passed in 1825, provided that in case of a contract between a landowner and a mechanic, the mechanic should have a lien upon the product of his labor for three months, after which the lien lapsed unless suit had been commenced. Three years later an unsuccessful attempt to secure such a law was made in New York.[1]

Two accounts on the records of the state are of sufficient interest to give at length. The first gives the amount of money received into the treasury during the two years ending December 27, 1822:

"The amount paid into the treasury by the
different sheriffs within the two years ending as aforesaid, is_____$ 7,121.09
The amount of a judgment obtained against
the former sheriff of Randolph [County]
for non-resident tax of 1818, is_____ 147.14
The amount from non-residents for the two
preceding years, including back taxes,
redemptions, interest, &c., is_____ 38,437.75
The amount from non-residents' bank stock, is   97.77
The amount from the Saline on the Ohio, is 10,563.09
The amount from the Saline on Muddy river, is   200.00
The amount from the sale of Lots in the town
of Vandalia, is_____ 5,659.86
Total amount of money paid at the Treasury
between the 1st of January, 1821, and the
27th of December, 1822_____$62,226.70"

The balance in the treasury was $33,661.11,[2] but Governor Edwards, in his message of December 2, 1828, reported a state indebtedness of $44,140.03 and taxes in Illinois as

1. "Revised Laws of Ill.," 1829, p. 106; McMaster, "Rights of Man in Am.," 97.

2. "Laws of Ill.," 1822-23, p. 222.

precisely eight times as high as those in Kentucky which were payable in the same kind of currency.[1] The rage for internal improvements was partly responsible, and for this in turn the wide dispersion of the settlements in Illinois, caused by the fact that all public lands were offered at the same minimum price and that the prairies were in large measure shunned, furnishes a partial explanation.

The second account of the state, above referred to, shows that in 1822 it cost $151.82 to make a trip from Vandalia to Shawneetown and return, and one from Vandalia to Kaskaskia and return, to convey to the capital some money paid by the United States on the three per cent fund due the state. The former trip occupied fourteen days, the latter eight days.[2]

Governor Cass' protection of Galena during the Winnebago War of 1827 may have been influenced by its uncertain governmental status. In 1828 miners in what is now southwestern Wisconsin voted for members of Congress from Illinois, and in 1829 Galena was enumerated among the thriving towns of Huron or Ouisconsin Territory. November 29, 1828, one hundred and eighty-seven inhabitants of Galena and vicinity sent a memorial to Congress asking that a separate territory be formed, the territory to be bounded on the south by a line drawn due west from the southern point of Lake Michigan to the Mississippi, and by the northern boundary of Missouri. The memorial began: "The undersigned, inhabitants of that portion of the 'Territory Northwest of the Ohio,' lying north of a due east and west line drawn through the southernmost end of Lake Michigan, and west of that lake to the British possessions, comprehending the mining district, more generally known as the Fever River Lead

2. "H. J.," Ill., 1828–29, p. 8.
1. "Laws of Ill.," 1822–23, pp. 229–30.

Mines." The petitioners referred to the violation of the Ordinance of 1787, and also stated that they were subject to two separate governments, each some hundreds of miles from them, and each unacquainted with their needs. The petition was read and tabled.[1] It is true that the situation of Galena was peculiarly difficult. No mail could be carried along the rude trail from Peoria to Galena during the wet season, and when the Illinois legislature, seeking to give relief, passed a bill for laying out a road between the "Illinois settlements and Galena," it was vetoed by the governor and council because the road would pass through lands of the United States and of the Indians. When the river was frozen provisions were very high, and mail was sent forward from Fort Edwards once a month. These conditions were more aggravating as the number of inhabitants increased, and in 1827, notwithstanding the trouble with the Winnebago Indians, there were about four thousand men at Galena, and they mined about fifteen times as much lead as had been mined in 1823. In January, 1828, a congressional committee reported favorably on a proposition to open a road to Galena.[2] In a letter written one year later by the delegate from Michigan Territory, to the committee on territories, the suggestion is made that a new territory, to be called Huron, should be formed, because the region at Galena was said to have received hundreds of settlers during the preceding summer and to have at the time of writing ten thousand or more, and government in the lead region could not be properly carried on from Detroit, which was eight hundred or one

---

1. Tenney, "Early Times in Wis.," in "Wis. Hist. Soc. Coll.," I., 97; "Niles' Register," XXXVII., 53; "State Papers," No. 35, 20th Cong., 2d Sess., II.

2. "Repts. of Com.," No. 177, 20th Cong., 1st Sess., III.; Meeker, "Early Hist. of the Lead Region of Wis.," in "Wis. Hist. Soc. Coll.," VI., 278-9.

thousand miles distant, by the routes commonly traveled. The legislature of Michigan was said to be compelled to meet in the summer in order to enable delegates to attend and that was the busy time at the mines.[1] A congressional act of February, 1829, provided for the laying out of a village at Galena. The plat was not to exceed one section of land, no lot was to be larger than one-fourth of an acre, unimproved lots were to be sold at not less than five dollars, improved lots were to be graded, without reference to their improvements, into three grades, to sell at the rate of twenty-five, fifteen, and ten dollars, respectively, per acre, the occupants having the right of preëmption.[2] Another mode of relief, which the inhabitants were working out for themselves, is described in a Galena paper of September 14, 1829: "Mr. Soulard's wagon and mule team returned, a few days since, from Chicago, near the southernmost bend of Lake Michigan; to which place it had been taken across the country, with a load of lead. This is the first wagon that has ever passed from the Mississippi River to Chicago. The route taken from the mines was, to Ogee's ferry, on Rock River, eighty miles; thence an east course sixty miles, to the Missionary establishment on the Fox River of the Illinois; and thence a north-easterly course sixty miles to Chicago, as travelled, two hundred miles. The wagon was loaded with one ton and a half of lead. The trip out was performed in eleven, and the return trip in eight days. The lead was taken, by water, from Chicago to Detroit. Should a road be surveyed and marked, on the best ground, and the shortest distance, a trip could be performed in much less time. And if salt could be obtained at Chicago, from the New

1. "State Papers," No. 66, 20th Cong., 2d Sess., II.
2. "Statutes at Large," IV., 334.

FIRST YEARS OF STATEHOOD.

York Salt Works, it would be a profitable and advantageous trade."[1]

As the life history of an individual recapitulates the history of the development of a species, so does the history of Galena, in respect to the difficulties of its early settlers, recapitulate the history of the several parts of the United States in their early days. As Illinois had sent petitions for relief to the governments of the Northwest Territory, of Indiana Territory, and of the United States, so did Galena send similar petitions to the governments of Illinois, of Michigan Territory, and of the United States. In each case the prayers of the petitioners were but partially granted. In each case the difficulties from Indians, lack of facilities for commerce, distance from the seat of government, inability to secure lands, were gradually mitigated until the steady onward sweep of settlement engulfed the outlying region and it ceased to be the frontier, and turned its energies to other questions—different, although probably as difficult. Galena, even at the close of 1830, was a frontier region on the outskirts of Illinois settlement.

TRANSPORTATION.

Transportation was long a difficult problem, although it became gradually less so. Travel by either water or land was slow and difficult. When a party of about one hundred men, conducted by Colonel R. M. Johnson, went, in six or eight boats, from St. Louis to the site of the present Galena, in 1819, to make an arrangement with the Indians which would permit the whites to mine lead, the upward voyage occupied some twenty days.[2] Doubtless the journey of Edward Coles from Albemarle county, Virginia, to

---

1. "Galena Advertiser," Sept. 14, 1829.
2. Bonner, "Life and Adventures of Beckwourth," 20, 21. Written from Beckwourth's dictation.

154   SETTLEMENT OF ILLINOIS.

Illinois, in 1819, was typical of that of the better class of immigrants. At the Virginia homestead, slaves, horses and wagons were prepared for the long journey. A trusty slave was put in charge of the caravan of emigrant wagons and started out on the long journey over the Alleghanies to Brownsville, Pennsylvania. Mr. Coles started a few days later, overtook the party one day's journey from Brownsville, and upon arriving at that place bought two flat-bottomed boats, upon which negroes, horses and wagons, with their owner, were embarked. The drunken pilot was discharged at Pittsburg, and Coles acted as captain and pilot on the voyage of some six hundred miles down the Ohio to a point below Louisville, whence, the boats being sold, the journey was continued by land to Edwardsville, Illinois.[1]

April 5, 1823, a party of forty-three started from Cincinnati in a keel-boat, arriving at Galena, June 1, 1823. Twenty-two days were required to stem the flooded Mississippi from the mouth of the Ohio to St. Louis, and twenty of these were rainy days.[2] In 1822 the English settlement in Edwards county sent several flat-boats loaded with corn, flour, beef, pork, sausage, etc., to New Orleans.[3] Improvement of the Wabash was entrusted to an incorporated company in 1825, and several years earlier a canal across the peninsula at the junction of the Ohio and the Mississippi was contemplated.[4]

Many immigrants came overland. The following is typical: "In the year 1819 a party of six men, and families

1. Washburne, "Sketch of Edward Coles," 48.
2. Meeker, "Early Hist. of the Lead Region of Wis.," in "Wis. Hist. Soc. Coll.," VI., 276-9.
3. Blaney, "Excursion through the U. S. and Canada," 159.
4. "Niles' Register," XXVIII., 168; Dana, "Sketches of Western Country," 1819, 154; "Laws of Ill. Ter.," 1817-18, pp. 57-64.

of three of them, started from Casey County, Kentucky, for Illinois. . . . The first three were young unmarried men, the last three had their wives and children with them. They came in an old-fashioned Tennessee wagon, that resembled a flat-boat on wheels. The younger readers of this sketch can form but a faint idea of the curious and awkward appearance of one of these old fashioned wagons, covered over with white sheeting, the front and rear bows set at an angle of forty-five degrees to correspond with the ends of the body, and then the enormous quantity of freight that could be stowed away in the hole would astonish even a modern omnibus driver! Women, children, beds, buckets, tubs, old fashioned chairs, including all the household furniture usually used by our log-cabin ancestors; a chicken coop, with 'two or three hens and a jolly rooster for a start,' tied on behind, while, under the wagon, trotted a full-blood, long-eared hound, fastened by a short rope to the hind axle. Without much effort on your part, you can, in imagination, see this party on the road, one of the men in the saddle on the near horse, driving; the other two, perhaps on horseback, slowly plodding along in the rear of the wagon, while the boys 'walked ahead,' with rifles on their shoulders 'at half-mast,' on the lookout for squirrels, turkey, deer, or '*Injin.*'"[1] Muddy roads sometimes caused emigrants to make long detours in the hope of finding better ones, and if the roads became impassable water transportation might be resorted to when the locality permitted.[2] The fear of breaking down was omnipresent and danger from professional bandits[3] was not

1. Henderson, "Early Hist. of the Sangamon Country," 13.
2. Reid, "Sketch of Enoch Long," "Chicago Hist. Soc. Coll.," II., 61-2.
3. "Pub. No. 8 of the Ill. State Hist. Lib.," 156; Strickland, "Autobiography of Peter Cartwright," 200-1; Faux, "Memorable Days in Am.," 310.

lacking. There was also danger of being lost on the enormous prairies in Illinois.[1]

The best road from North Carolina to Indiana, for loaded wagons, was that which crossed the Blue Ridge at Ward's Gap, in Western Virginia, led through East Tennessee and Kentucky, and reached the Ohio River at Cincinnati,[2] and this was a part of the route for some of the Illinois immigrants. Illustrations of the moving instinct, the ever-present desire to go frontierward, were constantly appearing.[3] Although the greater proportion of immigrants came by either wagon or boat, some came on horseback and some on foot.[4] One pioneer wrote: "My mother was a delicate woman and in the hope of prolonging her life, my father, in 1830, broke up his home at Windsor, Connecticut, and started overland for Jacksonville, Illinois. Most of the household furniture was shipped by water, *via* New Orleans and did not reach its destination until a year afterwards, six months after our arrival. The wagon for my mother was made strong and wide, drawn by three horses, so that a bed could be put in it and most of the way she lay in this bed. Most of the time the drive was pleasant but over the mountains it was rough and over the national corduroy road of Indiana, it was perfectly horrible."[5] A journey was made in 1827 in about four weeks over the same route that it had taken the same traveler seven and a half weeks to cover in 1822.[6]

1. "Reminiscences of Levi Coffin," 89-99.
2. *Ibid.*, 76.
3. *Ibid.*, 94-5; Mrs. Delilah Mullin-Evans, in "Trans. of the McLean Co. (Ill.) Hist. Soc.," II., 17; Hecke, "Reise durch die Vereinigten Staaten," I., 37-8.
4. Loomis, "Notes of a Journey to the Great West," pages unnumbered; "Niles' Register," XXII., 320.
5. "Stories of the Pioneer Mothers of Ill.," MS. in Ill. State Hist. Lib.
6. Tillson, "Reminiscences," 120.

FIRST YEARS OF STATEHOOD. 157

Within the state changes in facilities for transportation were constant. From Shawneetown to St. Louis, by way of Kaskaskia and Cahokia, passed the great western road. There was also a road from Shawneetown, by way of Carmi, to Birkbeck's settlement in Edwards county.[1] Frontier roads to different places seem to have been designated by different numbers of notches cut in the trees along the wayside.[2] New roads were in constant demand. In February, 1821, the legislature authorized the building of a turnpike road, one hundred feet wide, from the Mississippi, opposite St. Louis, across the American Bottom to the Bluffs. Toll was to be regulated by the county commissioners, but it must be not less than twelve and one-half cents for a man and horse, twenty-five cents for a one-horse wagon or carriage, six and one-fourth cents for each wheel and each horse of other wagons and carriages, six and one-fourth cents for each single horse or head of cattle, and two cents for each hog or sheep. If at any time the county should pay the cost of the road, plus six per cent, the county should become the owner.[3] A traveler writing late in 1822 says that a public road had just been opened between Vandalia and Springfield.[4] During the same year, Gurdon Saltonstall Hubbard, one of the most active of the agents of the American Fur Company in Illinois, established a direct path or track from Iroquois Post to Danville. In 1824 this path, which was known as "Hubbard's Trail," was extended northward to Chicago, and southward to a point about one hundred and fifty miles southwest of Danville. Along this trail trading-posts were established at intervals of forty or fifty miles.

1. Melish, "Information and Advice to Emigrants," 1819, 108.
2. Woods, "Residence in Ill.," 140.
3. "Laws of Ill.," 1820-21, pp. 94-6.
4. Tillson, "Reminiscences," 54.

The southern extremity of the trail was Blue Point, in Effingham county.[1] This became the regularly traveled route between points connected by it.

Springfield was the northern terminus of the mail route early in 1823, and the next year Sangamon county, in which the village lay, was almost entirely without ferries, bridges, or roads.[2] In 1830 mail was carried between Vincennes and St. Louis thrice a week; between Maysville and St. Louis, and between Belleville and St. Charles twice a week. No point in Illinois, not on one of these routes, received mail oftener than once a week. There was at this time a mail route from Peoria to Galena.[3] The legislatures of Indiana and Illinois petitioned Congress for an appropriation to improve the mail route from Louisville, Kentucky, to St. Louis, Missouri. The length of that part of the route which lay between Vincennes and St. Louis was one hundred and sixty miles, but a more direct route, recently surveyed by authority of the legislature of Illinois, reduced the distance to one hundred and forty-five miles. The distance between Vincennes and St. Louis was made up of about one-fourth of timber land and three-fourths of prairies, from five to twenty miles across. "The settlements are therefore scattered, and far between, and confined to the vicinity of the timbered land. More than nineteen-twentieths of the land, over which the road passes, is the property of the Federal Government. To make the necessary causeways and bridges, and to keep the road in a proper state of repair, is beyond the capacity of the people who reside upon it." Another writer says of the

1. Hamilton, "Incidents and Events in the Life of Gurdon Saltonstall Hubbard," 136.

2. Tillson, "Reminiscences," 81; Strickland, "Autobiography of Peter Cartwright," 250.

3. "State Papers," No. 77, 21st Cong., 1st Sess., III.

FIRST YEARS OF STATEHOOD. 159

route: "It must, for many years, be the channel of communication, through which the Government shall transmit, and receive, all its intelligence relative to the mines in the region of Galena, and Prairie Du Chien, the Military Posts of the Upper Mississippi, Missouri, and their tributary streams, and the whole northwestern Indian frontier."[1]

Galena remained much isolated. A man who had horses and cattle, purchased in southern Illinois and driven to Galena, by way of Springfield and Peoria, in 1823, says that there was no settlement between Peoria and Fever River. A year before, a traveler who went from St. Louis to Galena, on horseback, arrived in time to assist in completing the second cabin in the place.[2] Two travelers who walked from Upper Alton to Galena, in January and February, 1826, had to camp out several nights, because no residence was in reach. Much of the way no trail existed.[3] About 1827 it was common for men to go with teams of four yoke of oxen, and strong canvas-covered wagons from southern Illinois to the lead regions. In those regions they spent the summer in hauling from the mines to the furnaces or from the furnaces to the place of shipment, usually Galena, and taking back to the mines a load of supplies. In the fall the teamsters returned to their homes, sometimes, in the early days, taking a load of lead to St. Louis. These men lived in their wagons, and cooked their own food. The oxen lived by browsing at night.[4]

Transportation rates can be only approximately given,

1. "S. Doc.," No. 28, 21st Cong., 1st Sess., I.

2. Meeker, "Early Hist. of the Lead Region of Wis.," in "Wis. Hist. Soc. Coll.," VI., 278–9.

3. Reid, "Sketch of Enoch Long," Chicago Hist. Soc. Coll., II., 67-8. See also Owen, in "Deutsch-Amerikanische Geschichtsblätter," Jahrgang 2, Heft 2, 42.

4. Chetlain, "Recollections of Seventy Years," 10.

because they varied with the condition of the weather or of the roads, and were frequently agreed upon by a special bargain. In 1817 steamboats are said to have descended the Ohio and the Mississippi at the rate of ten miles per hour, and to have charged passengers six cents per mile. Freight, by steamboat, from New Orleans to Shippingport (Falls of the Ohio), and thence by boats to Zanesville, was about $6.50 per 100 pounds.[1] It took about one month to make the trip from New Orleans to Shawneetown—June 6 to July 10 in a specific case. Nine-tenths of the trade was still carried on in the old style—by flat-boats, barges, pirogues, etc.[2] In December, 1817, freight from Shawneetown to Louisville was $1.12½ per hundred weight; to New Orleans, $1.00; to Pittsburg, $3.50; to Shawneetown from Pittsburg, $1.00; from Louisville, $0.37½; from New Orleans, $4.50. The great difference between the rates up stream and those down stream was due to the difficulty of going against the current.[3] Cobbett estimated that Birkbeck's settlement, fifty miles north of Shawneetown, could be reached from the eastern seaboard for five pounds sterling per person.[4] In 1819, the passenger rate, by steamboat, from New Orleans to Shawneetown, was $110; the freight rate $0.04½ to $0.06 per pound, the high charges being attributed to a lack of competition, which the many new boats then building were expected to remedy.[5] A party of nine people with somewhat more than six thousand pounds of luggage, wishing to start from Baltimore

[1]. Hulme, in Cobbett, "Year's Residence in the U. S.," 279, 302.

[2]. Birkbeck, "Letters from Ill.," 113; Birkbeck, "Jour. from Va. to Ill.," 133-4.

[3]. Fearon, "Sketches of Am.," 260, repeated in Kingdom, "Am. and the British Colonies," 63. In the works of Fearon and Kingdom 4s. 6d. are equal to $1.00.

[4]. Cobbett, "A Year's Residence in the U. S.," 337.

[5]. Birkbeck, "Extracts," 4.

FIRST YEARS OF STATEHOOD.   161

for Illinois, in July, 1819, learned that the water was so low that large boats could with difficulty pass from Pittsburg to Wheeling. They accordingly went from Baltimore to Wheeling, a distance of two hundred and eighty miles, by land. They had two wagons with six horses and a driver to each wagon. The price for transportation was three hundred and fifty dollars. At Wheeling a contract was made for transportation to Louisville, six hundred miles distance. For this, fifty dollars was paid, the passengers agreeing to help navigate the boat. At Louisville an ark was bought for twenty-five dollars, and two men were hired for eighteen dollars and their board, to take the party to Shawneetown, about three hundred miles distant. At Shawneetown the master of a keel-boat was engaged to take the luggage of six thousand pounds to a point about eleven miles from Birkbeck's settlement, for 37½ cents per hundred pounds. The travelers proceeded on foot. The time occupied in the journey was: From Baltimore to Wheeling, sixteen days; from Wheeling to Shawneetown, thirty-eight days; from Shawneetown to the Birkbeck settlement, four days.[1] A traveler in Illinois, in 1819, said that the usual price of land carriage was fifty cents per hundred pounds for each twenty miles; sometimes higher, never lower, and that it would not pay to have corn transported twenty miles.[2] In 1820, the charge for carrying either baggage or persons from Baltimore to Wheeling was reported as from five to seven dollars per hundred weight. Persons wishing to travel cheaply had their luggage transported while they walked.[3]

In 1823 the following passenger rates, by steamboat, were quoted: From Cincinnati to New Orleans, $25.00; to

1. Woods, "Residence in Illinois," 33, 74, 111, 131, 133, 143-4.
2. Faux, "Memorable Days in Am.," 315.
3. Kingdom, "Am. and the British Colonies," 2.

Louisville, $4.00; to Pittsburg, $15.00; to Wheeling, $14.00; from New Orleans to Cincinnati, $50.00; from Louisville to Cincinnati, $6.00; from Pittsburg to Cincinnati, $12.00; from Wheeling to Cincinnati, $10.00. The time quoted for passage up stream was never less than twice that for passage down stream.[1] Early in 1825 the *Louisiana Gazette* (presumably of New Orleans) reported that a steamboat had made the 2200 miles from Pittsburg in sixteen days,[2] and a few weeks later another steamer arrived at Shippingport, at the Falls of the Ohio about two miles below Louisville, thirteen days from New Orleans, this time including three days detention from the breaking of a crank.[3] Rates quoted in 1826, per one hundred pounds, were: From Pittsburg to St. Louis, in keel-boats, $1.62½; to Nashville, $1.50; to Louisville, $0.75; to Cincinnati, $0.62½; to Maysville, $0.50; to Marietta, $0.40; to Wheeling, $0.18¾; in wagons, from Pittsburg to Philadelphia, $1.00 to $1.12½; from Philadelphia to Pittsburg, $3.00; from Philadelphia to Wheeling, $3.50.[4] A Columbus, Ohio, editor declared that it required thirty days and cost $5.00 per hundred to transport goods from Philadelphia to Columbus, while it required but twenty days and $2.50 to transport from New York.[5] No explanation was given, but the most probable one is the opening of the Erie Canal. Illinois buyers could, of course, take advantage of the cheaper rate as well as the inhabitants of Columbus. The freight schedule agreed upon by the owners, masters, and agents of steamboats in July, 1830, was, per 100 pounds, as follows: Pittsburg to Cincinnati, $0.45; Pittsburg to Louis-

1. "Niles' Register," XXV., 95.
2. "Cincinnati Emporium," Feb. 3, 1825.
3. "Cincinnati Gazette," Apr. 1, 1825.
4. "Niles' Register," XXXI., 58.
5. *Ibid.*, XXXI., 38.

ville, $0.50; Wheeling to Cincinnati, $0.40; Wheeling to Louisville, $0.45; Cincinnati to Louisville, $0.12½; in the reverse direction rates were the same, except that the rate from Louisville to Cincinnati was $0.16. Freight on pork, from Cincinnati to Louisville was $0.20 per barrel, and on flour and light (probably meaning empty) barrels, $0.15 per barrel. The schedule rates were not, however, generally adhered to, many boats carrying freight at from 2½ to 5 cents lower than the quoted rate.[1] At this time there were 213 steamboats in use in western waters—an increase of about three-fold since 1820.[2] Improved transportation caused a better market price for produce in the West. In 1819, at Cincinnati, flour sold at $1.37½ per barrel, corn at from $0.10 to $0.12 per bushel, and pork at $0.10½ per pound,[3] while in 1830, in the same market, flour from wagons sold at $2.65 per barrel, or from store at $3.00; corn at $0.18 to $0.20, and pork at $0.05 per pound ($10.00 to $10.50 per barrel).[4] The influence of improved transportation on emigration is obvious. In regard to steamboat navigation it should be noted that in 1817 rates upstream were more than three times as high as rates downstream, in 1823 the former were less than twice the latter, and in 1830 the two were about equal. During the same period the time of up-stream passage was diminished more than one-half. Steamboats had not driven out the ruder crafts, but more and more use was being made of the more expeditious means of transportation, and its effect on the future economic activity of the West could already be seen.

Naturally the difference in price of the same commodity

1. "Cincinnati Christian Journal and Intelligencer," July 27, 1830.
2. "Niles' Register," XXXVIII., 97.
3. *Ibid.*, XLIV., 36.
4. "Cincinnati Christian Journal and Intelligencer," July 27, 1830.

in two different markets was dependent in large measure on the ease or difficulty of transportation. In the latter part of 1817, corn was $0.24 to $0.30 and wheat $0.75, in Illinois, while corn was $0.50 and wheat $0.75 at Cincinnati.[1] In 1825 wheat was worth hardly $0.25 per bushel, while it sold for $0.80 to $0.87½ in Petersburg, Virginia, and flour was $6.00 per barrel at Charleston, South Carolina, and was scarce even at that price in Nashville, Tennessee. At the same time corn sold for from $0.08 to $0.10 in Illinois, and for $1.75 to $2.00 in Petersburg, Virginia.[2] In 1826 wheat sold in Illinois at $0.37½, and in England at $2.00 (nine shillings).[3] In 1829 flour was scarce at Galena. A supply from the more southern settlements in Illinois sold at $8.00 per barrel, and the farmers were urged to bring more.[4] This was in October. In November flour was quoted at Galena at $9.00 to $10.00 per barrel, while it sold at St. Louis for $4.50 to $5.50. In December, Cincinnati flour was from $10.00 to $10.50 and Illinois flour from $8.00 to $8.50, at Galena, whereas in the succeeding August they were $5.00 and $4.00, respectively. In November, 1829, the one article of food that was quoted as cheaper at Galena than at St. Louis was potatoes. They were $0.25 per bushel, at Galena, and from $0.37½ to $0.50 at St. Louis. Butter was $0.25 to $0.37½ at Galena, and $0.12½ to $0.20 at St. Louis; corn, $0.50 at Galena, and $0.25 to $0.31 at St. Louis; beef, $0.03½ to $0.04½ at Galena, and $0.01½ to $0.02 at St. Louis; whisky, $0.62½ per gallon at Galena, and $0.30 to $0.33 at St. Louis.[5]

1. Fearon, "Sketches of Am.," 217, 260. Reprinted in Kingdom, "Am. and the British Colonies," 55, 62.
2. "Niles' Register," XXIX., 165; "The Intelligencer" Petersburg, Va., Mar. 11, 1825; "Charleston (S. C.) Mercury," May 25, 1825; "Nashville (Tenn.) Republican," Apr. 16, 1825.
3. "Niles' Register," XXXI., 52.
4. "Miners' Journal," Galena, Oct. 4, 1829.
5. *Ibid.*, Nov. 3, 1829; Dec. 15, 1829; Aug. 14, 1830.

Life of the People.

Of the 13,635 persons who were following some occupation in Illinois in 1820, nearly 91 per cent (12,395) were engaged in agriculture.[1] To this pursuit the state was naturally well adapted. One of the most observant of German travelers in America wrote that the meaning of "fertile land" was very different in this region from its meaning in Germany. In America fertile land of the first class required no fertilizer for the first century and was too rich for wheat during the first decade, while fertile land of the second class needed no fertilizer during the first twelve to twenty years of its cultivation. Bottom-lands belonged to the first class.[2] The prairies remained unappreciated by the Americans, although some foreign farmers preferred to settle in Illinois, because there they could avoid having to clear land, and could raise a crop the first year, while coal could serve as fuel,[3] and a ditch and bank fence, requiring little wood, could be constructed, or a hedge could be grown.[4] A traveler of 1819 speaks of one of the largest prairies as not well adapted to cultivation, because of the scarcity of wood, and in the fall of 1825 there was

[1] "Twelfth Census of the U. S., Occupations," p. xxx.
[2] Duden, "Nordamerika," 61.
[3] Hecke, "Reise durch die Vereinigten Staaten," II., 134-5.
[4] The following describes a ditch and bank fence: "I very much admire Mr. Birkbeck's mode of *fencing*. He makes a ditch 4 ft. wide at top, sloping to 1 ft. wide at bottom, and 4 ft. deep. With the earth that comes out of the ditch he makes a bank on one side, which is turfed towards the ditch. Then a long pole is put up from the bottom of the ditch to 2 ft. above the bank; this is crossed by a short pole from the other side, and then a rail is laid along between the forks. The banks were growing beautifully, and looked altogether very neat as well as formidable, though a live hedge (which he intends to have) instead of dead poles and rails, upon top, would make the fence far more effectual as well as handsomer."—Hulme, in Cobbett, "Year's Residence in the U. S.," 282.

but one house on the way from Paris to Springfield, leading across eighty miles of a prairie ninety miles in length.¹

It was easy to obtain land. After 1820 it could be bought from the government of the United States at $1.25 per acre, it could be rented—sometimes for one peck of corn per acre per year²—, or the claim of a squatter could be purchased. When Peter Cartwright moved from Kentucky to Illinois in 1824, he gave as reasons for moving the fact that he had six children and but one hundred and fifty acres of land, and that Kentucky land was high and rising in value; the increase of a disposition in the South to justify slavery; the distinction in Kentucky between young people reared without working and those who worked; the danger that his four daughters might marry into slave families; and the need of preachers in the new country.³ The land being obtained, the first cultivation was difficult. Writers often give the idea that after a year or two the land which had been heavily timbered was left free from trees, stumps, or roots, but many a pioneer plowed for twenty years among the stumps. Stump fields are today no novelty in Illinois, and farming has not retrograded. Usually the settler's first need was a crop, and in order to hasten its production the trees were girdled, a process which might either precede or follow the planting, according to the time of year in which the immigrant arrived. If prairie land was plowed six horses, or their equivalent of power in oxen, were required for the first breaking, and a summer's fallow usually followed in order to allow the roots to decay. In 1819 five dollars per acre

1. Ernst in "Pub. No. 8 of the Ill. State Hist. Lib.," 156; "Jacksonville (Ill.) Weekly Journal," Apr. 18, 1877 (in "Ill. Local Hist.," III., in Wis. Hist. Soc. Lib.)

2. Faux, "Memorable Days in Am.," 213.

3. Strickland, "Autobiography of Peter Cartwright," 244.

was paid for the first plowing of the prairie, and three or four dollars for the second.[1]

Agricultural products exhibited considerable variety, although corn was the chief article raised, because it furnished food for man and beast, it gave a large yield, and it was more easily harvested than wheat. Wheat was raised without any great degree of care as to its culture, being frequently sowed upon ground that was poorly prepared, and being threshed in a most wasteful manner. Both wheat and flour were exported. Flour-mills, often of a rude sort, were found at inconveniently long distances from each other. Ferdinand Ernst, traveling in 1819, found a turbine wheel at the mill of Mr. Jarrott, a few miles from St. Louis, and mentioned the fact as a peculiar feature.[2] Some of the settlers in Sangamon county had to go sixty miles to mill in 1824.[3] In 1830 the first flour mill in northern Illinois was erected on Fox River. It was operated by the same power that ran a saw-mill, and the millstones were boulders, laboriously dressed by hand.[4] Tobacco of excellent quality was grown, and sometimes formed an article of export.[5] Cotton was an important article for home consumption. In the early years of the state hopes were entertained that cotton might become an article of export, but it was found that the crop required so much labor as to make raising it in large quantities unprofitable. It was after 1830, however, that it ceased to be cultivated in the state. It was raised at least as far north as the present Danville, about one hundred and

[1]. Faux, "Memorable Days in Am.," 273.
[2]. Ernst, in "Pub. No. 8 of the Ill. State Hist. Lib.," 155.
[3]. Strickland, "Autobiography of Peter Cartwright," 254.
[4]. Chapman, Lyde Grove, in "Stories of the Pioneer Mothers of Ill.," in MSS. in Ill. State Hist. Lib.
[5]. "Niles' Register," XXIX., 37; "Ill. Monthly Mag.," I., 127.

twenty-five miles south of Chicago.¹ A woman whose parents moved to Sangamon county in 1819 says that when in that county they raised, picked, spun, and wove their own cotton. The children had to seed the cotton before the fire in the long winter evenings. The importance of cotton as a factor in inducing immigration may have been considerable.² Large quantities of castor oil were made in the state from home-grown castor beans.³ Vegetables were large, although not always of good flavor.⁴ Peaches, apples, pears, quinces and cherries were cultivated successfully, while grapes, plums, crabapples, persimmons, mulberries, strawberries, raspberries and blackberries grew wild.⁵ An agricultural society was formed in 1819, a chief purpose being to rid the state of stagnant water.⁶

It is not easy to exaggerate the simplicity of the farming of pioneer times. When one reads that in 1817 a log cabin of two rooms could be built for from $50.00 to $70.00; a frame house, ten by fourteen feet, for $57.5.00 to $665.00; a log kitchen for $31.00 to $35.50; a log stable for $31.00 to $40.00; a barn for $80.00 to $97.75; a fence for $0.25 per rod, and a prairie ditch for $0.29 to $0.44 per rod; that a strong wagon cost $160.00; that a log house, eighteen by sixteen feet, was made by contract for $20, and ceiled and floored with sawn boards for $10 more;

1. "Niles' Register," XXII., 2, 67, 245, 386; "Ill. Monthly Mag.," I., 129; Loomis, "Journey to the Great West in 1825," ch. iv., pages unnumbered.
2. "Stories of the Pioneer Mothers of Ill.," in MSS. in Ill. State Hist. Lib.
3. "Niles' Register," XXX., 287; "Ill. Intelligencer," May 18, 1826.
4. "Ill. Monthly Mag.," I., 129.
5. *Ibid.*, I., 128–9.
6. Fearon, "Sketches of America," 1817, 261, reprinted in Kingdom, "Am. and the British Colonies," 63; Birkbeck, "Letters from Ill." 22, 32–3, 51–2, 69, 78, 85; Birkbeck, "Extracts," 24–5, shows that a honey-locust hedge could be made (1819) for less than 12 cents per rod.

that a cow and calf cost $12.00 to $16.00, and a breeding sow, $2.00 or $3.00; that laborers received $0.75 per day without board, and a man and two horses $1.00 per day; and that various other useful articles could be procured at certain prices, care is needed in order to avoid the conclusion that an immigrant must have had several dollars, if not a few hundreds of them. This need for care is increased by the fact that the most detailed statistical data for early Illinois is given by Birkbeck or his visitors, and is applicable to the English settlement in Edwards county—a settlement with enough unique features to make the data almost more of an obstacle than a help. As a matter of fact, many immigrants before 1820 had only enough money to make the first payment on their land ($80.00), or after July 1, 1820, only enough to buy the minimum tract offered for sale ($100.00), while in both periods hundreds had not even as much money as $80.00 or $100.00, and had to become squatters. A log house, and practically all of the first houses were of logs, was usually built without the expenditure of one cent in cash, being erected by the family which was to occupy it, or, if neighbors were within reach, on the "frolic" system. Ceilings and floors were both rare, and if a floor existed it was usually made of puncheons. The number of pioneers who actually paid as much as $31.00 for a log stable must have been small indeed. First fences were often of brush, or brush and logs, and many times crops were raised unfenced. Territorial laws prohibited allowing stock to run at large during the crop season. An immigrant often brought his cow and sow, and if not he either did without, which in the latter case was small privation in a region almost crowded with game, or secured the desired animals by barter or by working for a few days. Men frequently traded work, but the payment of cash wages was rare, the cheapness of land and the ease of securing a living leaving small inducement to anyone to become a day laborer;[1] while for the same reason those who were professional laborers were often of an undesirable type.[2] Foreigners were sometimes shocked at the utter carelessness of Illinois farmers. A soil of great fertility, a region so abundantly supplied with game and wild products as to make it almost possible to live from the forest alone, combined with a lack of efficient means of transportation, made such a temptation to a life of idle ease as many pioneers did not resist. Be it remembered, also, that although towns, retail trade, and export trade had begun in Illinois by 1830, these changes were not simultaneous throughout the state. As 1830 closed Illinois still had squatters many miles from a mill, it still had Indians, it still had unbridged streams, it still had regions far from a market—in a word, it had still persisting in some part of its wide extent each of the ills that had at various times confronted it in respect to personal danger and lack of inducements to farmers. The minority of really progressive farmers overcame the difficulties confronting them by raising cattle or hogs and driving them to distant markets, the price received being almost clear profit, or by constructing their own boats and shipping their produce.[3]

Although the great majority of the population of Illinois was engaged in agriculture, there were salt works in the southeast and lead mines in the northwest. The salt industry was important. Far the greater part of the salt made in the state was made at the Gallatin county saline, near Shawneetown. In 1819 the indefinite statement was made that these springs furnished between 200,000 and

1. Birkbeck, "Jour. from Va. to Ill.," 36; Duden, "Nordamerika," 319.
2. Faux, "Memorable Days in Am.," 315.
3. Birkbeck, "Letters from Ill.," 35-6.

300,000 bushels of salt annually, the salt being sold at the works at from fifty to seventy-five cents per bushel.[1] In 1822, the price of salt in Illinois was reported to have fallen from $1.25 to $0.50, because of the discovery of copious and strong salt wells.[2] The next year a strong well was reported twenty miles east of Carlyle.[3] In 1825, a visitor to the Vermilion county saline found twenty kettles in operation, producing about one hundred bushels of salt per week.[4] In 1828, an official report of the superintendent of the Gallatin county saline stated that about 100,000 bushels of salt was made annually, and sold at from $0.30 to $0.50 per bushel. The lessees paid $2,160.50 rent during the year.[5] In 1830, the salt works in Gallatin county had a capital of $50,000; a product of from 100,000 to 130,000 bushels, selling at from $0.40 to $0.50; and three hundred employees. The saline in Vermilion county had a capital of $3500; a product of 3000 to 4000 bushels, selling at $1.25 to $1.50 per bushel; and eight employees. The works in Jackson county produced 3000 to 4000 bushels, selling at $0.75 to $1.00; and had from six to eight employees. The difference in price is noteworthy as indicating what must have been the difficulty of transporting salt from Gallatin county to either Vermilion or Jackson counties. At the Gallatin county works fuel was becoming scarce and water had to be carried some distance in pipes, thus increasing the cost of production. At the springs in Indiana salt was $1.25 per bushel, and in Kentucky it was $0.50 to $1.00. The states of New York, Virginia, Massa-

1. Mackenzie, "View of the U. S.," 1819, 298.
2. "Niles' Register," XXII., 112.
3. *Ibid.*, XXV., 272.
4. Loomis, "Notes of a Journey to the Great West in 1825," ch. iv., pages unnumbered.
5. "H. J." (Ill.), 1828-29, 63.

chusetts and Ohio, respectively, produced more salt than did Illinois.[1]

The lead industry at Galena was still in its infancy, notwithstanding the fact that the richness of the mines was early known.[2] In 1822, a number of persons went to Galena from Sangamon county.[3] For some years it was a common practice to go to the mines in the summer and return to the older settlements for the winter.[4] The population of Galena was 74 in August, 1823;[5] about 100 on July 1, 1825; 151 on December 31, 1825; 194 on March 31, 1826; 406 on June 30, 1826;[6] and 1000 to 1500 in 1829.[7] In 1826 a part of Lord Selkirk's French-Swiss colony on the Red River moved to Galena and became farmers in that region.[8] The rush to the lead region began in 1826 and became intense in the next year.[9] In 1827, a rude log hut, sixteen by twenty feet, rented for $35.00 per month. Galena had then about two hundred log houses,[10] and in the same year the first framed house was raised.[11] In July, 1828, five hundred lead miners were wanted at $17.00 to $25.00 and board per month.[12]

1. "State Papers," No. 55, 21st Cong., 1st Sess., Vol. III.; "Niles' Register," XXVIII., 161.
2. "Niles' Register," XXII., 226.
3. Parkison, "Pioneer Life in Wis.," in "Wis. Hist. Soc, Coll.," II., 328-9.
4. Owen, "Ums Jahr 1819 und 1829," in "Deutsch-Amerikanische Geschichtsblätter," Jahrgang 2, Heft 2, S. 42.
5. Meeker, "Early Hist. of the Lead Region," in "Wis. Hist. Soc. Coll.," VI., 280.
6. "Pub. Lands," IV, 800.
7. "Narrative of Morgan L. Martin," in "Wis. Hist. Soc. Coll.," XI., 398.
8. Chetlain, "Recollections of Seventy Years," 6; Mrs. Adile Gratiot, in "Early Ill. Towns," Lib. of Chicago Hist. Soc.
9. Parkison, "Pioneer Life in Wis.," in "Wis. Hist. Soc. Coll.," II., 329.
10. "Ex. Doc.," No. 277, 20th Cong., 1st Sess., Vol. VII.
11. "Shattuck Memorials," 233-4.
12. "Niles' Register," XXXIV., 344.

FIRST YEARS OF STATEHOOD. 173

A pursuit that was once common and profitable is described by a lawyer who traveled the first Illinois circuit, consisting of the counties of Greene, Sangamon, Peoria, Fulton, Schuyler, Adams, Pike and Calhoun, in 1827, as follows: "On this circuit we found but little business in any of the counties—parties, jurymen and witnesses were reported in all the counties after Peoria, as being absent bee and deer hunting—a business that was then profitable, as well as necessary to the sustenance of families during the winter."[1]

Not until after 1830 was a common school system with effective provision for its support established, although subscription schools existed some years before the close of the eighteenth century. Instruction given in the earliest schools was slight, and in 1818 a most competent observer declared that he believed that in Missouri "at least one-third of the schools were really a public nuisance, and did the people more harm than good; another third about balanced the account, by doing about as much harm as good; and perhaps one-third were advantageous to the community in various degrees. Not a few drunken, profane, worthless Irishmen were perambulating the country, and getting up schools; and yet they could neither speak, read, pronounce, spell, or write the English language."[2] These schools closely resembled those of Illinois. Schoolbooks were rare and children carried to school whatever book they chanced to have, the Old Testament with its long proper names sometimes serving in lieu of a chart or primer.[3] In some schools pupils studied aloud. Reading, writing, spelling and arithmetic were the only branches commonly taught, although as early as 1806 surveying was

1. "Jacksonville (Ill.) Weekly Journal," Apr. 18, 1877.
2. Babcock, "Memoir of John Mason Peck," 123.
3. Peck, " 'Father Clark'; or, The Pioneer Preacher," 240.

taught in a "seminary" near the present Belleville.[1] In 1827 Rock Spring Seminary, now Shurtleff College, was opened by Baptists, and the following year instruction was begun in what was to become McKendree College (Methodist).[2] The teacher of the first school in McLean county (1825) received $2.50 per pupil for the term of four months.[3] The next year a teacher in Jacksonville was to be paid in cash or produce, or in pork, cattle, or hogs at cash prices, and to pay board in similar commodities at the rate of one dollar per week. This included washing, fuel and lights. School was open ten, and often twelve, hours per day.[4]

Religious societies were early organized, but the building of churches was not then common. In 1796 a Baptist society was organized, and previous to this time both Baptists and Methodists, without organized societies, had united in holding prayer-meetings in which the Bible and published sermons were read, prayers offered, and hymns sung.[5] Before the close of the century the Methodists organized. The Presbyterians were prominent in the early years of statehood, but in 1818 they were just beginning their work in Illinois.[6] Meetings were usually held in private houses until such time as the congregation felt that a church building should be erected, or at least until some one felt the need, for the first church was sometimes built by a few individuals.[7] Ministers were of two types—those who devoted all of their time to religious work and traveled over large areas, and those who

1. Reynolds, "Illinois—My Own Times," 59.
2. Babcock, "Memoir of John Mason Peck," 229.
3. "Trans. of the McLean Co. (Ill.) Hist. Soc.," II., 19.
4. "Jacksonville (Ill.) Weekly Journal," Apr. 18, 1877.
5. Peck, in Reynolds, "Pioneer Hist. of Ill.," 259.
6. *Ibid.*, 272–3.
7. Strickland, "Autobiography of Peter Cartwright," 386–7.

combined ministerial duties with farming, hunting, or some other frontier occupation. Neither class received much money. Peter Cartwright, one of the most famous pioneer preachers, received $40 one year (1824-25) and $60 the next—and this he considered good wages.[1] Pioneer energy was displayed in the overcoming of difficulties. For more than ten years the Baptists held meetings on alternate months at two places thirty-six miles apart, and several families regularly traveled that distance to the two-days' meeting, even in unfavorable weather—and this, too, after Illinois had become a state.[2] In 1829, the Presbyterians, true to their missionary spirit, occupied the extreme frontier at Galena.[3] Catholicism increased but slowly.[4] Divisions such as were found in the East or South reached Illinois, and at one time the Baptists were divided into three factions, which had about the same kind of fraternal relations as the Jews and the Samaritans. The chief questions for contention were whether or not missionaries should be sent out by the church and whether fellowship with slaveholders should be maintained.[5] An association of anti-slavery Baptists was formed, as also Bible societies and temperance societies.[6] Camp-meetings, with their well-known phenomena, were common in the early years of statehood, and it is no reflection upon their value to say that they were one of the chief diversions for the pioneers.

1. Strickland, "Autobiography of Peter Cartwright," 254.
2. Babcock, "Memoir of John M. Peck," 96-7.
3. Reynolds, "Illinois—My Own Times," 128.
4. *Ibid.*, 116-7.
5. Babcock, "Memoir of John M. Peck," 94-5.
6. *Ibid.*, 183, *et seq.*, 203, 209.

In general, on the subject of religion in early Illinois, see: Peck, in Reynolds, "Pioneer Hist. of Ill.," 253-75, and the above mentioned works.

CHAPTER VI.

SLAVERY IN ILLINOIS AS AFFECTING SETTLEMENT.

SLAVERY, as well as indentured servitude, existed in Illinois as late as 1845,[1] and the "Black Laws" of the state were repealed on February 7, 1865.[2] From 1787 until years after 1830 the slavery question was an unsettled one. In addition to the arguments for or against the institution that were used everywhere, the pro-slavery party in Illinois asserted that as the Ordinance of 1787 guaranteed to the French inhabitants their property, the French could hold slaves, and that as all citizens of a state had equal rights other persons in Illinois could hold slaves. The reply was that the Ordinance plainly forbade slavery.[3]

Whatever the merits of the argument, slavery did exist in Illinois. The fear of the French that they might lose their slaves, and the desire to attract slaveholders to Illinois, led to determined and repeated efforts to legalize slavery. Early in 1796 a petition was sent from Kaskaskia to Congress, praying that the anti-slavery article in the Ordinance of 1787 might be either repealed or so altered as to permit the introduction of slaves from the original states or elsewhere into the country of Illinois, that a law might be enacted permitting the introduction of such slaves as servants for life, and that it might be declared

[1]. Harris, "Negro Servitude in Ill.," 116-9, note 3, p. 118.
[2]. "Public Laws" (Ill.), 1865, 105.
[3]. The question of the binding effect of the Ordinance received much attention, especially from state courts, but early petitions show that the discussion was not early important. In general, see Haight, "Ordinance of 1787," in "Mich. Pol. Sci. Ass'n Pub.," II., 343-402; Cooley, "Michigan," 137-9; Washburne, "Sketch of Edward Coles," 67-71.

for what period the children of such servants should serve the masters of their parents. This petition was signed by four men, including some of the largest landowners in Illinois, but as the petition, while purporting to come from Illinois alone, concerned the entire Northwest Territory, as there was no indication that the four petitioners represented Illinois sentiment, and as the congressional committee was informed that many of the inhabitants of the territory did not desire the proposed change, the prayer of the petition was denied.[1]

In 1800, two hundred and sixty-eight inhabitants of Illinois, chiefly French, petitioned Congress to repeal the anti-slavery provision of the Ordinance, stating that many of the inhabitants were crossing the Mississippi with their slaves. The petition was not considered.[2] A similar request, presented late in 1802, was twice reported upon by committees, one report (Randolph's) declaring that the growth of Ohio proved that a lack of slavery would not seriously retard settlement, while the other was in favor of suspending the anti-slavery article for ten years, the male descendants of immigrating slaves to be free at the age of wenty-five years, and the females at twenty-one.[3] In 1805 a majority of the members of the respective houses of the Indiana legislature petitioned for the repeal of the anti-slavery article, and this petition was closely followed by a memorial from Illinois expressing the hope that the general government would not pass unnoticed the act of the last legislature authorizing the importation of slaves into the territory. It violated the Ordinance, the memorialists declared, and although they desired slavery they

1. "Pub. Lands," I., 68-9; "Ind. Hist. Soc. Pub.," II., 447-52, 452-5.
2. "Ind. Hist. Soc. Pub.," II., 455-61; "Annals of Cong.," 6th Cong., 735.
3. "Ind. Hist. Soc. Pub.," II., 461-70; "A. S. P. Misc.," I., 387; "Annals of Cong.," 8th Cong., 1st Sess., 1023-4; *ibid.*, 9th Cong., 1st Sess., 466-8.

professed themselves to be law-abiding.[1] A committee report on the petition and memorial recommended that permission to import slaves into Indiana (then including Illinois) for ten years be granted, in order that the evil effects of slavery might be mitigated by its dispersion, but no legislation resulted from the report,[2] and the next year petitioning was resumed. The legislature sent resolutions asking for the suspension of the anti-slavery article, and elaborating the argument for such suspension. A committee of which the territorial delegate from Indiana was chairman, presented a favorable report.[3]

In September, 1807, a petition for the suspension of the anti-slavery article was sent to Congress from the Indiana legislature. It was signed by Jesse B. Thomas, later author of the Missouri Compromise, but then Speaker of the territorial House of Representatives, and resident in what was to become the State of Indiana, and by the president *pro tem.* of the Legislative Council. Action in committee was adverse,[4] Congress being then busied with the question of the abolition of the slave trade.

During the territorial period in Illinois (1809–1818), the slavery question was not much agitated. The Constitution of 1818 provided that slaves could not be thereafter brought into the State, except such as should be brought under contract to labor at the Saline Creek salt works, said contract to be limited to one year, although renewable, and the proviso to be void after 1825, but existing slavery was not abolished, and existing indentures—and some were

1. "Ind. Hist. Soc. Pub.," II., 476–83, 498–506.
2. *Ibid.*, II., 494–7; "A. S. P., Misc.," I., 450; "Annals of Cong.," 9th Cong., 1st Sess., 293, 466–8.
3. "Ind. Hist. Soc. Pub.," II., 507–10; "A. S. P., Misc.," I., 467, 477; "Annals of Cong.," 9th Cong., 2d Sess., 375, 482.
4. "Ind. Hist. Soc. Pub.," II., 515–21; "A. S. P., Misc.," I., 484; "Annals of Cong.," 10th Cong., 1st Sess., 23, *et seq.*, 816.

SLAVERY AS AFFECTING SETTLEMENT.

for ninety-nine years[1]—should be carried out. Male children of slaves or indentured servants should be free at the age of twenty-one and females at eighteen.[2] In Congress, as has been seen, Tallmadge, of New York, objected to admitting Illinois before she abolished slavery, but his objection was ineffectual.

In March, 1819, a slave code was enacted. Any black or mulatto coming into the State was required to file with the clerk of a circuit court a certificate of freedom. Slaves should not be brought into the state for the purpose of emancipation. Resident negroes, other than slaves and indentured servants, must file certificates of freedom. Slaves were to be whipped instead of fined, thirty-nine stripes being the maximum number that might be inflicted. Contracts with slaves were void. Not more than two slaves should meet together without written permission from their masters. Any master emancipating his slaves must give a bond of $1000 per head that such emancipated slaves should not become public charges, failure to give such a bond being punishable by a fine of $200 per head. Colored people must present passes when traveling.[3]

Stringent as was the code of 1819, it was of a type that was common in the slave states. Its passage may have kept some negroes, both free and slave, from coming into the state upon their own initiative without certificates of freedom. From 1810 to 1820 the number of slaves in Illinois increased from 168 to 917, Illinois being the only state north of Mason and Dixon's line having an increase in the number of slaves during the decade, although in the Territory of Missouri, during this time, the number increased from about 3000 to over 10,200. At the same

1. Harris, "Negro Servitude in Ill.," 11, note 3.
2. Poore, "Charters and Constitutions," Pt. I., 445-6.
3. "Revised Laws of Ill.," 1833, 457-62.

time the number of free blacks in Illinois decreased from about 600 to some 450, while they increased in Indiana from nearly 400 to over 1200. Of the slaves in Illinois in 1820 precisely 500 were in the counties of Gallatin and Randolph, the former being the center of the salt-making industry, and the latter the seat of the early French settlement at Kaskaskia.[1]

Whether the anti-slavery clause of the Ordinance of 1787 freed the slaves of the old French settlers was long a disputed question, and it is certain that a strict construction of the Illinois Constitution of 1818 made further importation of slaves illegal. Many slave-owners passed through southern Illinois to Missouri, because the main road for emigration by land to that territory crossed the Ohio River at Shawneetown. Many of the slaves who produced the large increase in the number of slaves in Missouri from 1810 to 1820 must have gone over this route. In 1820 more than one-seventh of the population of Missouri was slave.[2] The people of Illinois could not fail to see that they were losing a certain class of emigrants— the prosperous slaveholders. The loss became greater as the likelihood of Missouri's admittance as a slave state increased. As early as 1820 there was a rumor of the formation of a party in Illinois to introduce slavery into the state in a legal manner.[3] The next year an editorial in a leading newspaper of Illinois said: "Will the admission of slavery in a new state tend to increase its population?—is a question which has been of late much discussed both within and without this state. It has been contended that its admission would induce the emigration of citizens of states as well where slavery was, as where it

1. "Ninth Census of U. S., Population and Social Statistics," 5, 7, 24–5; Melish, "Geog. Desc. of the U. S.," 1822, 359.
2. "Ninth Census of U. S., Population and Social Statistics," 3, 7.
3. J. Q. Adams, "Memoirs," V., 9.

was not tolerated—that while it would attract the attention of the wealthy southern planter, it would not deter the industrious northern farmer." The editor cites Ohio and Kentucky as proof against the above argument. In 1810 Ohio had a population, in round numbers, of 230,700 and Kentucky one of 406,500; in 1820 Ohio had 581,400, while Kentucky had 563,300, giving a difference in favor of Ohio of over 18,000; and an access of gain during the decade, in favor of Ohio, of 93,847. "We are willing to take into consideration the unsettled titles of land in the last-mentioned state [Kentucky], and admit that in this respect Ohio had a decided advantage—we will therefore deduct the fraction of 93,847, believing it equivalent to the loss of population from this cause—there is still a difference of 100,000."[1] The editor's figures for 1810 were correct and those for 1820 were approximately so. It is also true, and in line with his argument, that during the same decade Indiana showed an increase from 24,500 to 147,200, while Missouri's increase was from 20,800 to 66,500; the increase in Illinois being between the two in proportion of increase—from 12,282 to 55,162.[2] The passing of the slaveholders to Missouri continued and the discussion of the slavery question became animated.

In the gubernatorial election of 1822 there were four candidates for governor, two being anti-slavery and two pro-slavery in belief. Edward Coles, from Virginia, an anti-slavery man, was elected by a plurality of but a few votes. His election was due to a division in the ranks of the opposite party, as is shown by the fact that the pro-slavery party polled over 5300 votes, while the anti-slavery party polled only some 3300.[3] In his message of Decem-

1. "Illinois Intelligencer" (Vandalia), Apr. 24, 1821.
2. "Ninth Census of the U. S., Population and Social Statistics," 3.
3. The vote for governor given by W. H. Brown, "Early Movement in Illinois for the Legalization of Slavery," ("Fergus Hist. Ser.," No. 4, p. 15),

ber 5, 1822, Governor Coles strongly urged the passage of a law to prevent kidnapping[1]—then a regular trade. This was referred to a select committee which reported as follows: "Your committee have carefully examined the laws upon the subject, and with deep regret announce their incapability of devising a more effectual plan than the one already prescribed by law for the suppression of such infamous crimes. It is believed that the benevolent views of the executive and the benign purposes of the statutes can only be realized by the redoubled diligence of our grand juries and our magistrates, aided by the well-directed support of all just and good men."[2] The legislature was politically opposed to the governor, and the committee's report sounds like the baldest irony. With the report was presented a scheme for introducing slavery into the state,[3] a scheme which eventually led to the vote of 1824.[4]

The Constitution of Illinois provided that upon the vote of two-thirds of the members of each house of the legislature, the question of calling a convention for the revision of the Constitution should be submitted to the people. For calling a convention only a majority vote from the people was necessary. This method of procedure the pro-slavery party determined upon. The two-thirds in favor of the project could be secured without difficulty in the senate, but in the house the desperate expedient of

differs from that by Washburne, "Sketch of Edward Coles," 58, and Bonham, "Fifty Years Recollections," 22, while neither gives Coles a plurality of 46 votes, as Harris in "Negro Servitude in Ill.," 31, says the official returns show him to have received. For the purposes of this work the differences are so slight as to be negligible.

1. "House Journal" (Ill.), 1822–23, pp. 25–7; "Senate Journal" (Ill.), 1822–23, pp. 29–30.
2. "Senate Journal" (Ill.), 1822–23, pp. 43–6; "House Journal" (Ill.), 1822–23, pp. 68, 134, 147–8.
3. "House Journal" (Ill.), 1822–23, pp. 44, 45.
4. Davidson and Stuvé, "Hist. of Ill.," 320.

SLAVERY AS AFFECTING SETTLEMENT. 183

reconsidering the right of a member to a contested seat and seating his opponent was resorted to.[1] This being done the resolution to submit the question of a constitutional convention to the people was passed by a bare two-thirds vote in each house.[2] Of the eighteen men who voted against the resolution, eleven were natives of southern states, two of New York, two of Connecticut, one of Massachusetts, one of Vermont, and one of Sweden. There were some northern men who voted in favor of the resolution.[3]

The campaign resulting from the passage of the convention resolution was waged for eighteen months with great vigor. Press and pulpit were actively employed.[4] A large anti-slavery society was formed in Morgan county,[5] and it was in all probability one of many such organizations. In August, 1824, came the final vote, and the official count of the votes showed a majority of 1668 against calling a constitutional convention.[6]

1. "House Journal" (Ill.), 1822–23, p. 272.
2. *Ibid.*, 1822–23, p. 276; "Senate Journal" (Ill.), 1822–23, p. 252.
3. Washburne, "Sketch of Edward Coles," *passim.*
4. "Edwardsville Spectator," Jan. 27, 1824; Nov. 29, 1823.
5. Eames, "Historic Morgan and Classic Jacksonville," 12.
6. "House Journal" (Ill.), 1824–25, p. 64. The corrected official vote (Aug. 2, 1824), by counties, is as follows:

	For.	Against.		For.	Against.		For.	Against.
Alexander	75	51	Hamilton	173	85	Pope	273	124
Bond	63	240	Jackson	180	93	Randolph	357	284
Clark	31	116	Jefferson	99	43	Sangamon	153	722
Crawford	134	262	Johnson	74	74	St. Clair	408	506
Edgar	3	234	Lawrence	158	261	Union	213	240
Edwards	189	391	Madison	351	563	Washington	112	173
Fayette	125	121	Marion	45	52	Wayne	189	111
Franklin	170	113	Montgomery	74	90	White	355	326
Fulton	5	60	Monroe	141	196	Totals	4972	6640
Gallatin	597	133	Morgan	42	432			
Greene	164	379	Pike	19	165			

The vote as here given is from Moses, "Illinois," I., 324. It is also given in

It is noteworthy that in this struggle the governor of the state was an anti-slavery southerner; eleven of the eighteen anti-slavery men in the legislature were southern; the pro-slavery party, which polled 1971 more votes than its opponents in 1822, was defeated by 1668 votes in 1824. It is also true that of the leaders in the campaign some of the most noted were southern anti-slavery or northern pro-slavery men.

The history of settlement suggests several explanations for the votes of 1822 and 1824. The legislature which passed the convention resolution had not been chosen with the avowed purpose of doing so. Some designing politicians had such an object in view and secured the election of pro-slavery men by anti-slavery constituents. The number of such cases was not large, but as the resolution passed by the minimum vote they are important.[1] In 1822, however, there was almost without doubt a pro-slavery majority in the state, but it is improbable that there was a two-thirds majority. In the election of 1822, there were 8635 votes cast, while in that of 1824 there were 11,612 votes cast. This great increase indicates a large immigration. Immigration at this time was largely to the northern counties of the state, and it is a point of prime significance that each of the seven northern counties gave large majorities against the calling of the convention,

Harris, "Negro Servitude in Illinois," 48. It differs to a slight degree from that given by William H. Brown in his "Historical Sketch of the Early Movement in Illinois for the Legalization of Slavery," read at the annual meeting of the Chicago Hist. Soc., Dec. 5, 1864 ("Fergus Hist. Ser.," No. 4), and in Washburne, "Sketch of Edward Coles," 191. Brown was one of the leaders in the struggle and his work is of especial value. It is probable that the vote appended to his address was prepared by some one else. The work of Moses is of later date and his figures correspond to the official report in respect to the majority against the convention, as the others do not.

1. Brown, "Early Movement in Illinois for the Legalization of Slavery," in "Fergus Hist. Series," No. 4, pp. 16-17.

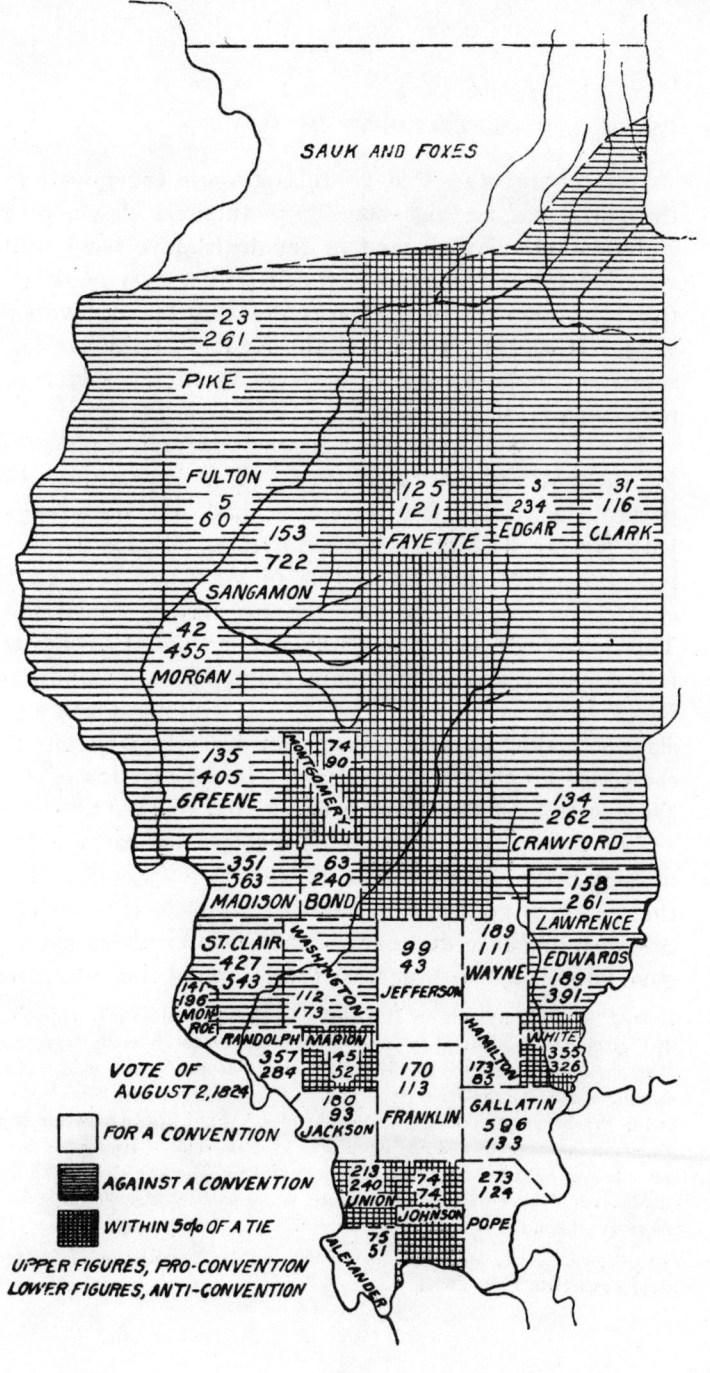

and that without the vote of these seven counties the vote would have been 4523 for a convention and 4408 against a convention, thus changing the decision of the state. This vote of the northern counties can not be explained by an increased immigration from the north, because no such increase to any significant degree is discoverable. The admission of Missouri as a slave state would naturally lead pro-slavery emigrants to go to that state instead of to Illinois. Another event which tended to influence the vote in Illinois was the decision of Indiana against slavery, in the summer of 1823, in the midst of the campaign in Illinois.[1] The unjust action of the Illinois House of Representatives in unseating an anti-convention member was a powerful argument against the pro-slavery party.

In his message to the legislature, on November 16, 1824, Governor Coles said: "In the observations I had the honor to make to the last Legislature, I recommended that provision should be made for the abolition of the remnant of African slavery which still existed in this state. The full discussion of the principles and policy of personal slavery, which has taken place since that period, resulting in its rejection by the decided voice of the people, still more imperiously makes it my duty to call your attention in an especial manner to this subject, and earnestly to entreat you to make just and equitable provision for as speedy an abolition of this remnant of slavery, as may be deemed consistent with the rights and claims of the parties concerned.

"In close connection with this subject, is my former recommendation, to which I again solicit your attention, that the law as it respects those held in service should be rendered less severe, and more accordant with our political

[1]. "Niles' Register," XXV., 39; "The Columbian Star" (Washington, D. C.), Feb. 21, 1824.

institutions and local situation; and that more severe penalties should be enacted against the unnatural crime of kidnapping, which then prevailed to a great extent and has since considerably increased, in consequence of the defects of the present law. Regarding the former, our laws in general are a mere transcript of those of the more southern states, where the great number of slaves makes it necessary for the safety of the whites, that the laws for their government, and concerning free blacks, should be very strict.—But, there being no such motive here, the necessity of such laws ceases, and consequently their injustice and cruelty are the more apparent. The latter are found every day more and more defective and inefficient; and kidnapping has now become a regular trade, which is carried on to a vast extent to the country bordering on the lower Mississippi, up the Red River, and to the West Indies. To put an immediate and effectual stop to this nefarious traffic, is the imperious duty of the Legislature."[1]

The house of representatives referred the governor's remarks concerning kidnapping to a select committee. A bill was reported, but after being weakened by amendments it was tabled.[2] In his message in 1826 the governor renewed his recommendations,[3] and a section of the criminal code of January, 1827, provided that kidnapping should be punishable by confinement in the penitentiary for not less than one nor more than seven years.[4] An act of January, 1825, provided that anyone who had failed to give the bond required by the black code of 1819 from

1. "H. J." (Ill.), 1824–25, p. 13; on kidnapping see Harris, "Negro Servitude in Ill.," 53 ff.
2. *Ibid.*, 1824–25, pp. 26, 27, 151.
3. *Ibid.*, 1826–27, pp. 9–10.
4. "Revised Laws of Ill.," 1833, 180–1.

SLAVERY AS AFFECTING SETTLEMENT.   187

those who emancipated slaves, should be released from any verdict or judgment arising from such failure, upon indemnifying the county for any money expended for the relief of the freedmen.[1] By an act of 1829 relating to slaves, whites were not to marry blacks, slaves were not to come to the state in order to be free, and runaway slaves should be advertised in the newspapers of the state.[2] The number of slaves in Illinois decreased after 1820. In 1820 there were 917 slaves in the state; in 1830, 747; in 1840, 331,[3] and before the next census slavery in the state was abolished.

The vote of 1824 against calling a constitutional convention marked the end of the slavery question as an obstacle to the immigration of an anti-slavery population. Slaveholders, never a large proportion of the immigrants, practically ceased to come to the state, while the immigration of anti-slavery southerners continued, and the aggregate immigration greatly increased. The population of the state was 55,162 in 1820; 72,817, in 1825; and 157,445 in 1830. Missouri, more populous than Illinois by more than 11,000 in 1820, was less so by 17,000 in 1830.[4] Governor Coles, in his message of January 3, 1826, said: "The tide of emigration, which had been for several years checked by various causes, both general and local, has again set in, and has afforded a greater accession of population during the past, than it had for the three preceding years. This addition to our population and wealth has given a new impulse to the industry and enterprise of our citizens, and has sensibly animated the face of our country. And as the causes which have impeded the

1. "Laws of Ill.," 1824-25, p. 50.
2. "Revised Laws of Ill." 1833, 463-65.
3. "Ninth Census of the U. S., Population and Social Statistics," p. 7.
4. Ibid., 3; "H. J." (Ill.), 1826, 11.

prosperity of the state are daily diminishing, and the inducements to emigration are increasing, we may confidently anticipate a more steady and rapid augmentation of its population and resources."[1]

From 1820 to 1825 the increase of population in Illinois was 17,655, while from 1825 to 1830 it was 84,628. Contemporaries have left some interesting records of immigration during the latter five years—a period in which the population of the state increased more than 116 per cent. Immigration had begun to be brisk by the fall of 1824. At the general election in August, 1820, there were 1132 votes cast in Madison county, while at a similar election in August, 1824, there were 3223 votes cast in the same tertory, Madison county having been divided into Madison, Pike, Fulton, Sangamon, Morgan and Greene counties. A Madison county newspaper said: "That country bordering on the Illinois River is populating at this time more rapidly than at any former period. Family wagons with emigrants are daily passing this place [Edwardsville], on their way thither."[2] During the five weeks ending October 28, 1825, about two hundred and fifty wagons, with an average of five persons to each, passed through Vandalia, bound chiefly for the Sangamo country.[3] The unsettled condition of the slavery question from 1820 to August, 1824, is given as the cause of the slight increase in population during that period, and the settlement of the question is thought to have been a chief cause for the increase after 1824.[4] It must not be supposed, however, that any one cause excludes all others. The country as a whole had scarcely recovered from the great financial depression of 1819;

1. "H. J." (Ill.), 1826, 11.
2. "Edwardsville (Ill.) Spectator," Oct. 5, 1824.
3. "Niles' Register," XXIX., 208.
4. *Ibid.*, XXIX., 422.

SLAVERY AS AFFECTING SETTLEMENT. 189

Kentucky was in turmoil over her bank, land titles and old and new courts;[1] early in 1825 over 65,000 acres in a single county in Tennessee were advertised for sale for the delinquent taxes of 1824;[2] and in 1826 a great drought in North Carolina caused a marked emigration from that state.[3]

In 1829 emigration was great. Some forty English families from Yorkshire came by way of Canada and settled near Jacksonville, Illinois. They brought agricultural implements and some money.[4] The *Kentucky Gazette* lamented the fact that a large number of the best families of Lexington were removing to Illinois.[5] An Illinois newspaper reported: "The number of emigrants passing through our Town [Vandalia] this fall, is unusually great. During the last week the waggons and teams going to the north amounted to several hundred. At no previous period has our State encreased so rapidly, as it is now encreasing."[6] Another editor estimated the annual increase in population from 1826 to 1829 at not less than 12,000[7]—a figure which was almost certainly too low. In 1830 a meeting of gentlemen from the counties of Hampshire and Hampden (Massachusetts) was held at Northampton to consider the expediency of forming a colony to remove to Illinois. After a discussion it was voted to adjourn to meet on the 10th of October at Warner's Coffee House in Southampton. Similar meetings were held at Pawtucket and Worcester.[8]

1. Shaler, "Kentucky," 176–85.
2. "Nashville (Tenn.) Republican," Apr. 16, 1825.
3. "Niles' Register," XXX., 449.
4. "Galena Advertiser," July 20, Aug. 10, Sept. 21, 1829.
5. "Niles' Register," XXXVI., 222.
6. "Illinois Intelligencer" (Vandalia), Oct. 31, 1829.
7. "Niles' Register," XXXVI., 271.
8. "Illinois Intelligencer" (Vandalia), Nov. 27, 1830.

The immigration to Illinois was but part of a general westward movement. From Charleston, Virginia, we hear: "The tide of emigration through this place is rapid, and we believe, unprecedented. It is believed that not less than eight thousand individuals, since the 1st September last [written on November 6, 1829], have passed on this route. They are principally from the lower part of this state and South Carolina, bound for Indiana, Illinois, and Michigan.—They jog on, careless of the varying climate, and apparently without regret for the friends and the country they leave behind, seeking forests to fell, and a new country to settle." The editor attributes this movement to the fact that slavery had rendered white labor disreputable.[1] Three thousand persons bound for the West arrived at Buffalo in one week and six thousand per week were reported as passing through Indianapolis, bound for the Wabash country alone.[2] The great northern tide was chiefly bound to Ohio and Michigan,[3] northern Illinois not being open to settlement. Five years after Detroit received three hundred arrivals per week, Chicago had about a dozen houses, besides Fort Dearborn. This was the Chicago of 1830.[4]

1. "Niles' Register," XXXVII., 195.
2. "Galena Advertiser," July 20, 1829; "Niles' Register," XXXVII., 230.
3. "Niles' Register," XXVIII., 161.
4. "State Papers," No. 69, 21st Cong., 1st Sess., Vol. III.

CHAPTER VII.

SUCCESSFUL FRONTIERSMEN.

THE character of the men who succeed in gaining the favor of those among whom they live indicates the character of those whose favor has been gained. Preachers, land dealers, lawyers, town builders, and politicians can not thrive in a hostile community. It is worth while in studying Illinois in its frontier stage to notice some of the chief traits of its leaders.

No better type of the pioneer preacher need be sought than the Rev. Dr. Peter Cartwright. He preached in the West for nearly seventy years, during which time he delivered some eighteen thousand sermons, baptized some fifteen thousand persons, received into the church nearly twelve thousand members, and licensed preachers enough to make a whole conference. He was for fifty years a presiding elder in the Methodist Episcopal church. His home was in Illinois from 1824 until his death in 1872. Aside from his ministerial duties he twice represented Sangamon county in the Illinois House of Representatives; was a candidate for congressman against Abraham Lincoln in 1846; and was a member of an historical society founded as early as 1827.

Cartwright had a number of traits that attracted frontiersmen. In person he was about five feet ten inches high, and of square build, having a powerful physical frame and weighing nearly two hundred pounds. "The roughs and bruisers at camp-meetings and elsewhere stood in awe of his brawny arm, and many anecdotes are told of his courage and daring that sent terror to their ranks. He felt that he was one of the Lord's breaking plows, and that he had to drive his way through all kinds of roots and stubborn soil. . . . His gesticulation, his manner of listening, his walk, and his laugh were peculiar, and would command attention in a crowd of a thousand. There was something undefinable about the whole man that was attractive to the majority of the people, and made them linger in his presence and want to see him again." He had a remarkable power to read men, his first impressions being quickly made and almost always correct. He was often gay, but never frivolous; often eccentric, but never silly. A Cumberland Presbyterian, after attending a communion service administered by Cartwright and at which the Baptist, Rev. John M. Peck, was present, wrote: "After meeting, I invited these two men to spend the night with me, which they did; and such a night!—of all Western anecdotes and manners, flow of soul and out-spoken brotherhood— we had never seen, and never expect to enjoy again. These were, then [1824 c.], the two strongest men of mark in the ministry, in this State [Illinois]." Cartwright's vitality was remarkable. In the sixty-sixth year of his ministry, and the eighty-sixth of his life, he dedicated eight churches, preached at seventy-seven funerals, addressed eight schools, baptized twenty adults and fifty children, married five couples, received fifteen into the church on probation and twenty-five into full connection, raised twenty-five dollars missionary money, donated twenty dollars for new churches, wrote one hundred and twelve letters, delivered many lectures, and sold two hundred dollars worth of books. Many frontier preachers of the time were lacking in common sense, but they were not popular. This is the testimony of a contemporary (1828) writer whose analysis of western character has rarely been excelled.[1]

[1]. Thomas S. Hinde, writing over the signature of "Theophilus Arminius," in "Methodist Magazine," XI., 1828, 154--8. The identity of the writer is shown by a note on p. 33 of the same volume.

SUCCESSFUL FRONTIERSMEN.

John Edgar, a native of Ireland, was one of the largest landholders who ever lived in Illinois. At the outbreak of the American Revolution he was a British officer living at Detroit, but becoming implicated in the efforts of his American wife to aid British soldiers in deserting, he was imprisoned. He escaped, and in 1784 settled in Kaskaskia, where his wife joined him two years later, having saved from confiscation some twelve thousand dollars. This made Edgar the rich man of the community. "In very early times, he erected, at great expense, a fine flouring mill on the same site where M. Paget had built one sixty years before. This mill was a great benefit to the public and also profitable to the proprietor. Before the year 1800, this mill manufactured great quantities of flour for the New Orleans market which would compare well with the Atlantic flour." Edgar built a splendid mansion in Kaskaskia and entertained royally. At a time when hospitality was common he improved upon it. His home was the fashionable resort for almost half a century. It was here that Lafayette was entertained. In addition to his flour mill, which attracted settlers to its vicinity near Kaskaskia and which for many years did most of the merchant business in flour in the country, Edgar owned and operated salt works near the Mississippi, northwest of Kaskaskia, and also invested largely in land. Before the commissioners appointed to settle land claims he claimed thirty-six thousand acres in one claim as the assignee of ninety donation-rights, while he and John Murry St. Clair

Among the many writings concerning Peter Cartwright, the best are Strickland, "Autobiography of Peter Cartwright"; Cartwright, "Fifty Years as a Presiding Elder," and the obituary notice in "Minutes of the Annual Conferences of the M. E. Church," 1873, 115–7. See also Moses, "Illinois," I., 348, 379, 395, 506, 1166.

For the character of John M. Peck, also a noted pioneer preacher and founder of Rock Spring Seminary in Illinois, see "Memoir of John Mason Peck, D. D.," edited by Rufus Babcock.

claimed 13,986 acres which proved upon survey to cover almost thirty thousand acres. In territorial times Edgar paid more taxes than any one else in the territory. In 1790 Edgar was appointed chief justice of the Kaskaskia district of St. Clair county; in 1800 he was "Lieutenant-Colonel Commandant of the First Regiment of Militia of the County of Randolph"; in 1802 he was commissioned an associate judge of the Criminal Court of Randolph county, by Governor Harrison. He had never studied law "but common sense, a good education, and experience in business with perfect honesty made him a very respectable officer." Edgar's correspondence with Clark and Hamtramck show him to have been a leader in Illinois during its period of anarchy preceding the establisment of government in 1790. He offered to board a garrison on the credit of the United States, if a garrison should be sent to protect Illinois. At a time when slaveholding was regarded as eminently respectable by the people of Illinois, Edgar held slaves, and in 1796 he was one of four who petitioned Congress to introduce slavery into the territory. He was a member of the legislature of the Northwest Territory, was worshipful master of the first Lodge of Ancient Free and Accepted Masons in Illinois, constituted at Kaskaskia in 1806, and was major-general of militia, in which capacity he presided at reviews with much dignity. In person Gen. Edgar was large and portly. He was definitely charged with forgery by the commissioners to settle land titles at Kaskaskia. In one case a letter signed in a fair hand by one who had made his mark to a deed was produced by Edgar. The letter was an offer of the illiterate owner to sell his land to Edgar. There is no indication that this conduct of the hospitable and popular man changed the esteem in which he was held by his contemporaries.[1]

1. "Pub. Lands," I., 69-70; II., 203-4; "Early Chicago and Illinois," in

John Rice Jones, the first lawyer in Illinois, was eminently successful. He was born in Wales in 1759, received a collegiate education at Oxford, England, and afterward took regular courses in both medicine and law. In 1783 he was a lawyer in London and owned property in Wales. The next year he came to Philadelphia where he practiced law and became acquainted with Benjamin Rush, Benjamin Franklin, Myers Fisher, and other distinguished men. In 1786 he came to Kentucky and joined Clark's troops against the Wabash Indians. A garrison was irregularly established at Vincennes and Jones was made commissary-general. He sold seized Spanish goods to partially indemnify those whose goods had been seized by the Spanish. In 1790 Jones removed to Kaskaskia, bringing to his residence on the frontier a mind well trained by education and experience. He early became a large landowner, in 1808 paying taxes on 16,400 acres in Monroe county alone. The list of offices held by Jones shows him to have been prominent wherever he went. He was attorney-general of the Northwest Territory, a member and president of the legislative council of the same, joint-revisor with John Johnson, of the laws of Indiana Territory, one of the first trustees, as well as a chief promoter, of Vincennes University, official interpreter and translator of French for the commissioners appointed to settle land claims at Kaskaskia, and after his removal to Missouri, about 1810, a

"Chicago Hist. Soc. Coll.," IV., 145, 159, 167, 169–70, 178–9, 209; Reynolds, "Pioneer Hist. of Ill.," 110, 116–8, 180, 215; John Edgar to Clark, from Kaskaskia, Nov. 7, 1785, in "Draper's Notes, Trip 1860," VI., 214–5; Edgar to Clark, from Kaskaskia, Oct. 23, 1786, "Draper Coll., Clark MSS.," LIII., 56; Petition from Kaskaskia, Sept. 14, 1789, "Draper Coll., Harmar Papers," II., 124–7; Offer of John Edgar, from Kaskaskia, Oct. 3, 1789, "Draper Coll., Harmar Papers," II., 127–8; Hamtramck's reply to the Kaskaskia petition of Sept. 14, 1789, from Vincennes, Oct. 14, 1789, "Draper Coll., Harmar Papers," II., 128–30; Edgar to Hamtramck, from Kaskaskia, Oct. 28, 1789, *ibid.*, II., 132–6; "Draper Coll., Kenton MSS.," Edgar Papers.

member of the Missouri Constitutional Convention of 1820, and, upon the admission of the state, justice of its Supreme Court until his death in February, 1824. In Missouri he engaged in lead mining and smelting with Moses Austin and later with Austin's sons. He made an exhaustive report on the lead mines of Missouri in 1816. Jones was well versed in English, French and Spanish law, especially in regard to land titles. He was an excellent mathematician, and had also a thorough acquaintance with the Greek, Latin, French, Spanish, English, and Welsh languages. The pioneers recognized his peculiar fitness for a legal career on the frontier. Governor Reynolds, a fellow-townsman of Jones, says: "Judge Jones lived a life of great activity and was conspicuous and prominent in all the important transactions of the country. . . . His integrity, honor, and honesty were always above doubt or suspicion. He was exemplary in his moral habits, and lived a temperate and orderly man in all things."[1]

The founding of the towns of Mt. Carmel, Alton and Springfield illustrates the work of successful town building on the frontier. Mt. Carmel was laid out in 1817, Alton in 1818, and the land where Springfield now stands was entered in 1823.

The town of Mt. Carmel was founded by three ministers, Thomas S. Hinde, William McDowell and William Beauchamp, the first two being proprietors and the last agent and surveyor. McDowell probably never settled in Illinois. Hinde and Beauchamp were men of more than ordinary ability. The former was a son of the well-known Dr. Hinde, of Virginia, who was a surgeon in the British navy during the French and Indian war. Dr.

[1] Reynolds, "Pioneer Hist. of Ill.," 170–2; W. A. Burt Jones, in "Chicago Hist. Soc. Coll.," IV., 230–70; Jones to Hamtramck, from Kaskaskia, Oct. 29, 1789, "Draper Coll., Harmar Papers," II., 136–41.

Hinde moved to Kentucky and there the boy Thomas grew up. At one time he was a neighbor of Daniel Boone, and later of Simon Kenton. He was in the office of the Superior Court of Kentucky for some time, during which he became well acquainted with Governor Madison and his nephew, John Madison, kinsmen of President James Madison. He was well informed as to some of the obscure movements of Aaron Burr. This led him to send copies of the *Fredonian*, which he published in order to oppose Burr, to Henry Clay, then secretary of state, although the copies later unaccountably disappeared; and, in 1829, to write to James Madison, who was reported as contemplating the writing of a political history, offering to furnish information which he possessed at first hand concerning the conspiracy. Madison denied any intention of writing a history, but asked Hinde to furnish an account of Burr's transactions to be filed with Madison's papers. This was done. In 1806, Hinde moved to Ohio to get away from slavery.

William Beauchamp was born in Kent county, Delaware, in 1772. He became a minister in the Methodist Episcopal Church in 1794, but located in 1801 on account of ill health. His ministry had been markedly successful and he had been stationed in New York and Boston. In 1807 he settled on the Little Kanawha River in Virginia, and in 1815 moved to Chillicothe, Ohio, where he acted as editor of the *Western Christian Monitor*, Hinde being a contributor. Beauchamp knew Latin, Greek and Hebrew, was a writer of considerable ability, and was well fitted to be editor. In 1816, however, the General Conference decided to establish a magazine, and in the following year Beauchamp retired from the editorship of the *Monitor*, having successfully established the first Methodist magazine in America. Beauchamp, Hinde and McDowell were now fellow-townsmen. They resolved to establish a town where their ideas of rectitude might be applied.

The site chosen for the town was a point on the west bank of the Wabash, opposite the mouth of the White River, and twenty-four miles southwest of Vincennes. This point was selected because of the available water power and of the likelihood that main roads from east to west would pass here. The town became a railroad and manufacturing center and justified the wisdom of its founders. An elaborate circular, called the "Articles of Association, for the City of Mount Carmel," was issued at Chillicothe in 1817. The purpose of the association was announced to be "to build a city on liberal and advantageous principles, and to constitute funds for the establishment of seminaries of learning and for religious purposes." The proprietors reserved for themselves one-fourth of the lots, these being called "proprietors' lots;" one-fourth were called "public donation lots;" and one-half were called "private donation lots." The plan of survey and sale was described as follows: "The front street is 132 feet wide; the others 99. The in-lots are six poles in front, and eleven and a half back; containing each sixty-eight perches, nearly half an acre. The most of the out-lots contain four acres and eight square poles; some of them more, (five and six acres on the back range); and a few of them less. There are 748 in-lots, and 331 out-lots—1079 in the whole.

"The lots are offered at private sale, at the following prices:

IN-LOTS ON FRONT STREET.

Corners ------------------------------- $150 each
Not corners ----------------------- 100

THE REST OF THE IN-LOTS.

Corners ------------------------------- $120 each
Not corners ------------------------ 80
The out-lots ---------------------- $100 each

"The payments are to be made in four annual instalments; the first at the time of sale.

"A bank is to be constituted by the sale of the lots.

"One-fourth of the lots are appropriated to the use of schools and religious purposes.

"One-half of the lots are to be given away to those who will improve them according to the articles of association. A person may have as many gift, or private donation out-lots, as he has such in-lots; the out-lots not required to be improved. The gift lots are to be disposed of on the following terms: the persons receiving them pay the prices above stated, and receive for the money thus paid, stock in the aforesaid bank. They are to improve the in-lots thus given to them, by building one dwelling-house for every such in-lot; one-half of the houses to be built within five years, and the other half within ten years, from the sale of said lots. The houses to be framed, brick, or stone, and to contain two rooms, and two fire-places each."

The bank referred to was "The Bank of Mount Carmel." Its shares were ten dollars each. The proprietors might put into the stock one-half of the money received from the sale of proprietors' lots; all the money received for public donation lots was to be divided into three equal parts, one part to be funded in the bank in the name of the trustees (to be appointed) of the Methodist Episcopal Church, the proceeds to be applied to the building of "Methodist Episcopal meeting houses in the city of Mount Carmel, and to other religious purposes," not including ministers' salary; the second part to be funded in the name of the trustees (to be appointed) of a male academy; the third part to be similarly funded for a female academy; the money from private donation lots to be funded in the name of the purchasers, after deducting ten per cent for expenses, which ten per cent should remain in the bank as permanent stock. The articles of association were elaborate. The 18th article became known as the "Blue Laws." It read as follows: "ART. 18. No theatre or playhouse shall ever be built within the bounds of this city. No person who shall be guilty of drunkenness, profane swearing or cursing, Sabbath breaking, or who shall keep a disorderly house, shall gamble, or suffer gambling in his house, or raise a riot, or break the peace within the city, or be guilty of any other crime of greater magnitude in guilt than those here mentioned, and shall be convicted thereof before the mayor, council, or any other court having cognizance of such crime or crimes, shall be eligible to any office of the city of Mount Carmel or its bank, or be entitled to vote for any such officer, within three years after such conviction, nothwithstanding anything in these articles to the contrary."

The plan for a town was successful. Beauchamp was surveyor, pastor, teacher, and lawyer in the beginning of settlement. By 1819 a school was established; four or five years later a school-house was built; by 1820 Mt. Carmel circuit of the M. E. church had been formed; in 1825 a brick church was erected; the same year the town was incorporated by the state on the plan laid down in the articles of association; in 1827 the annual conference of the Illinois Conference was held at Mt. Carmel.

Beauchamp's health having improved he reëntered the ministry in 1822, and at the General Conference two years later he lacked but two votes of being chosen bishop. He died in 1824.

Hinde, in 1825, was a member of the Wabash Navigation Company, consisting of seventeen prominent Indiana and Illinois men, and having a capital stock of one million dollars. He was one of the nine directors for the first year. He continued to be a contributor to periodical literature and became the biographer of his friend Beauchamp. In a letter from Mt. Carmel, of May 6, 1842, Hinde says: "I have just returned from the East, having visited the Atlantic cities generally for the first time, after forty-five years pioneering in the wilderness of the West. I have been three times a citizen of Kentucky, twice of Ohio, and twice of Illinois." Hinde died in 1846 and was buried at Mt. Carmel. Among his writings is found one of the most acute analyses of frontier character that has appeared. The writer points out that eastern ministers have often been unsuccessful and eastern immigrants unpopular, because they have underrated the people of the West, among whom there are many people of culture. They prefer "the *useful* to the shining or showy talent." In the West the best work has been done by westerners. The English spoken in the West is the purest to be found, because the various provincialisms of the immigrants are mutually corrective. The Virginian, who retained his unbounded hospitality, was the most prominent character in the West. "If we expect to find on crossing the mountains a people either illiterate or ignorant as a body, we will assuredly, in many instances, be happily disappointed. It too often happens, that one puffed up with self importance, and possessing a conceited and heated imagination, will form wild conjectures as to men and things. We have been amused at the bewildered minds of such, with the 'whys' and 'wherefores'; and one of the most ridiculous whims of some, is to endeavour to press every thing into their own *mould;* and shape it, be it what it may, if possible, after their own manner, custom, or operation, forgetting that 'we have to take the world as it is, and not as we would have it to be.' The fact is, an emigrant should come forth as an inquirer, and set himself down to learn at the threshold of experience. On this rock thousands have been injured, and none have suffered more than the English emigrants. Oh! with what poignant grief have I heard the English emigrant exclaim with the bitterest invectives on his own course and conduct, as to this particular. Conceiving that he knew every thing, when he came here to test his experience, he soon found that he 'knew nothing.' This circumstance I have found too to have its bearings upon American emigrants from different states; upon families, upon individuals, and upon preachers also. How often have I heard the old settler complaining, (who having himself learned by *experience*) of the impertinent conduct of an emigrant, who sometimes carries his local policy through all the ramifications of his life, and often into the religious society, as well as elsewhere; he wishing every thing done, as he saw it done in Boston, New-York, Philadelphia, Baltimore, and very often 'Old England' and 'Ireland!' as if men who have to act, and reflect upon the circumstances of the case, different from any ever before presented except among themselves, are to be governed by acts and doings of people in the moon!"[1] A man who

[1]. "Methodist Magazine," XI., 1828, 154-8. The remarks of Hinde recall the difficulty which was experienced by the men who governed the Northwest Territory under the Ordinance of 1787 when they attempted to use only such laws as had been adopted by some state. The attempt was early and finally abandoned. Hinde gives the following in a foot-note: "A gentleman, a Virginian, a physician of eminence who was educated in Paris, visited a western state many years ago [written in 1827], and lost all his money by gambling, (playing at cards). Meeting a friend on the mountains on his return, he was thus addressed: 'Well, doctor, you have been to see the new country.' 'Yes,' replied the doctor, biting his lips, 'it is a new country, it is true; but there are some of the oldest people in it that I ever saw.' "—See above reference, p. 155.

On Mt. Carmel and its founders, in general, see: "Articles of Association for the City of Mount Carmel"; Bangs, "Hist. of the M. E. Church," IV., appendix, 3, 25; III., 230, 308-14; "Minutes of Conferences" (Annual, M E.), I., 347, 474, 516; "American Pioneer," I., 327; II., 363-8; "Laws of Ill., 1824-25," 72-5; Simpson, "Cyclopædia of Methodism," 97-8; "Meth-

thus knew the frontier was fitted to be the founder of a western town.

Rufus Easton was the founder of the town of Alton. Like Hinde, he brought to his work a fund of experience gained on the frontier and in public affairs. Easton was born at Washington, Litchfield county, Connecticut, in 1774. He descended from pioneers, being a direct descendant of Joseph Easton, who came from England to Newtowne, now Cambridge, Massachusetts, about 1633, and was later one of Rev. Thos. Hooker's colony which founded Hartford, Connecticut, of which Easton was an original proprietor. In 1792 Rufus Easton's father, a Tory, obtained a large grant of land near Wolford, now Easton Corners, Ontario. Rufus received a good education before studying law. In 1798 he was practicing law in Rome, New York, then a frontier town. November, 1801, Easton, with thirteen other prominent men, held a banquet to celebrate the election of Thos. Jefferson as President. The prominence of the young lawyer at this time is shown by the fact that he was consulted in regard to federal appointments, and that he was in 1803 a confidential correspondent of De Witt Clinton. The winter of 1803–4 Easton spent in Washington, where he became a friend of Aaron Burr, Postmaster-General Granger, and others. In the spring of 1804 he started for New Orleans. Aaron Burr gave him a letter of introduction to Abm. R. Ellery, Esq., of New Orleans, in which he said: "You will certainly be greatly amused to converse with a man who has passed the whole winter in this city—who has had free intercourse

---

odist Magazine," VIII., 17, 49, 86. Less reliable data is given in "Hist. of Edwards, Lawrence, and Wabash Counties, Ill.," 85, 162, 189–90, 236, 238, 239. Mount Carmel is now (1908) the county seat of Wabash county. The "Hinde MSS." in the "Draper Coll." are large in volume, but have slight historic value, being chiefly musings of the author's later years.

with the officers of Govt. & members of Congress—who has discernment to see beyond the surface, and frankness and independence enough to speak his own sentiments." Easton did not, however, go to New Orleans. He stopped for a short time at Vincennes and then located at St. Louis. He was appointed by Jefferson judge of the Territory of Louisiana and first postmaster of St. Louis. In September, 1805, Burr, Wilkinson and Easton had a conference at St. Louis. Easton turned a deaf ear to Burr's questionable proposals and from this time Wilkinson was hostile to Easton. Easton corresponded with Jefferson and Granger concerning the Burr conspiracy. Jefferson appointed him United States attorney, 1814–18 he was delegate to Congress from Missouri, 1821–26 he was attorney-general of Missouri. Easton was very prominent, entertaining almost all visitors of note. Edward Bates, Lincoln's attorney-general, read law in Easton's office.

Soon after coming to St. Louis, Easton began to buy up claims to land in Missouri and Illinois. When seeking to find a suitable place for a town in Illinois, he selected a point on the east bank of the Mississippi, twenty-five miles north of St. Louis and twenty miles south of the mouth of the Illinois. There was here a good landing place for boats, and also extensive beds of coal and limestone. The town was named Alton in honor of the founder's son. One hundred lots in the new town were donated to the support of the gospel and public schools, one-half of the proceeds to be devoted to each. This provision was confirmed by the act of incorporation of January 30, 1821, and the trustees were given the right to tax undonated lots for the support of schools. This latter provision was in advance of public sentiment and two years later it was repealed. Alton, like Mt. Carmel and to a much greater extent, proved the wisdom of its location.

SUCCESSFUL FRONTIERSMEN.   205

It has long been noted for its manufactures and is a thriving modern city.[1]

The town of Springfield, since 1839 the capital of Illinois, was laid out in 1822, before the land upon which it stood was offered for sale. When the land was sold in November, 1823, the section upon which the town stood was bought by Elijah Iles, Pascal Paoli Enos, Thomas Cox, and Daniel P. Cook, each purchasing one quarter, but the title being vested by agreement in Iles and Enos. Cook, like McDowell in the founding of Mt. Carmel, seems to have been a non-resident proprietor.

Elijah Iles was a child of the wilderness. He was born in Kentucky in 1796, and died at Springfield, Illinois, in 1883, leaving valuable reminiscences of his long experience on the frontier. His mother was Elizabeth Crockett Iles, a relative of David Crockett. Elijah attended school two winters and taught two winters. In 1812, although but sixteen years of age, he acted as deputy for his father, who was sheriff of Bath county, Kentucky. Some three years later his father gave him three hundred dollars, with which he bought one hundred head of yearling cattle. For three years he herded these cattle among the mountains of Kentucky, about twenty miles from civilization, having as his only companions his horse, dog, gun, milk cow, and the cattle. His meals usually consisted of a stew made of bear meat, venison, or turkey, and a piece of fat bacon. At the end of the three years the cattle were sold for about ten dollars a head, and the youthful dealer having attained his majority went to Missouri and became a land agent for eastern speculators, and soon began to speculate

[1]. Bay, "Reminiscences of the Bench and Bar of Mo.," 78-91; "Pub. Lands," II., index under Easton, Rufus; Easton, "Descendants of Joseph Easton, Hartford, Conn.," 1, 37, 65; Moses, "Illinois," I., 272; "Laws of Ill., 1820-21," 39-45; *ibid.*, "1822-23," 147.

for himself. In 1821, concluding that Missouri was too far from a market, he sold some of his land and resolved to move to Illinois. At that time the site upon which Springfield was to stand had been chosen as the temporary county seat of Sangamon county, because eight men, some of whom had families, lived within a radius of two miles from the site, and at no other place in the county could the lawyers and judge secure board and lodging. Iles quickly discerned the advantages of the Sangamon country as a place of settlement, and straightway built a log store sixteen feet square, went to St. Louis and bought fifteen hundred dollars worth of goods, which he loaded on a keel-boat and had towed up the Mississippi and the Illinois by six men, whom he paid seventy-five dollars for their services. When the land was offered for sale, in 1823, Iles bought a quarter-section.

Another quarter-section of the town site was bought by Pascal Paoli Enos. The fact that the frontier is a great social leveler is well illustrated by the combination of Enos and Iles as joint owners of a town site. The Enos family had come from England in 1648, and Pascal Paoli Enos, son of Major-General Roger Enos, was born in Windsor, Connecticut, in 1770. He was graduated from Dartmouth College in 1794, studied law, was a member of the Vermont legislature in 1804, married in Vermont and moved to Cincinnati in 1815, later to St. Charles, Missouri, then to St. Louis, then to Madison county, Illinois, and in 1823 was appointed by President Monroe receiver of public moneys for the land-office in the District of Sangamo. Thus the elderly scholar joined the shrewd but youthful frontiersman.

Col. Thomas Cox was the third of the trio of the resident proprietors of Springfield. He had signed a petition for the division of Randolph county in 1812, represented

SUCCESSFUL FRONTIERSMEN. 207

Union county as a senator in the first general assembly of Illinois, and in 1820 was appointed register of the land-office at Vandalia. In 1823 he came to Springfield as register of the land-office at that place. Col. Cox was six feet tall, weighed two hundred and forty pounds, and was a drunkard within a short time after the founding of Springfield.

The most important thing about the founding of the town is the heterogeneous character of its founders. A few incidents in their subsequent history will emphasize this, and also show how well they worked together when surrounded by the same conditions. When the commissioners came to locate a permanent county seat Springfield, then called Calhoun, had a formidable rival for the honor. Iles and Enos managed to have a mutual friend engaged as guide to the commissioners. The guide conducted them to the rival settlement by a long and rough route and upon being requested to take them back over a shorter route he took a course more difficult still. The commissioners decided that the rival settlement was inaccessible. Iles was twice state senator, major in the Winnebago war, and captain in the Black Hawk war, in which he served with Zachary Taylor, Jefferson Davis, Abraham Lincoln, John T. Stuart, Robt. Anderson, of Fort Sumter fame, and others. Iles was also a large stock dealer, selling hogs and cattle in St. Louis and mules in Kentucky, until 1838, in which year he lost ten thousand dollars on hogs packed at Alton. In 1838-9 he built the American House in Springfield. This was then the largest hotel in the state and its erection created a great sensation. He was four times state senator, and was an officer of the Bank of Edwardsville. Enos held his position as receiver until removed for political reasons by Jackson in 1829. Cox had an eventful career. He was removed from his position of register, under charges of misconduct, early in 1827; the next year he was keeping a hotel in Springfield; later he removed to Iowa, then Wisconsin, having secured a contract for the survey of public lands. He was three times a member of the Iowa territorial House of Representatives and twice a member of the territorial Council. A band of murderers, horsethieves, counterfeiters, and blacklegs, having gained possession of the town of Bellevue, on the Mississippi, in Jackson county, Iowa, Col. Cox led the citizens in a successful attack in which seven men were killed outright and some ten or fifteen wounded. At this time Cox was recognized as a pronounced drunkard, but his undoubted courage, ability to command, and strong physique secured him a following.[1]

Shadrach Bond, the first governor of Illinois, and Pierre Menard, the first lieutenant-governor, were both poorly educated, but they had a good knowledge of men and a large fund of information concerning practical affairs.[2] Edward Coles, the second governor of the state, is a good example of the polished, well-educated gentleman succeeding with a rude constituency. Coles was born in 1786, in Albemarle county, Virginia, fitted for college by private

---

1. For information concerning Iles, see: "Reminiscences of Elijah Iles," in "Hist. of Sangamon County, Ill.," 580-3; Power, "Hist. of the Early Settlers of Sangamon Co., Ill.," 397-400 (practically a short autobiography of Iles, written in 1876); Moses, "Illinois," I., 344; II., 1174. Concerning Enos, see: Stiles, "Ancient Windsor," (Conn.), II., 245, 246; "Executive Journal," Senate, 1815-29, pp. 325, 328, 551, 553, 555; *ibid.*, 1829-37, pp. 50, 391; "Edwards Papers," in "Chicago Hist. Soc. Coll.," III., 205, 391. Concerning Cox, see: Moses, "Illinois," II., 1168; "Executive Journal," Senate, 1815-29, pp. 216-7, 325, 328, 551, 553, 555; Washburne, "Sketch of Edward Coles," 128-30; "Edwards Papers," in "Chicago Hist. Soc. Coll.," III., 76, 211, 336-7; Gue, "Hist. of Iowa," I., 205, 211; Fairall, "Manual of Iowa Politics," 107; "Hist. of Jackson County," Iowa, 360-403. On Springfield, see: Peck, "Gazetteer of Illinois," 1834, 337.

2. Moses, "Illinois," I., 287, 289-90; Reynolds, "Pioneer Hist. of Ill.," 291-4, 323-7.

tutors, educated at Hampden Sidney and later at William and Mary College. His father's home was visited by Patrick Henry, Jefferson, Madison, Monroe, the Randolphs, Tazwell, Wirt, and others. For six years Coles was the private secretary of President Madison, and during this time he became an intimate friend of Nicholas Biddle. In 1815 he visited Illinois in what must have seemed at that time great state, for he traveled not only with a horse and buggy, but with a servant and a saddle-horse as well In 1816–17 he was sent as a special messenger to Russia, stopping at Paris on his return, meeting Louis XVIII. of France and becoming a friend of Lafayette. In 1819 he came to Edwardsville, Illinois, emancipated his slaves, and assumed his duties as register of the land-office. The rough pioneers were very anxious to get a title to their lands. "When the settler reached Edwardsville, dressed in jeans and wearing moccasins, with his money in his belt, having traveled on foot or on horseback long distances, and first presented himself to the Register of the Land Office, there he found Edward Coles, who had recently emigrated into the State from Virginia. It was known to some of them that he had been the private secretary for President Madison, and had been on an important mission to Europe.

"They found him a young man of handsome, but somewhat awkward personal appearance, genteelly dressed, and of kind and agreeable manners. The anxious settler was at once put at ease by the suavity of his address, the interest he appeared to feel in aiding him, and the thoroughly intelligent manner in which he discharged his duty. No man went away who was not delighted with his intercourse with the 'Register.' And herein is illustrated the great mistake so often made by politicians and candidates for popular favor. Too many candidates for the suffrage of the people in our early political contests thought it necessary, in order to make themselves popular, to affect slovenly and unclean dress and vulgar manners in their campaigns. There was never a greater mistake. However rough, ill-clothed and unintelligent the voter might be, he always preferred to vote for the man who was dressed and acted like a gentleman to the one who dressed like and acted like himself."[1] Coles was always dignified, always gentlemanly, and always respected. His brief residence in Illinois affected its history for all time to come. Like Coles in several respects was his successor as governor, Ninian Edwards. Born in Maryland in 1775, educated by the celebrated William Wirt, and later graduating from Dickinson College, Pennsylvania, at nineteen years of age he came to Kentucky. Here he served two terms in the Kentucky legislature, was presiding judge of the general court, circuit judge, and chief-justice of the court of appeals. Henry Clay gave as Edwards' marked characteristics, good understanding, weight of character, and conciliatory manners. In his campaign for governor of Illinois, Edwards presented himself as the highest type of a polished and well-dressed gentleman, always riding in his own carriage and driven by his negro servant, and dressing in all the style of an old-fashioned gentleman with broadcloth coat, ruffled shirt, and high-topped boots. The people were not repelled by such a display, but considered it an honor to vote for such a man. The egotistical Adolphus Frederick Hubbard, who was one of the two opponents of Edwards, intermingled bad grammar and poor attempts at wit in his electioneering speeches, and

---

[1]. Washburne, "Sketch of Edward Coles," 16 *et seq.*, 54-7. Washburne, the writer, came to Galena, Illinois, when it still had many frontier characteristics, and for seventeen years represented his district in Congress.

received less than one-tenth of the number of votes cast for either of the two other candidates.[1]

[1] Moses, Illinois," I., 242-3, 336, 340-1, 351; Washburne, "Sketch of Edward Coles," 54-7; and for a general view of Edwards, see: N.W. Edwards, "Hist. of Ill. and Life of Ninian Edwards," and "The Edwards Papers," in "Chicago Hist. Soc. Coll.," III.

WORKS CONSULTED.

I.
SOURCES.

American Historical Association, Annual Report of the. Washington: Government Printing Office.
Report for 1893, pp. 199-227, see Turner, Frederick Jackson; Report of 1896, Vol. I., pp. 930-1107, has "Selections from the Draper Collection in the possession of the State Historical Society of Wisconsin, to elucidate the proposed French expedition under George Rogers Clark against Louisiana, in the years 1793-94."

American monthly Magazine and critical Review. New York: H. Biglow, editor.
Volumes I.-III. (1817-18) give information of much value concerning European conditions inducing emigration. A few of the notices concern emigration from east to west in the United States.

American Register; or, Summary Review of History, Politics, and Literature. Philadelphia.
Volume II., 202, 203, 216 (1817), tells of improvements in steamboat navigation.

Americans as they are; described in a Tour through the Valley of the Mississippi. London: Hurst, Chance & Co., 1828. vi. + 218 pp.
Observations on Illinois are more suggestive than accurate.

ATWATER, CALEB. *Remarks made on a Tour to Prairie du Chien.* Columbus, Ohio: Isaac N. Whiting, 1831. 296 pp.
The tour was from Circleville, Ohio, to Prairie du Chien, in 1829, and thence to Washington. The writer's remarks give valuable material for the history of the time.

—— *Writings.* Columbus, Ohio: Caleb Atwater, 1833. 408 pp.
The author was one of a commission to treat with the Indians at Prairie du Chien for the cession of the lead region. In 1829 he went from St. Louis to Prairie du Chien. He gives good descriptions of Quincy, Galena, and a few other places. The part of the Writings describing this journey was separately printed in 1831. The edition of 1833 is somewhat better than the previous one.

BALESTIER, JOSEPH N. *Annals of Chicago: a Lecture delivered before the Chicago Lyceum, Jan. 21, 1840. Republished from the original Edition of 1840, with an Introduction, written by the Author in 1876.* Chicago: Fergus Printing Co., 1876. In *Fergus historical Series,* I., No. 1. 48 pp.

Contains a copy of Capt. Heald's letter of 1812, describing the massacre at Fort Dearborn.

BIGGS, WILLIAM. *Narrative of William Biggs, while he was a Prisoner with the Kickepoo Indians . . . on the west Bank of the Wabash River . . . Printed for the author, June,* 1826. 22 pp.

Biggs was captured on March 28, 1788, and remained a captive for several weeks. This very rare book gives valuable insight into the revolting customs of the Indians.

BIRKBECK, MORRIS. *Extracts from a supplementary Letter from the Illinois: an Address to British Emigrants, and a Reply to the Remarks of William Cobbett, Esq.* 2d ed. London: *James Ridgway,* 1819. 36 pp.

Birkbeck had issued an address to British emigrants, advertising the virtues of his English settlement in Illinois. William Cobbett declared that Birkbeck's account of the fertility and salubrity of Illinois was not true. Birkbeck issued a somewhat scathing reply, showing Cobbett's ignorance.

—— *Letters from Illinois.* Philadelphia: *M. Carey & Son,* 1818. 12mo. vii. + 154 pp.

Twenty-two letters written from November, 1817, to March, 1818, by Morris Birkbeck, from the English settlement in Edwards county, Ill., of which settlement he was the founder. Very valuable for notes concerning transportation and the manner of life of the early settlers of Illinois.

—— *Notes on a Journey in America from the Coast of Virginia to the Territory of Illinois.* Philadelphia: Richardson, 1817.

Passed through several editions in England.

A graphic account of the journey of Birkbeck from 500 miles east of Cape Henry, Va. (April 26, 1817), to Shawneetown, Ill., where on August 2, 1817, he bought 1440 acres of land as a site for his English settlement. Very valuable for information concerning transportation and western conditions.

BLANEY, Capt. *An Excursion through the United States and*

Canada during the years 1822–23. By an English Gentleman. London: Baldwin, Cradock, and Joy, 1824. 16mo. 511 pp.

Pages 156-92 tell of the author's trip across Illinois. He visited Albion and then went to St. Louis overland. The descriptions of Birkbeck's settlement, the difficulties of prairie travel, and of the frontier life encountered are much above the average of travelers' reports.

BONNER, T. D. *Life and Adventures of James P. Beckwourth, Mountaineer, Scout, and Pioneer, and Chief of the Crow Nation of Indians. Written from his own Dictation. New York: Harper & Bros.*, 1858. 16mo. 535 pp.

The book deals almost entirely with the region west of the Mississippi, but in 1820 Beckwourth visited Galena. He went from St. Louis with a party led by Col. R. M. Johnson, the object of the party being to gain a mining concession from the Sauk Indians.

BRANNAN, JOHN *(Editor). Official Letters of the military and naval Officers of the United States, during the War with Great Britain in the Years 1812, 13, 14, & 15. Washington: Way & Gideon,* 1823. 510 pp.

A valuable collection. Printed without comment. Pages 84-5 give Capt. Heald's official report of the massacre at Fort Dearborn, August 15, 1812. The report is in a letter to Thos. H. Cushing, Adjutant General, written from Pittsburg, October 23, 1812.

BRODHEAD, COL. DANIEL. *A Letter from Brodhead to Gen. Washington referring to La Balme's Expedition.*

In *The olden Time*, II., 390–91.

BUTRICKE, GEORGE. *Affairs at Fort Chartres, 1768–1781. Albany: J. Munsell,* 1864. 10 pp.

Reprinted from *Historical Magazine*, VIII., No. 8. Valuable. Several letters written by Geo. Butricke, then stationed at Fort Chartres. Contains interesting notes on Indians, Spaniards, and British. Tells of epidemic.

Calendar of Virginia State Papers and other Manuscripts. Richmond, Va., 1875–1900. 9 vols.

The early volumes have documents of great value concerning the period when Illinois was a part of Virginia.

CARTWRIGHT, PETER, *Autobiography of Peter Cartwright, the*

backwoods Preacher. Ed. by W. P. Strickland. New York: Carlton & Porter, 1857. 16mo. 525 pp.

The author was from 1803 to the time of writing his book (1856) one of the most famous circuit riders. His first work was in Kentucky. He came to Illinois in 1823. His views on slavery, which caused his removal, are interesting. A valuable work, especially for giving an insight into the social life of the time.

CHETLAIN, Gen. AUGUSTUS LOUIS. *Recollections of seventy Years.* Galena: The Gazette Pub. Co., 1899. 304 pp.

The author was one of the first settlers in Galena, and gives valuable information concerning that important region — 1821 ff.

Chicago Historical Society's Collections. Chicago, 1882-90: —
 I. History of the English Settlement in Edwards County, Illinois, by George Flower, 1882. 408 pp.
 II. Sketch of Enoch Long, by Harvey Reid, 1884. 112 pp.
 III. The Edwards Papers, edited by E. B. Washburne, 1884. 632 pp.
 IV. Early Chicago and Illinois, 1889. 400 pp. Of great value.

CHILDS, Col. EBENEZER. *Recollections of Wisconsin since 1820.* In Wis. Hist. Coll., IV., 1859, 153-95.

The writer describes Chicago as it was in 1821, at which time he visited it.

Christian Spectator, V., 1823, 20-26. *Remarks on the States of Illinois and Missouri,* by Edward Hollister.

The author had recently completed a missionary tour in these states, and his remarks give an insight into the social conditions of the time.

COBBETT, WILLIAM. *A Year's Residence, in the United States of America.* 3d ed. London: William Cobbett, 1828. 370 pp.

Cobbett was in the United States in 1817-18. He declared that Birkbeck and Fearon had deceived the people of England by portraying America as better than it was. His book is unfair.

COFFIN, LEVI. *Reminiscences of Levi Coffin, the reputed President of the Underground Railroad.* . . . Cincinnati: Western Tract Society [c. 1876]. 2d ed. with appendix. Cincinnati: Robert Clarke & Co., 1880. 732 pp.

Pages 89-99 describe the author's visit to a Quaker settlement in Sangamon county, Ill., in 1823. Lost on the prairies.

COLLOT, VICTOR. *A Journey in North America, containing a Survey of the Countries watered by the Mississippi, Ohio, Missouri, and other affluing Rivers . . . . Illustrated by 36 Maps, Plans, Views, and divers Cuts.* Paris: Arthus Bertrand, 1826. 2 vols. and atlas in one. iv.+310; v.+272 pp.

The author traveled through Illinois in 1796. His observations were acute and are more helpful than would be expected from a soldier of fortune. The New Orleans *Picayune* of March 18, 1901, has a valuable article on the journey of Collot and its purpose. See his *Map of the Country of the Illinois,* in pocket.

Columbian Centinel. Boston, June–December, 1790; 1791–1801; 1802–1829.

The issue for June 16, 1790, has a note on the current experiments with steamboats. In Library of Wisconsin State Historical Society.

CROGHAN, GEORGE, *Journal,* 1765. In Thwaites, *Early western Travels,* I., 126–73. Cleveland, Ohio: Arthur H. Clark Company, 1904.

The Journal is of a trip to the West, and characterizes the early French settlers.

CUMING, FORTESCUE. *Sketches of a Tour to the western Country, . . . commenced at Philadelphia in the Winter of 1807 and concluded in 1809.* Pittsburg: Cramer, Spear & Eichbaum, 1810. 12mo. 504 pp.

Describes Shawneetown and gives some information in regard to routes. Very slight, however, in respect to Illinois. Criticism: *The Inter Ocean,* August 3, 1904.

CUTLER, JULIA PERKINS. *Life and Times of Ephraim Cutler. Prepared from his Journals and Correspondence.* Cincinnati: Robert Clarke & Co., 1890. 353 pp.

Cutler early settled in Ohio. This work gives good examples of the difficulties of travel, between 1795 and 1809, on some of the Alleghany routes frequented by emigrants to Illinois. The driving of western cattle to market is also described.

CUTLER, WILLIAM PARKER, *and* CUTLER, JULIA PERKINS. *Life, Journals and Correspondence of Rev. Manasseh Cutler,*

LL. D. Cincinnati: Robert Clarke & Co., 1888. 2 vols. 9 + 524; 495 pp.

Considerable information concerning early eastern opposition to western settlement is given. Dr. Cutler kept a diary from 1765 to 1823, of which nine years are missing.

DE PEYSTER, J. WATTS, LL. D. *Miscellanies, by an Officer* [Colonel Arent Schuyler de Peyster, B. A.], 1774–1813. *New York: A. E. Chasmar & Co.*, 1888. 80 pp., and an appendix of cci. pp.

Pages xxvi.–xxvii. contain a letter from Arent De Peyster to Capt. McKee describing an Illinois expedition against St. Josephs in 1780 or 1781. Letter dated Detroit, Feb. 1, 1781.

Draper Collection of Manuscripts.

This collection, made by Lyman C. Draper, is the property of the State Historical Society of Wisconsin. It has been of more value to the writer than any other single source, being especially helpful for the hitherto obscure period immediately succeeding the expedition of George Rogers Clark, 1779–1790. Most important of all are the Harmar Papers, although the Illinois MSS., the Clark MSS., and Draper's Notes were much used. The Hinde MSS. have little historical value, consisting as they do, largely of religious musings of the writer's old age.

DUDEN, GOTTFRIED. *Bericht über eine Reise nach den westlichen Staaten Nordamerika's und einen mehrjährigen Aufenthalt am Missouri (in den Jahren 1824–1827) in Bezug auf Auswanderung und Uebervölkerung. 1st ed. of 1500 copies. 2d ed. Bonn, In Commission bei Eduard Weber*, 1834. lviii. + 404 pp.

Contains a prediction of Illinois' future greatness. Gives valuable information concerning the cost and manner of transportation, and concerning social life. Comparison of American and European conditions.

DUNN, JACOB PIATT, *Compiler. Slavery Petitions and Papers.* In *Indiana Hist. Soc. Pub.*, II., 443–529. *Indianapolis: The Bowen-Merrill Company*, 1894.

"The following papers are the petitions to Congress from Northwest and Indiana Territories for the suspension of the sixth article of compact of the Ordinance of 1787, and the admission of slavery to the Territory, together with the counter-petitions, the reports on them, and the accompanying documents."—Compiler's introduction.

WORKS CONSULTED. 219

Edwardsville Spectator. Edwardsville, Ill.: Hooper Warren, pub., Apr. 18, 1820—*Feb.* 8, 1825, *and* 1820–22.

Material has been gleaned from the issues of Nov. 7, 1820; August 31, 1822; Nov. 30, 1822; Nov. 29, 1823; Jan. 27, 1824; and Oct 5, 1824. In Library of Chicago Historical Society.

ERNST, FERDINAND. *Travels in Illinois in 1819. Translation from the German Original.* In *Pub.* No. 8 *of the Ill. Hist. Lib.*, pp. 150–65. *Springfield, Ill.: Phillips Bros*, 1904.

Ernst was the leader of a party of German immigrants who settled at Vandalia soon after his journey to Illinois. He gives a vivid picture of the rapidly settling Illinois with its squatters and its fertile and inviting land. He visited the Sangamo country and the Kickapoo United States treaty conference.

FAUX, W. *Memorable Days in America: being a Journal of a Tour to the United States, principally undertaken to ascertain, by positive Evidence, the Condition and probable Prospects of British Emigrants; including Accounts of Mr. Birkbeck's Settlement in the Illinois . . . London: W. Simpkin & R. Marshall,* 1823. 488 pp.

Sufficiently pessimistic to require cautious use. The journey was performed in 1819–20.

FAY, H. A. *Collection of the official Accounts, in Detail, of all the Battles fought by Sea and Land, between the Navy and Army of the United States, and the Navy and Army of Great Britain, during the Years* 1812, 13, 14, & 15. *New York: E. Conrad,* 1817. 295 pp.

Contains Capt. Heald's official report of the massacre at Fort Dearborn, August 15, 1812, and Col. Russell's official report of Gov. Edwards' attack on the Indians near Peoria in 1812.

FEARON, HENRY BRADSHAW. *Sketches of America. A Narrative of a Journey of five thousand Miles through the eastern and western States of America . . . With Remarks on Mr. Birkbeck's "Notes" and "Letters." 3d ed. London: Strahan and Spottiswoode,* 1819. xv.+ 454 pp.

The work gives a glimpse of Illinois through a foreigner's eye. Fearon paints in sober colors, but his values are fairly true. Of considerable value as a work on society in the U. S. in 1817-18.

FLINT, JAMES. *Letters from America, containing Observations on the Climate and Agriculture of the western States, the Manners of the People, and the Prospects of Emigrants, &c., &c. Edinburgh: W. & C. Tait*, 1822. 16mo. 330 pp.

The author probably did not reach Illinois, but his letters from Ohio, Indiana and Kentucky give interesting bits of information in regard to the manner and cost of travel—1818 to 1820.

FLOWER, GEORGE. *History of the English Settlement in Edwards County, Illinois, founded in 1817 and 1818, by Morris Birkbeck and George Flower. Chicago: Fergus Printing Co.*, 1882. 16mo. 401 pp.

The work is volume I. of the Chicago Historical Society's Collections. The best book on this important episode in immigration to Illinois.

FLOWER, RICHARD. *Letters from Lexington and the Illinois, containing a brief Account of the English Settlement in the latter Territory, and a Refutation of the Misrepresentations of Mr. Cobbett. London: J. Rigdway*, 1819. iv. + 32 pp.

Two letters—one from Lexington and the other from New Albion, Ill. Highly colored.

FORSYTH, Maj. THOMAS, *Indian Agent. Journal of a Voyage from St. Louis to the Falls of St. Anthony, in 1819.* In *Wis. Hist. Coll.*, VI., 188-215. *Madison, Wis.: Atwood & Culver, State Printers*, 1872.

Incidentally the writer gives an account of the atrocities committed in 1812 by Capt. Thomas E. Craig upon the inhabitants of Peoria. Forsyth was an eye-witness of the barbarities described.

Galena Advertiser. Galena, Ill. Pub. by H. Newhall, Philleo and Co., July 20, 1829—*May* 24, 1830, *and July* 20, 1829—*May* 10, 1830.

July 20, July 27, August 10, Sept. 14, Sept. 21, 1829, have been used. In Library of Chicago Historical Society.

Galena (Ill.) Weekly Gazette.

The issue for May 2, 1879, contains reminiscences of Mrs. Adile B. Gratiot, whose husband settled in Galena, Ill., in 1825. This account furnishes a valuable bit of reliable history. It describes Galena, northern Illinois, a Fourth of July celebration (1826), the coming of Lord Selkirk's colonists, and the trouble with the Sauk Indians (1827).

GILLESPIE, Hon. JOSEPH. *Recollections of early Illinois and her noted Men. Fergus hist. Series,* No. 13. 51 pp. Chicago: Fergus Printing Co., 1880.

Valuable because of the author's direct knowledge of persons and events.

GOODRICH, SAMUEL GRISWOLD. *Recollections of a Life Time; or, Men and Things I have seen: in a Series of Letters to a Friend, historical, biographical, anecdotal, and descriptive.* New York: Miller, Orton & Co., 1857. 2 vols. 542, 563 pp.

Letter XXXIII. describes the emigration from East to West in 1816-17.

GRATIOT, Mrs. ADILE. *In early Illinois (Towns).*

A volume of newspaper clippings in the Library of the Chicago Historical Society. Mrs. Gratiot, who early lived in Galena, gives reminiscences of her life there. Describes the trouble with the Winnebago Indians.

HALL, JAMES. *Letters from the West; containing Sketches of Scenery, Manners, and Customs; and Anecdotes connected with the first Settlements of the western Sections of the United States.* London: Henry Colburn, 1828. 16mo. 385 pp.

Verbose, but not without value. One of the twenty-two letters is from Shawneetown and describes the vicinity. Illinois is defended from her foreign detractors. Routes and manner of travel receive much attention.

HAMILTON, HENRY EDWARD. *Incidents and Events in the Life of Gurdon Saltonstall Hubbard, collected from personal Narrations and other Sources, and arranged by his Nephew, Henry E. Hamilton.* Chicago: Rand, McNally & Co., 1888. 189 pp.

Very valuable for the history of northern and eastern Illinois from 1818 to the close of the Black Hawk war. Most of the work is autobiographical. Mr. Hubbard was an employee of the American Fur Company. Later he was in business in Danville and Chicago.

HARDING, BENJAMIN. *A Tour through the Western Country, A. D. 1818 & 1819.* New London: Samuel Green, 1819. 8vo. 17 pp.

The inducements which Illinois offered to emigrants are described with a degree of sense rarely displayed in the period to which the work belongs by writers of advice to emigrants. The American Bottom and the prairies are described.

HARRIS, WILLIAM TELL. *Remarks made during a Tour through the United States of America, in the Years 1817, 1818, and 1819.*

Describes Shawneetown (1818), and speaks of the great number of wagons, horses, and passengers which crossed the ferry there.

HECKE, J. VAL. *Reise durch die Vereinigten Staaten von Nord-Amerika in den Jahren 1818 und 1819. Nebst einer kurzen Uebersicht der neuesten Ereignisse auf dem Kriegs-Schauplatz in Süd-Amerika und West-Indien. Berlin: H. Ph. Petri,* 1820–21. 2 vols. 16mo. I., 228; II., xvi. + 326. pp.

Interesting and incorrect. The author tells well both of what he knows and what he does not know. Tells foreigners how to reach Illinois.

HENRY, WILLIAM WIRT. *Patrick Henry. Life, Correspondence, and Speeches. New York: Charles Scribner's Sons,* 1891. 3 vols. I., 20 + 622; II., 652; III., 672 pp.

The third volume contains instructions issued by Gov. Henry to officers of the County of Illinois, and some correspondence of those officers.

Historical Register of the United States. Philadelphia: G. Palmer, 1814–1816.

II., 60–62 (second pagination) gives Capt. Heald's official report of the massacre at Fort Dearborn on August 15, 1812.

HODGSON, ADAM. *Remarks during a Journey through North America in the Years 1819–21, in a Series of Letters: with an Appendix, containing an Account of several of the Indian Tribes, and the principal missionary Stations, &c. New York: Samuel Whiting,* 1823. 8vo. iv. + 335 pp.

The author did not visit Illinois, but he gives an interesting criticism of Mr. Birkbeck's venture in Illinois. He conversed with persons who had visited Birkbeck's settlement. Criticism rather unfavorable.

HOLMES, ISAAC. *An Account of the United States of America,* [1823] *derived from actual Observation, during a Residence of four Years in that Republic: including original Communications. London: Caxton Press,* 1823. 16mo. viii. + 476 pp.

WORKS CONSULTED. 223

Most of the author's remarks are general. He, however, mentions Birkbeck and advises emigrants to settle in the East rather than to go West as Birkbeck advised.

HULME, THOMAS. *Journal.* In Cobbett, "A Year's Residence in the United States of America," 259–309. 3d ed. *Andover: B. Bensley,* 1828.

The Journal was of a journey through the West in 1817. Birkbeck's settlement and the manner of traveling were described. Some information in regard to prices was given.

HUTCHINS, Capt. THOMAS. *A topographical Description of Virginia, Pennsylvania, Maryland, and North Carolina, comprehending the Rivers Ohio, Kenhawa, Sioto, Cherokee, Wabash, Illinois, Mississippi, etc.* . . . *With a Plan of the Rapids of the Ohio, a Plan of the several Villages in the Illinois Country* . . . *and an Appendix containing Mr. Patrick Kennedy's Journal up the Illinois River. London: T. Hutchins,* 1778. 8vo. 67 pp.

Valuable for its map of the Illinois country and a description of the settlements.

ILLINOIS AND WABASH LAND COMPANIES:—

An Account of the Proceedings of the Illinois and Ouabache Land Companies, in Pursuance of their Purchases made of the independent Natives, July 5th, 1773, and 18th October, 1775. Philadelphia: William Young, 1796. 55 pp.

Memorial of the Illinois and Wabash Land Company, 13th January, 1797. Referred to Mr. Jeremiah Smith, Mr. Kittera, and Mr. Baldwin. Published by Order of the House of Representatives. Philadelphia: Richard Folwell, [c. 1797.] 26 pp.

An Account of the Proceedings of the Illinois and Ouabache Land Companies, in Pursuance of their Purchases made of the independent Natives, July 5th, 1773, and 18th October, 1775. Philadelphia: William Duane, 1803. 74 pp.

Memorial of the Illinois and Ouabache Land Companies to the honorable Congress of the United States. Intended as a full Recapitulation and clear Statement of the former Addresses, Peti-

tions, Memorials, &c., of the Company; and their short and final Prayer for Redress, without Delay: presented at the Sessions, 1802. 20 pp.

Memorial of the United Illinois and Wabash Land Companies, to the Senate and House of Representatives of the United States. Baltimore: *Joseph Robinson,* 1816. 48 pp.

Illinois, House Journal, 1824–25. Vandalia, Ill.: *Robert Blackwell & Co.,* 1824. 305 pp.

Contains items on slavery (pp. 13, 151–2), and tells of the election of a U. S. senator to succeed Ninian Edwards (pp. 38–9).

Illinois Intelligencer. Edwardsville, Ill.: *Hooper Warren, ed.,* 1826–30.

In St. Louis Mercantile Library.

Illinois Laws, 1824–25. 190 pp.

Pages 50–51 give the text of an act to amend an act entitled "An act respecting free Negroes, Mulattoes, Servants, and Slaves," approved 30th March, 1819.

Illinois monthly Magazine. Vandalia, Ill.: *conducted by James Hall.*

Notes on Illinois in Volumes I. and II. (1830–1832) and the History of St. Louis in Volume II. are of some service. The articles are, however, unsigned, and are of too popular a type to be wholly relied upon.

Illinois Revised Laws of 1833. Vandalia, Ill.: *Greiner & Sherman,* 1833. 677 pp. and index.

Contains the negro codes of 1819 and 1829, respectively.

IMLAY, GILBERT. *A topographical Description of the Western Territory of North America, containing a succinct Account of its Climate, natural History, Population, Agriculture, Manners and Customs.* London: *J. Debrett,* 1792. 8vo. xv.+247 pp. *3d ed.,* 1797, enlarged. More valuable.

The best early authority on the subject treated. Not very full in regard to Illinois. Predicts western state-making.

KEATING, WILLIAM H. *Narrative of an Expedition to the Source of St. Peter's River, Lake Winnepeek, Lake of the Woods,*

&c., &c., *performed in the Year 1823* . . . *compiled from the Notes of Major Long, Messrs. Say, Keating, and Colhoun.* Philadelphia: Carey & Lea, 1824. 2 vols. 8vo. I., xii.+439; II., 459 pp. Same, *London: Whittaker,* 1825.

Contains an extremely interesting and important description of Chicago and its vicinity, and in less detail, of northern Illinois.

KINZIE, Mrs. JOHN H. (Juliette A. McGill Kinzie). *Wau-Bun, the "Early Day" in the North-West.* New edition with an introduction and notes by Reuben Gold Thwaites. Chicago: The Caxton Club, 1901. xxvii.+451 pp.

This work, which first appeared in 1856, has the best account, not by an eye-witness, of the massacre at Fort Dearborn in 1812. Mrs. Helm gives this account.

———— *Narrative of the Massacre at Chicago, August 15, 1812, and of some preceding Events.* Chicago: Ellis & Fergus, 1844. 34 pp.

A valuable account, written by Mrs. Kinzie from the dictation of her mother-in-law, who was an eye-witness of the massacre. Incorporated almost verbatim in Mrs. Kinzie's "Wau-Bun." The edition of 1844 was the first, not the second, as stated in the Chicago Magazine, I., 103, and repeated by Dr. Thwaites.

LAUSSAT, Count. *The military Title of Louisiana and the Territory of Illinois, dated New Orleans, Jan. 12, 1804, and signed by Count Laussat, Napoleon's Ambassador. It is also the order to Gen. De Lassus to deliver the Territory over to Capt. Amos Stoddard, of the U. S. Artillery.*

Original manuscript letter, in French, in the Illinois State Historical Library, Springfield, Ill.

LOOMIS, CHESTER A. *The Notes of a Journey to the Great West in 1825.* 28 unnumbered pages, six chapters. Printed without place, name of publisher, or date.

The writer entered Illinois in the present Vermilion county, went south to the Wabash, west to Vandalia, then to Kaskaskia. His observations are acute and readable. Describes Vermilion county salines, Illinois farm products, pioneer homes, and the inconvenience attendant upon traveling on horseback. Bound with other pamphlets in the Champaign (Illinois) Public Library.

—— *A Journey on Horseback through the Great West, in 1825. Visiting Alleghany Towns, Olean, Warren, Franklin, Pittsburg, New Lisbon, Elyria, Norfolk, Columbus, Zanesville, Vermilion, Kaskaskia, Vandalia, Sandusky, and many other places.* Bath, N. Y.: Plaindealer Press. 27 unnumbered pages.

The writer was from Rushville, Ontario county, N. Y. Same as the preceding. In Library of State Historical Society of Wisconsin.

McLean County Historical Society, Transactions of the. Vol. II. Bloomington, Ill.: Pantagraph Printing and Stationery Co., 1903. 695 pages.

Some facts of interest concerning the first school in the county, and the early settlers and their manner of living, are given by those old settlers who were chief actors.

Mandements des Évêques de Québec. Québec: Imprimérie Générale A. Coté et Cie., 1887–88. I., (1659–1740), 588; II., (1741–1806), 566; III., (1806–1850), 635; IV., (1850–1870), 794 pp.

A valuable collection of manuscripts. They tell of a monopoly on sending missionaries to Illinois, and one letter (II., 205) gives a good idea of the worldliness of the Kaskaskians of 1767. The first two volumes alone concern us.

MASON, EDWARD G. *(Editor). Early Chicago and Illinois.* Chicago: Fergus Printing Co., 1890. 521 pp.

This volume is the fourth of the collections of the Chicago Historical Society. It is one of the most valuable collections for the study of early Illinois history. Contains, among other things, Pierre Menard Papers, John Todd Papers, John Todd's Record-Book, Lists of Early Illinois Citizens, and Rocheblave Papers.

MEEKER, Dr. MOSES. *Early History of the Lead Region of Wisconsin.* In *Wis. Hist. Coll.,* VI., 271–96. Madison, Wis.: Atwood & Culver, State Printers, 1872.

Very valuable. Dr. Meeker came to Galena in 1822 and settled there in 1823. The article gives the history of the settlement of the lead region to 1825.

Michigan pioneer and historical Collections. Lansing, Mich., 1877–1900. 29 vols.

Valuable for the French and British periods of Illinois history.

Mount Carmel, Articles of Association, for the City of. Chillicothe: *John Bailhache*, 1817. 4to. 22 pp.

Mt. Carmel was to be, and now is, on the west bank of the Wabash in what is now Wabash county, Illinois. The articles drawn up by the proprietors and their agent contain curious provisions in regard to the support of church and school. Some Puritanic rules are given. (In *Ill. Local Hist. Pam.*, VII., in Library of Wisconsin State Historical Society.)

Niles' weekly Register, Baltimore.

Of great value for the period 1811-1830. Its notices of foreign immigration are extensive.

OGDEN, GEORGE W. *Letters from the West.* New-Bedford: Melcher & Rogers, 1823. 126 pp.

Describes several of the Illinois towns, and characterizes their inhabitants. A part of the work is plagiarized from Harding, *Tour through the western Country*. Reprinted in Thwaites, *Early western Travels*, XIX.

Olden Time, I., 1846, 403-15. *George Croghan's Journal of his Route.*

Interesting sketches of the French.

OWEN, A. R. *Ums Jahr 1819 und 1829.* In *Deutsch-Amerikanische Geschichtsblätter*, Jahrgang 2, Heft 2, pp. 41-43. *Chicago: April*, 1902.

Not sufficiently definite, reliable, or extensive to be of much value.

PALMER, JOHN. *Journal of Travels in the United States of North America and in Lower Canada, performed in the year 1817.* London: Sherwood, Neely, and Jones, 1818. vii.+456 pp.

Pages 411-20 are on Illinois. Too inaccurate to be of great value, although some information in regard to roads may be used. Tells of routes, methods, and cost of travel.

PALMER, JOHN McCAULEY. *Personal Recollections of John M. Palmer.* Cincinnati: The Robert Clarke Co., 1901. 631 pp.

The writer came to Illinois in 1831, but he had previously lived in Kentucky, and he gives some facts concerning slavery that are of value.

PARKISON, Col. DANIEL M. *Pioneer Life in Wisconsin.* In *Wis. Hist. Coll.*, II., 326-64. *Madison, Wis.:* Calkins & Proudfit, 1856.

The author came from Tennessee to Madison county, Illinois, in 1817; in 1819, to Sangamon county, Illinois; in 1827, to Galena, Illinois. Gives a valuable statement concerning the feeling of Yankees toward Southerners, tells of the first sermon in Sangamon county, and of the Winnebago war of 1827.

PECK, Rev. JOHN MASON. *A Guide for Emigrants* (1831), *containing Sketches of Illinois, Missouri, and the adjacent Parts.* Boston: Lincoln & Edmands, 1831. 336 pp.

Contains a great amount of fairly accurate information. Its description of cities is especially useful. Page 184 gives an amusing and instructive illustration of the need of energy and work in even a frontier settlement (1829).

―――― *Memoir of John Mason Peck, D. D.*, edited from his *Journals and Correspondence*. By Rufus Babcock. Philadelphia: Am. Baptist Pub. Soc., 1864. 12mo. 360 pp.

Not in good literary form. Throws much light upon the moral and religious life in Illinois and Missouri from 1817 to 1857.

―――― *The Religion and Morals of Illinois prior to 1818.* In Reynolds, *Pioneer History of Illinois*. Pp. 253–275.

The writer came to Illinois before 1818, and knew many of the persons of whom he wrote.

Pennsylvania Packet and daily Advertiser. Philadelphia, 1785–89; Apr., 1789; Mar., 1790; Apr.-Dec., 1790. In Library of Wisconsin State Historical Society.

August 23, 1790, the expression of apprehension of the depopulation of the East by emigration to the West is said not to be well founded.

Peoria County, Illinois, Marriage Licences, 1825–1855. On file in the court house in Peoria, Ill.

The early names show the French origin of the inhabitants. The absence of clergymen is noticeable.

PIKE, Lieut. ZEBULON MONTGOMERY. *An Account of a Voyage up the Mississippi River, from St. Louis to its Source; made under the Orders of the War Department, by Lieut. Pike, of the U. S. Army, in the Years 1805 and 1806. Compiled from Mr. Pike's Journal.* A 68 page pamphlet without place, publisher, or date.

Locates the largest Sauk village. These reports are of extreme importance.

An edition including the trip of 1807 was issued in 1895 by Harper, F. P., New York. 3 vols. $10.00.

Pioneer of the Valley of the Mississippi, The.   Rock Spring, Ill.: Rev. *J. M. Peek, editor.*

Issue of April 24, 1829, in St. Louis Mercantile Library.

PITTMAN, Capt. PHILIP.   *The present State of the European Settlements on the Mississippi, with a geographical Description of that River; illustrated by Plans and Draughts. London: J. Nourse,* 1770.   viii.+99 pp.   8 maps.

Describes the settlements in Illinois and gives a map of the region. Of great value.

Criticism in *Narrative and Critical History of America,* VI., 702.

Regulators of the Valley.

Charles M. Eames, in his *Historic Morgan and Classic Jacksonville* (1885), says that a vigilance committee with the above title was formed in 1821, or thereabouts, to rid the country of horse-thieves and robbers. "A regular constitution was drawn up and subscribed to, and this paper is still in existence." C. M. Eames, son of the now deceased author, in a letter of Oct. 7, 1903, said that he had made an unsuccessful search for the manuscript.

REYNOLDS, JOHN.   *My own Times, embracing also, the History of my Life.   Belleville, Ill.,* 1855.   Reprinted, *Chicago: Fergus Printing Co.,* 1879.   iv.+395 pp. $7.50.

Verbose, but has much wheat among the chaff. Covers the period from 1800 to 1853. The first edition is now very rare.

Ross, HARVEY LEE.   *The early Pioneers and pioneer Events of the State of Illinois.   Chicago,* 1899.

A medley of facts, written by a pioneer of 1820. The author was acquainted with both Cartwright and Lincoln, and speaks of them and of pioneer events with authority. Tells of a trip from New Jersey by wagons.

SCHOOLCRAFT, HENRY ROWE.   *Summary Narrative of an exploratory Expedition to the Sources of the Mississippi River, in 1820; resumed and completed, by the Discovery of its Origin in Itasca Lake, in 1832.   By authority of the United States.   Philadelphia: Lippincott, Grambo, & Co.,* 1855.   596 pp.

The book is chiefly of interest to us because of its description of Chicago.

—— *Travels in the central Portions of the Mississippi Valley: comprising Observations on its mineral Geography, internal Resources, and aboriginal Population. Performed under the Sanction of Government, in the Year 1821.* New York: Collins & Hannay, 1825. 459 pp.

The writer descended the Wabash, the Ohio, and then ascended the Mississippi and the Illinois to Chicago. His descriptions of places, peoples and things are well written and are a chief historical source.

SCHULTZ, CHRISTIAN. *Travels on an inland Voyage through the States of New-York, Pennsylvania, Virginia, Ohio, Kentucky, and Tennessee, and through the Territories of Indiana, Louisiana, Mississippi and New-Orleans; performed in the Years 1807 and 1808.* New York: Isaac Riley, 1810. 2 vols. I., xviii.+206; II., 224 pp.

Has an interesting description of Illinois settlements.

SMITH, WILLIAM HENRY, Editor. *The St. Clair Papers. The Life and public Services of Arthur St. Clair . . . with his Correspondence and other Papers.* Cincinnati: Robert Clarke & Co., 1882. 2 vols. I., viii.+609; II., 649 pp.

Much information concerning Illinois under the Ordinance of 1787. Criticisms: *Nation*, XXXIV., 383; *New York Tribune*, June 16, 1882.

Stories of the pioneer Mothers of Illinois. A collection of Manuscript Letters from the pioneer Women of the State, giving their early Experiences. Collected for the World's Columbian Exposition and afterward deposited in the Illinois State Historical Library.

Especially valuable for information on reasons for immigration and on methods of traveling.

STORROW, SAMUEL A. *The North-West in 1817.* In *Wis. Hist. Coll.*, VI., pp. 154–87. Madison, Wis.: Atwood & Culver, State Printers, 1872.

The narrative, which is in the form of a letter to Maj.-Gen. Brown, was first published in pamphlet form. The letter is dated Dec. 1, 1817. It deals chiefly with the country to the north of Illinois, but the author visited Chicago, was entertained at Fort Dearborn, and wrote of the desirability of an Illinois-Michigan canal.

TENNEY, H. A. *Early Times in Wisconsin.* In *Wis. Hist. Coll.,* I., pp. 94–102. Madison, Wis.: Beriah Brown, 1855.

Written in 1849. Gives considerable information concerning the Galena region. Tells of the size of Galena and of Springfield, Ill., in 1822. Criticism: *Draper MSS.*, Z 24.

THOMAS, Judge WILLIAM. *Reminiscences.* Printed in the *Jacksonville, Ill., Weekly Journal,* Apr. 18, 1877. Clipping bound in *Ill. Local Hist. Pamphlets,* V., in Library of Wisconsin State Historical Society.

The article is of extreme interest to a student of early society in Illinois. The author settled in Jacksonville, Ill., in 1826. His observations were unusually acute. He was a lawyer and a teacher. He tells of Yankees *vs.* Southerners, of early lawlessness, and of early Galena.

—— *Winnebago Outbreak of 1827.* In *Chicago Tribune,* Apr. 7, 1877. Reprinted from the *Jacksonville (Ill.) Journal* of Aug. 17, 1871.

The article is important because the writer was a volunteer in the campaign against the Winnebagoes.

THWAITES, REUBEN GOLD. *Narrative of Morgan L. Martin. In an Interview with the Editor* [Thwaites]. In *Wis. Hist. Coll.,* XI., pp. 385–415. Madison, Wis.: Democrat Printing Co., State Printers, 1888.

Page 398 gives an estimate of the population of Galena, which Martin visited in 1829.

TILLSON, CHRISTIANA HOLMES. *Reminiscences of early Life in Illinois.* Privately printed—as late as 1870. iv.+138 pp.

A very rare book. Copy in the Chicago Historical Society Library. The best book I know of from which to secure a knowledge of life in Illinois from 1822 to 1827. The writer was observant, and her command of English is far superior to that of many old persons who write reminiscences. Of great value.

VAN ZANDT, NICHOLAS BIDDLE. *A full Description of the Soil, Water, Timber, and Prairies of each Lot, or quarter Section of the Military Lands between the Mississippi and Illinois Rivers.* Washington City: P. Force, 1818. 8vo. 127 pp.

Rare and valuable. Pages 109–25 contain a venomous account of Birkbeck's settlement in Illinois. In Library of Wisconsin State Historical Society.

Vermont. Records of the Council of Safety and Governor and Council of the State of Vermont, to which are prefixed the Records of the general Conventions from July, 1775, to December, 1777. Montpelier: J. & J. M. Poland, 1873–80. 8 vols.

Vol. VI., 431–2 contains remarks of Governor Galusha on the scarcity of food in 1816.

Virginia Patriot and Richmond mercantile Advertiser. Richmond, Va., Apr.–Dec., 1816. In Library of Wisconsin State Historical Society.

Sept. 7, 11, 21, 1816, tell of the cold in New England and the drought in the South.

VOLNEY, CONSTANTIN FRANÇOIS CHASSE-BŒUF. *A View of the Soil and Climate of the United States of America: with supplementary Remarks upon Florida; on the French Colonies on the Mississippi and Ohio, and in Canada; and on the aboriginal Tribes of America. Philadelphia*, 1804. *London*, 1804. xxv.+446 pp.

Translated by C. B. Brown. The author gives a moderately full description of the Illinois of the close of the 18th century. Valuable for characterization of the inhabitants.

WASHBURNE, ELIHU BENJAMIN. *Sketch of Edward Coles, second Governor of Illinois, and of the slavery Struggle of 1823–4. Prepared for the Chicago Historical Society. Chicago: Jansen, McClurg & Co.*, 1882. 253 pp.

Indispensable for a specialist in this period of Illinois history. Well written. Quotes many letters.

—— Editor. *The Edwards Papers.* (*Volume II. of the Chicago Historical Society's Collections.*) *Chicago: Fergus Printing Co.*, 1884. 8+xxviii.+633 pp.

Pages 86–90 give Capt. Thos. E. Craig's official report to Governor Edwards of the attack on Peoria in 1812. The volume has a description of Peoria in 1827, and considerable information concerning the Indian troubles of that year.

WELBY, ADLARD, Esq. *A Visit to North America and the English Settlements in Illinois, with a winter Residence at Phila-*

delphia; solely to ascertain the actual Prospects of the emigrating Agriculturist, Mechanic, and Commercial Speculator. London: *J. Drury*, 1821. 16mo. xii.+224 pp.

Wheeling, Va. Report of a Meeting of Workingmen in the City of Wheeling, Virginia, on forming a Settlement in the State of Illinois. 12 pp.

The report is dated Oct. 4, 1830. Printed without place and publisher's name. In Library of Chicago Historical Society. Rare. It set forth a scheme for purchasing and settling a county in Illinois.

WILLIAMS, SAMUEL. *Sketches of the War, between the United States and the British Isles: intended as a faithful History of all the material Events from the Time of the Declaration in 1812 to and including the Treaty of Peace in 1815.* Rutland, Vt.: *Fay & Davison*, 1815. 496 pp.

Contains Capt. Heald's official account of the massacre at Fort Dearborn, August 15, 1812.

WOODS, JOHN. *Two Years' Residence in the Settlement on the English Prairie, in the Illinois Country, U. S. With an Account of its animal and vegetable Productions, Agriculture, &c. &c. A Description of the principal Towns, Villages, &c. &c. With the Habits and Customs of the Back-woodsmen.* London: *Longman & others*, 1822. 310 pp.

Of great value. Unusually conservative as to Illinois advantages, but apparently truthful.

WRIGHT, JOHN S. *Letters from the West; or, A Caution to Emigrants.* Salem, N. Y.: *Dodd & Stevenson*, 1819. 72 pp.

A series of letters from one who traveled through the West in 1818-19. In a fair manner the discouragements which emigrants may expect to meet are portrayed. In Library of Chicago Historical Society.

II.

SECONDARY WORKS.

ABBOTT, JOHN STEVENS CABOT. *History of Maine from the earliest Discovery of the Region by the Northmen until the present Time.* Boston: B. B. Russell, 1875. 556 pp.

Tells of the "Ohio fever," which raged about the close of the war of 1812, and which furnished some settlers to Illinois.

AGNEW, Hon. DANIEL, LL. D. *History of the Region of Pennsylvania north of the Ohio and west of the Allegheny River . . . also, an Account of the Division of the Territory for public Purposes, and of the Lands, Laws, Titles, Settlements, Controversies, and Litigation within this Region.* Philadelphia: Kay & Brother, 1887. 4+246 pp.

The work shows the price at which Pennsylvania public lands sold at the time Illinois was being settled.

ALLEN, J. A. *American Bisons, living and extinct.* Cambridge, Mass.: Welch, Bigelow, & Co., 1876. ix.+246 pp. and 12 plates.

Carefully done. Tells of the great herds of buffalo early found in Illinois and of their extermination in that region.

ALLEN, WILLIAM FRANCIS. *The Place of the North-West in general History.* Pages 92-111 of the author's *Essays and Monographs.* Boston: Geo. H. Ellis, 1890. 392 pp. Found also in *Papers of the Am. Hist. Ass'n,* III., pp. 329-48.

Good for a view of our subject as connected with larger portions of the world's history.

Alton city Directory, 1858. Alton, Ill.: McEvoy & Bowron, 1858. 156 pp.

A short historical sketch of Alton is given. Its authority is on a par with that of county histories.

American historical Review. New York. Vol. IV., 623-35. See Boyd, Carl Evans, below.

ANDREAS, A. T. *History of Chicago from the earliest Period to the present Time.* Chicago: A. T. Andreas, 1884. I., 648; II., 780; III., 876 pp.

Only pages 31–111 of Volume I. concern the period before 1830. The narrative is written with considerable care, and the work is especially rich in copies of old maps, having not fewer than two dozen before 1830.

ASBURY, HENRY. *Reminiscences of Quincy, Illinois, containing historical Events, Anecdotes, Matters concerning old Settlers and old Times, etc.* Quincy, Ill.: D. Wilcox & Sons, 1882. 224 pp.

Tells of the first settlement of Adams county, under the congressional act of Jan. 13, 1825. The large number of New Englanders is suggestive of the increase of northern over southern immigration.

Atlantic Monthly. Boston and London. Vol. II., 579–95. (May, 1861.) See Clarke, S. C.

BARBER, JOHN WARNER, and HOWE, HENRY. *All the Western States and Territories, from the Alleghanies to the Pacific, and from the Lakes to the Gulf.* Cincinnati: Howe's Subscription Book Concern, 1867. 16mo. 733 pp.

Pages 195–250 are on Illinois. Early settlement, Clark's campaign, and the Chicago Massacre of 1812 are described. The work is popular in character, yet its citation of sources makes it of some value.

BARRY, Hon. P. T. *The first Irish in Illinois. Reminiscent of Old Kaskaskia Days.* In *Trans. of the Ill. State Hist. Soc.*, 1902. Springfield, Ill.: Phillips Bros., State Printers, 1902. pp. 63–70.

Almost exclusively concerned with the period before 1830. Tells of the work of Chevalier Makarty, George Croghan, John Reynolds, and of the Irish soldiers under George Rogers Clark.

BARSTOW, GEORGE. *The History of New Hampshire, from its Discovery, in 1614, to the Passage of the Toleration Act in 1819.* 2d ed. New York: G. P. Putnam & Co., 1853. 8vo. iv.+ 456 pp.

Gives a short account of the unusual cold of 1816–17, which affected western immigration. There is nothing to indicate that the second edition is not an exact reprint of the first. Copyright, 1842.

BECK, LEWIS C. *A Gazetteer of the States of Illinois and Missouri; containing a general View of each State, a general View of their Counties, and a particular Description of their Towns, Villages, Rivers, &c., &c.* Albany: Charles R. and George Webster, 1823. 352 pp.

165 pages are devoted to Illinois. Much interesting material is given, but the nature of the publication makes caution in its use necessary.

BECKLEY, HOSEA, A. M. *The History of Vermont; with Descriptions, physical and topographical.* Brattleboro: George H. Salisbury, 1846. 16mo. 396 pp.

Describes the effects of the unusual cold of 1816–17, which greatly affected western emigration.

BECKWITH, HIRAM WILLIAMS. *Historic Notes on the Northwest, gleaned from early Authors, old Maps and Manuscripts, private and official Correspondence, and other authentic, though, for the most part, out-of-the-way Sources.* (In *Hist. of Vermilion County, Ill.* Chicago: H. H. Hill & Co., 1879. 11–304 pp).

Deals with the period before Illinois became a state (1818). "The authorities consulted show a large range of acquaintance with the very best sources of information extant"—Lyman C. Draper. Strong on French and Indians.

—— *A brief History of Danville, Illinois, with a concise Statement of its mining, manufacturing, and commercial Advantages.* Danville, Ill.: Danville Printing Co., 1874. 11 pp. (unnumbered).

Slight, but tells of the beginnings of the city in the third decade of the 19th century.

BECKWITH, PAUL. *Creoles of St. Louis.* St. Louis: Nixon-Jones Printing Co., 1893. 169 pp.

The genealogy of the five branches of the Chouteau family is given. As many of this family were prominent in early Illinois the work is of some interest, although not wholly reliable.

BEGGS, Rev. STEPHEN R. *Pages from the early History of the West and North-West: embracing Reminiscences and Incidents of Settlement and Growth, and Sketches of the material and religious Progress of the States of Ohio, Indiana, Illinois, and Missouri, with especial Reference to the History of Methodism.* Cincinnati: Methodist Book Concern, 1868. 325 pp.

Good upon the beginnings of northern Illinois. Tells of the Chicago massacre (1812), of the work of Rev. Jesse Walker, and of early pioneer life. No clerical bias, in the bad sense.

BERNHEIM, G. D. *History of the German Settlements and of*

the *Lutheran Church in North and South Carolina, from the earliest Period of the Colonization of the Dutch, German and Swiss Settlers to the Close of the first Half of the present Century.* Philadelphia: The Lutheran Book Store, 1872. ix.+557 pp.

Pages 471-3 tell of the North Carolina Synod sending a missionary to Illinois in 1827.

BIRNEY, WILLIAM. *James G. Birney and his Times. The Genesis of the Republican Party with some Account of abolition Movements in the South before 1828.* New York: D. Appleton & Co., 1890. 24mo. x.+443 pp.

Chapter 12 is on abolition in the South before 1828. The work is helpful in learning the conditions from which southern emigrants moved.

BLANCHARD, RUFUS. *Discovery and Conquest of the Northwest, with the History of Chicago.* Wheaton: R. Blanchard & Co., 1879. Chicago: Cushing, 1880. 768 pp. 8vo.

A well-written and valuable book for discovery and conquest, but of little value for a study of mere immigration before 1831. What it has of immigration is almost exclusively confined to immigration to the region of the present Chicago.

——— *History of Illinois, to accompany an historical Map of the State.* Chicago: National School Furnishing Company, 1883. 128 pp.

The text is a disconnected symposium, and has in some cases been superseded by later research. The map is the most valuable part of the work. It is 27½x42½ inches in size, mounted on heavy cloth, and shows, with dates, Indian trails, routes of exploring and military expeditions, early stage and mail routes, historic sites, dates of settlement of the principal towns.

BONHAM, JERIAH. *Fifty Years' Recollections with Observations and Reflections on historical Events, giving Sketches of eminent Citizens—their Lives and public Services.* Peoria: J. W. Franks & Sons, 1883. 536 pp.

The "fifty years" seem to have begun shortly after 1830. The biographical sketches, however, give several facts in regard to the origin and immigration of such early leaders as Coles, Edwards, Reynolds, Carlin, and others.

BOYD, CARL EVANS. *County of Illinois, The.* Am. Hist. Rev., IV., 623-35. July, 1899.

A scholarly history of Virginia's ephemeral County of Illinois, although in error as to the dates of its beginning and ending, respectively.

BRACKENRIDGE, HENRY MARIE, Esq. *History of the late War between the United States and Great Britain. Containing a minute Account of the various military and naval Operations. Baltimore: Cushing,* 1817. *4th ed. Baltimore: Cushing & Jewett,* 1818. xxiv.+348 pp. *6th ed. Philadelphia: James Kay,* 1839. 298 pp.

Valuable. Several times translated. Impartial. Gives a short account of the massacre at Fort Dearborn, August 15, 1812.

BROWN, CHARLES R. *The Old Northwest Territory: its Missions, Forts, and trading Posts. Kalamazoo, Mich.: Brown, Moore & Quale,* 1875. 32 pp.

The work consists of an historical and chronological map (14½ x 15 inches), and notes upon the 94 sites located upon it. Eleven of the sites are in Illinois. Valuable and suggestive, although deficient in citation of authorities.

BROWN, HENRY. *The History of Illinois from its first Discovery and Settlement to the present Time. New York: J. Winchester,* 1844. vi.+492 pp.

The author confesses to having written in haste and to having borrowed stories from other states simply to amuse his readers. Worthless except to furnish a few topics which one may wish to verify. Criticism: *Draper MSS.*, Z No. 2.

BROWN, SAMUEL R. *The Western Gazetteer, or, Emigrant's Directory, (1817) containing a geographical Description of the western States and Territories, viz., the States of Ky., Ind., La., O., Tenn., and Miss., and the Territories of Ill., Mo., Ala., Mich., and N. Western, with an Appendix containing Sketches of some of the western Counties of N. Y., Pa. and Va.; a description of the Gt. Northern Lakes; Indian Annuities, and Directions to Emigrants. Auburn, N. Y.: H. C. Southwick,* 1817. 360 pp.

Pages 17-35 give an inaccurate description of Illinois' population and resources.

BROWN, WILLIAM HUBBARD. *An historical Sketch of the early Movement in Illinois for the Legalization of Slavery, read at the annual Meeting of the Chicago Historical Society, Dec. 5, 1864.*

Chicago: Fergus Printing Co., 1876. 31 pp. *Fergus hist. Series*, No. 4. 8vo. 25 cents.

Especially valuable for the great struggle over slavery in Illinois in 1822-24. First printed in 1865, under the auspices of the Chicago Historical Society.

BUCKLEY, JAMES MONROE. *A History of Methodists in the United States.* (Volume V. of *American Church History.*) *New York: The Christian Literature Co.*, 1896. xix.+714 pp.

Tells of the founding of Lebanon Seminary, later McKendree College, at Lebanon, Ill., in 1828.

Chicago City Directory, for the Year 1855-56, and Northern Illinois Gazetteer. *Chicago: Robert Fergus*, 1855. 150+xxxii.+208+128 pp.

Of slight value for our purpose, although the historical introductions to the directories of the various cities and towns have a few usable statements.

Chicago daily Democratic Press. Railroads, History and Commerce of Chicago, three Articles. 2d ed. *Chicago: Democratic Press Job and Book Steam Print*, 1854. 80 pp.

Of considerable interest, although many statements are of too late a date to be used.

Chicago Magazine. Chicago, Ill.

I., 103–16 (1857), gives an account of the massacre at Fort Dearborn, August 15, 1812, largely taken from the Kinzie narrative.

Chicago Sunday Tribune, Nov. 28, 1897.

New light thrown on Old Fort Dearborn. An account of the finding of important records in the archives of the U. S. government. The archives contained the original order for building a fort where Fort Dearborn later stood (order of 1803), and sketches of Fort Dearborn as early as January, 1808. The sketches are reproduced.

CLARKE, S. C. *Prairie State, The.* (*Atlantic Monthly*, VII., 579-595, *May*, 1861.)

Well written and treats a large number of subjects.

COPELAND, LOUIS ALBERT, B. L. *The Cornish in southwest Wisconsin.* Pages 301–334 of *Wis. Hist. Coll.*, XIV. *Madison, Wis.: Democrat Printing Co., State Printer*, 1898.

Gives several facts concerning the early history of the Galena region. Most of the Cornish, however, came after 1830.

DANA, E. *Geographical Sketches on the Western Country: designed for Emigrants and Settlers: being the Result of extensive Researches and Remarks. To which is added a Summary of all the most interesting Matters on the Subject, including a particular Description of the unsold public Lands, . . . also, a List of the principal Roads. Cincinnati: Looker, Reynolds & Co.*, 1819. 312 pp.

Pages 133-156 are devoted to Illinois. A suggestion of the fraudulent count in the census of 1818 is given.

—— *A Description of the bounty Lands in the State of Illinois: also, the principal Roads and Routes, by Land and Water, through the Territory of the United States. Cincinnati: Looker, Reynolds & Co.*, 1819. 12mo. 108 pp.

Gives very few references to settlement and few descriptions of historic sites.

DAVIDSON, ALEXANDER, *and* STUVÉ, BERNARD. *A complete History of Illinois from 1673 to 1873; embracing the physical Features of the Country; its early Explorations, aboriginal Inhabitants; French and British Occupation; Conquest by Virginia; territorial Condition and the subsequent civil, military and political Events of the State. Springfield, Ill.: Ill. Journal Co.*, 1874. 944 pp.

Crude, but no specialist in Illinois history should be without it. Not minute in treatment of immigration.

Decatur, Macon County, Illinois, History of. Decatur, Ill.: Compiled and published by Wiggins & Co., Cleveland, O., 1871. 51 pp.

A symposium without historical merit. Almost exclusively of a later period than 1830, but tells of the first settlement of the county in 1820.

DRAKE, SAMUEL ADAMS. *The Making of the Ohio Valley States, 1660-1837. New York: Charles Scribner's Sons*, 1894. 16 mo. 269 pp.

A very few pages are devoted to Illinois, and naturally the larger events alone are noted.

WORKS CONSULTED. 241

DREW, BENJAMIN. *The Refugee; or, The Narratives of fugitive Slaves in Canada. Related by themselves, with an Account of the History and Condition of the colored Population of Upper Canada.* Boston: *John P. Jewett & Co.*, 1856. 12mo. 387 pp.

A few of the refugees whose escapes are narrated passed through Illinois on the Underground Railroad.

EAMES, CHARLES M. *Historic Morgan and Classic Jacksonville. Jacksonville, Ill.: Daily Journal Steam Job Printing Office*, 1885. 336 pp. In Library of Chicago Historical Society.

Of great interest because of its details concerning early methods of travel and concerning the beginnings in Morgan county. Deals with pioneer and slavery history.

EDWARDS, NINIAN WIRT. *History of Illinois, from 1778 to 1833; and Life and Times of Ninian Edwards. Springfield, Ill.: Ill.. State Journal Co.*, 1870. 549+iii. pp.

Written by the son of Gov. Ninian Edwards. Not in good form, but has much authentic material.

Family Magazine; or, Monthly Abstract of general Knowledge. New York, Boston, Cincinnati.

Volumes IV. (1837) and V. (1839) have short articles on Illinois, which are too light to be taken seriously.

FARMER, SILAS. *The History of Detroit and Michigan, or the Metropolis illustrated. A chronological Cyclopedia of the Past and Present, including a full Record of territorial Days in Michigan and the Annals of Wayne County. Detroit: Silas Farmer & Co.*, 1884. Revised and enlarged, 1890. 2 vols.

Valuable for information concerning Clark, Hamilton, Vigo, and La Balme.

FLAGLER, Major D. W. *A History of the Rock Island Arsenal from its establishment in 1863 to December, 1876; and of the Island of Rock Island, the Site of the Arsenal, from 1804 to 1863. Washington: Government Printing Office*, 1877. 483 pp. 13 plates, 2 pictures.

The first chapter of the book refers to the first white settlement in the region of Rock Island, about 1828.

FORD, GOV. THOMAS. *A History of Illinois, from its Com-*
19

mencement as a State in *1818 to 1847*. Containing a full Account of the Black Hawk War, the Rise, Progress, and Fall of Mormonism, the Alton and Lovejoy Riots, and other important and interesting Events. Chicago: S. C. Griggs & Co., 1854. 447 pp.

As the title indicates, the book is chiefly valuable for a period later than 1830. It is also largely political. The first one hundred and ten pages will be found useful and deal to some extent with the social life when the state was young. Criticism: *Draper MSS.*, Z 13.

GERHARD, FRED. *Illinois as it is; its History, Geography, Statistics, Constitution, Laws, Government, Finances, Climate, Soil, Plants, Animals, State of Health, Prairies, Agriculture, Cattle-breeding, Orcharding, Cultivation of the Grape, Timber-growing, Market-prices, Lands and Land-prices . . . etc.* Philadelphia: Charles Desilver, 1857. 451 pp.

Pages 13–137 are devoted to the historyi of Illnois. The author is conspicuously accurate and treats a large number of topics. A valuable secondary work.

Glimpses of the Monastery. Scenes from the History of the Ursulines of Quebec during two hundred Years, 1639–1839. By a Member of the Community. Second edition, completed by Reminiscences of the last fifty Years, 1839–1889. Quebec: L. J. Domers & Frère, 1897. ix.+418+184 pp.

Pages 84–93 of the first pagination give a suggestive discussion of the capability of the Indian for civilization.

GREEN, THOMAS MARSHALL. *Historic Families of Kentucky. (First Series.)* Cincinnati: Robert Clarke & Co., 1889. 304 pp.

Gives a few facts concerning John Todd and John Todd Stuart, who were active in Illinois. The latter was a cousin of Mary Todd Lincoln and had much early influence upon Lincoln. The volume deals with McDowells, Logans, and Allens. Well written and valuable.

HAIGHT, WALTER C., B. L. *The Ordinance of 1787.* (pp. 343-402 of *Pub. of the Mich. Pol. Sci. Ass'n*, II.), 1896, 1897.

A discussion of the binding effect of the Ordinance of 1787. The question has a close connection with slavery in Illinois.

HALL, B. F. *The early History of the North Western States, embracing New York, Ohio, Indiana, Illinois, Michigan, Iowa and Wisconsin, with their land Laws, etc., and an Appendix containing the Constitutions of those States.* Buffalo: Geo. H. Derby & Co., 1849. Duodecimo. 477 pp.

Statements made in this book must be carefully verified. The rise of conflicting land titles is fairly well treated.

HARRIS, N. DWIGHT, Ph. D. *The History of Negro Servitude in Illinois and of the slavery Agitation in that State 1719–1864.* Chicago: A. C. McClurg & Co., 1904. 276 pp.

An erudite work, compiled from many sources previously unused.

HAYES, A. A., Jr. *The Metropolis of the Prairies.* (*Harper's New Monthly Mag.,* LXI., 711–730, Oct. 1880).

A readable popular article. Chiefly concerned with events later than 1830.

HEATON, JOHN L. *The Story of Vermont.* Boston: D. Lothrop Co., 1889. 319 pp.

Has an interesting chapter of twenty pages on The Great West. More reliable than so popular a book usually is.

HENDERSON, JOHN G. *Early History of the "Sangamon Country," being Notes on the first Settlements in the Territory now comprised within the Limits of Morgan, Scott and Cass Counties.* Davenport, Iowa: Day, Egbert & Fidlar, 1873. 33 pp.

Of great interest for a study of early troubles with the Indians. Treats of East *vs.* South in Illinois and of Regulators. Deals almost exclusively with the period before 1830. Compiled largely from interviews with old settlers, hence not wholly reliable.

HINSDALE, BURKE AARON. *The Old Northwest with a View of the thirteen Colonies as constituted by the royal Charters.* New York: Townsend MacCoun, 1888. 8vo. 440 pp. 2d ed., rev. New York: Silver, Burdett & Co., 1899. $2.50.

In general only the boldest outlines of immigration to Illinois are sketched. The slavery struggle in Illinois (1822–24) is treated with comparative fullness. Criticism: *Boston Herald, July* 2, 1888.

HOSKINS, NATHAN. *A History of the State of Vermont, from its Discovery and Settlement to the Close of the Year 1830.* Vergennes: J. Shedd, 1831. 12mo. 316 pp.

Tells of the unusually cold summer of 1816.

HOWE, HENRY. *Historical Collections of the great West: containing Narratives of the most important and interesting Events in western History—remarkable individual Adventures—Sketches of frontier Life—Descriptions of natural Curiosities: to which is appended historical and descriptive Sketches of Oregon, New Mexico, Texas, Minnesota, Utah and California.* Cincinnati: Henry Howe, 1853. 8vo. 440 pp.

Compiled from a large number of sources, largely secondary.

HUBBARD, GEORGE D. *A Case of geographic Influence upon human Affairs.* Pages 145–157 of *Bulletin of the American Geographical Society*, XXXVI., No. 3, March, 1904. Pub. by the Society, New York.

A scientific discussion of the effect of glaciation upon the character of the people of different portions of Illinois.

HULBERT, ARCHUR BUTLER. *Red-Men's Roads. The Indian Thoroughfares of the central West.* Columbus, Ohio: Fred J. Heer & Co., 1900. 37 pp.

The book has many maps and is a help toward an understanding of the ways by which early settlers reached Illinois.

HYNES, REV. THOMAS W. *History of a Century. An Address delivered at Greenville, Bond Co., Ill., on July 4, 1876.*

A newspaper clipping, bound, without the name of the paper from which it was taken, in *Illinois Local History Pamphlets*, V., in Library of the Wisconsin State Historical Society. It contains a valuable historical letter from Mrs. Almira Morse, a resident as early as 1820.

Illinois. Historical Encyclopedia of Illinois. Chicago and New York: Munsell Pub. Co., 1900. 608 pp.

Edited by Newton Bateman, LL. D., and Paul Selby, A. M. Much more reliable than many books of the same literary type.

International Monthly. Burlington, Vt., IV., 794–820. See Turner, Frederick Jackson.

JAMES, EDMUND JANES, and LOVELESS, MILO J. *A Bibliography of Newspapers published in Illinois prior to 1860.* Springfield, Ill., Phillips Bros., State Printers, 1899. 94 pp.

A very valuable work. An appendix gives a list of the Illinois and Missouri papers (1808-1897) in the St. Louis Mercantile Library, while a second appendix enumerates the county histories of Illinois and tells where they may be found.

JOHNSON, ERIC and PETERSON, C. F. *Svenskarne i Illinois.* Chicago: W. Williamson, 1880. 471 pp.

Chiefly valuable for a later period. The salient points of early Illinois history are canvassed.

KINGDOM, WILLIAM, Jr. *America and the British Colonies, an abstract of all the most useful Information relative to the United States of America, and the British Colonies of Canada, the Cape of Good Hope, New South Wales, and Van Diemen's Island.* London: G. and W. B. Whittaker, 1820. 16mo. 359 pp.

Pages 61-73 describe Illinois and give some judicious advice to emigrants. Conservative, but not cynical. Entire pages are reprinted from other authors, notably Fearon, without the use of quotation marks.

KINGSTON, Hon. JOHN T. *Early Western Days.* (In *Wis. Hist. Coll.*, VII., 297-344). Madison, Wis.: E. B. Bolens, 1876.

Gives a short account of the slavery struggle in Illinois in 1822-24.

——— *Slavery in Illinois.* Necedah, Wis.: Necedah Republican. 6 pp. Reprinted, without date, in pamphlet form. In Library of State Historical Society of Wisconsin.

A very short sketch of slavery in Illinois from its introduction in 1719-20.

KIRKLAND, JOSEPH. *The Story of Chicago.* Chicago: Dibble Pub. Co., 1892. 470 pp.

The book makes large reference to authorities and is in consequence valuable for reference.

KÖRNER, GUSTAV. *Das deutsche Element in den Vereinigten Staaten von Nordamerika*, 1818-1848. Cincinnati: A. E. Wilde & Co., 1880. 16mo. 461 pp.

The 12th chapter (pp. 244-81) treats of German settlement in Illinois. Tells of the first German and Swiss settlements in the state. Naturally this chapter and the work as a whole is largely concerned with a period later than 1830.

LAW, Judge JOHN. *Address delivered before the Vincennes Historical and Antiquarian Society, February 22, 1839.* Louisville,

Ky.: *Prentice & Weissinger*, 1839. 48 pp. Enlarged and reprinted as *The colonial History of Vincennes*. Vincennes: *Harvey, Mason & Co.*, 1858. 156 pp.

Of great value on account of its description of Clark's campaign, and its notes on Mermet, Gibault, Hamilton, Tecumseh, La Balme, and on the public lands.

LAWRENCE, JOHN. *The History of the Church of the United Brethren in Christ*. Dayton, Ohio: *W. J. Shuey*, 1868. 2 vols. I., vi.+416; II., vii.+431 pp.

The book contains many facts concerning early emigration and settlement. Its bearing on early Illinois history is, however, slight.

LEATON, REV. JAMES. *History of Methodism in Illinois, from 1793 to 1832*. Cincinnati: *Walden & Stowe*, 1883. 410 pp.

Very interesting notes on Peter Cartwright, Jesse Walker, and other pioneers.

LEE, FRANCIS BAGLEY. *New Jersey as a Colony and as a State*. New York: *The Publishing Soc. of New Jersey*, 1902. 4 vols. I., 422; II., 456; III., 400; IV., 402 pp.

The work is superbly printed and illustrated and contains a vast amount of information, but is totally lacking in bibliography or references, except a few indications in the index to the illustrations.

LÖHER, FRANZ. *Geschichte und Zustände der Deutschen in Amerika*. Cincinnati: *Eggers & Wulkop*, 1847. v.+544 pp.

The chapters of especial interest to us are "Ausströmen der Yankees," pp. 237–41; "Einwanderung von 1815 bis 1830," pp. 253–58; "Die Wohnsitze" (Illinois and Missouri), pp. 337–40. The author cites many authorities, and his book is of very great value in the study of the assimilation of an expatriated people.

LOTHROP, J. S. *J. S. Lothrop's Champaign County (Ill.) Directory for 1870–1, with History of the same, and of each Township therein*. Chicago: *J. S. Lothrop*, 1871.

Tells a great many things—several of which are false—concerning the early period of Illinois history.

LUSK, D. W. *Eighty Years of Illinois Politics and Politicians, Anecdotes and Incidents. A succinct History of the State, 1809–1889*. 3d ed. Revised and enlarged. Springfield, Ill.: *H. W. Rokker*, 1889. 609+109 pp.

The 609 pages are political. The 109 pages have a great interest, dealing as they do with the beginnings of Illinois. Secondary sources are largely quoted. Not exact enough for critical work, yet very suggestive.

M'AFEE, ROBERT B. *History of the late War in the Western Country, comprising a full Account of all the Transactions in that Quarter, from the Commencement of Hostilities at Tippecanoe, to the Termination of the Contest at New Orleans on the Return of Peace.* Lexington, Ky.: Worsley & Smith, 1816. 8vo. 534 pp.

Very rare. In the Chicago Historical Society Library. A valuable book. Describes the attack on Fort Dearborn in 1812.

MACKENZIE, E. *An historical, topographical, and descriptive View of the United States of America, and of Upper and Lower Canada . . . the present State of Mexico and South America, and also of the native Tribes of the New World.* Newcastle-upon-Tyne: Mackenzie & Dent, 1819. viii.+432 pp.

The four pages devoted to Illinois are interesting and fairly reliable, though scarcely up to date. The author mentions eighteen works used in compiling his book.

McLAUGHLIN, ANDREW C. *Lewis Cass.* Boston: Houghton, Mifflin & Co., 1891. 363 pp. $1.25.

Describes the expedition of General Cass to northern Illinois during the Sauk outbreak of 1827. Criticism: *Nation*, LIII., 204.

MARIETTA, O. *Report of the Commissioners of the National Centennial Celebration of the Early Settlement of the Territory North West of the Ohio River, . . . held at Marietta, O., July 15–19, inclusive, 1888.* Columbus, O.: The Westbote Company, State Printers, 1889. 292 pp.

Contains many speeches of varying historical accuracy and importance.

MASON, EDWARD GAY. *Chapters from Illinois History.* Chicago: Herbert S. Stone, 1901. 322 pp.

Scholarly and accurate, and rich in citation of sources. Tells of Old Fort Chartres, John Todd's Record-Book, the march of the Spaniards across Illinois, and the Chicago massacre.

—— *March of the Spaniards across Illinois.* (In his *Chapters of Illinois History*, Chicago, 1901; also in *Mag. of Am. Hist.* N. Y., XV., 457–469, 1886.)

Refers to a number of sources. The march is that of 1781 against St. Joseph.

MATHER, IRWIN F. *The Making of Illinois.* Chicago: A. Flanagan, 1900. 292 pp.

The work is strong in the number of subjects which it treats. The Illinois of our period is well covered. The bibliography cites many valuable sources, but no references are given in the body of the work. The date of the founding of the village of Kaskaskia is given as 1695—a confusion of the mission on the Illinois River with the later village of the same name.

MAYO, A. D. *Western Emigration and Western Character.* (*Christian Examiner*, N. Y., LXXXII., 265–82, 1867.)

The subject is well treated, but the value of the article for our purpose is not so great as it would have been if confined to the early period.

MEIGS, WILLIAM M. *The Life of Thomas Hart Benton.* Philadelphia and London: J. B. Lippincott Company, 1904. 535 pp.

The work throws much light upon the policy of the United States in regard to the sale of public lands, and the attitude of the West towards that policy.

MELISH, JOHN. *A geographical Description of the United States, with the contiguous British and Spanish Possessions.* Philadelphia: John Melish, 1816. 182 pp.

A trifle over one page is devoted to Illinois. Of interest only as showing what was presented to the East at the time concerning Illinois. Melish was a professional map and gazetteer maker. His work typifies that of the geographers of the time, who described the world with marvelous audacity.

—— *A geographical Description of the United States, with the contiguous Countries, including Mexico and the West Indies.* Philadelphia: John Melish, 1822. v.+491 pp.

Seven pages are devoted to Illinois. The description of several Illinois towns is useful. This was a second and much improved edition of the author's similar work of 1816.

—— *Information and Advice to Emigrants to the United States: and from the Eastern to the Western States: illustrated by a Map of the United States and a Chart of the Atlantic Ocean.* Philadelphia: John Melish, 1819. 12 mo. v.+144 pp.

An entire chapter of twenty-six pages is devoted to Birkbeck's settlement in Illinois. The map shows several routes in Illinois, but it must have been old. The book is a good type of its class.

MOORE, CHARLES. *The Northwest under three Flags, 1635-1796.* New York: Harper & Bros., 1900. xxiii.+402 pp.

Many facts concerning the Illinois of the period are given. This work is of considerable historical value. References to sources, although not abundant, are helpful.

MOSES, JOHN. *Illinois, historical and statistical. Comprising the essential Facts of its Planting and Growth as a Province, County, Territory, and State. Derived from the most authentic Sources, including original Documents and Papers. Together with carefully prepared statistical Tables . . . Chicago: Fergus Printing Co.,* 1889-93. 2 vols. 1316 pp.

The author was secretary and librarian of the Chicago Historical Society. His work is perhaps the best that has appeared.

MOWRY, WILLIAM AUGUSTUS. *The territorial Growth of the United States. New York: Silver, Burdett & Co., 1902.* 225 pp.

The chapter on the Northwest Territory tells of various cessions of land comprised in the present Illinois.

MURAT, ACHILLE. *America and the Americans. New York: William H. Graham,* 1849. Duodecimo. vii.+260 pp.

Too late in date to be of much service, although some valuable suggestions as to the social and political development of the frontier can be obtained. The writer was an acute observer. He treats politics, slavery, society, religion, justice, etc. The book was written about 1829. Describes customs and extra legal proceedings in the West.

Nashville, Tennessee, History of, with full Outline of the natural Advantages. . . . Nashville, Tenn.: Pub. House of the M. E. Church, South, 1890. 656 pp.

Tells of passage of emigrants from North Carolina to Illinois in 1780, of French traders from Illinois to Tennessee in 1779, of Tennesseeans getting head rights from George Rogers Clark.

North American Review, Boston.

Volume LI., 92-140 (July, 1840) has an exhaustive review of Peck's Gazetteer of Illinois. The review is probably of much more historical interest than the Gazetteer.

PALMER, B. M. *Slavery in Illinois. (Dubuque semi-weekly Telegraph, Tues., Sept. 19,* 1899.)

Gives the bill of sale, taken from the county records of Jo Daviess County, Ill., and executed in that county in 1830, of a negro mother and child.

PATTERSON, ROBERT WILSON. *Early Society in southern Illinois.* Chicago: Fergus Printing Co., 1879. Pp. 103–131 of *Fergus historical Series* No. 14.

A characterization, in general terms, of early Illinois society, its manners and its origin. This was a lecture read before the Chicago Historical Society, Oct. 19, 1880.

PECK, Rev. JOHN MASON, *Editor.* *"Father Clark," or the pioneer Preacher. Sketches and Incidents of Rev. John Clark, by An Old Pioneer.* New York: Sheldon, Lamport & Blakeman, 1855. 287 pp.

Gives considerable religious and Indian material for Illinois history from 1790 to 1833, but chiefly on the earlier part of that period.

—— *An historical Sketch of the early American Settlements in Illinois, from 1780–1800.* Read before the Ill. State Lyceum, at it's anniversary, Aug. 16, 1832. *(Western monthly Mag., I., 73–83. Feb. 1833.)*

Popular, but of some value.

POST, Rev. T. M. [Author of pp. 93–102.] *Contributions to the ecclesiastical History of Connecticut; prepared under the Direction of the General Association, to commemorate the Completion of one hundred and fifty Years since its first annual Assembly.* New Haven: Wm. L. Kingsley, 1861. xiv.+562 pp.

A symposium. The article by Rev. Mr. Post is on "The Mission of Congregationalism at the West." It is suggestive on the moral effects of frontier life.

POWELL, J. W., Director. *Eighteenth annual Report of the Bureau of American Ethnology to the Secretary of the Smithsonian Institution, 1896–97.* Washington: Government Printing Office, 1899. Part 2. *Indian land Cessions in the United States compiled by Charles C. Royce, with an Introduction by Cyrus Thomas.* 521–997 pp. and 67 plates.

Valuable. The work was used in preparing the outline maps of Indian cessions contained in this work.

REID, HARVEY. *Biographical Sketch of Enoch Long, an Illinois Pioneer.* Chicago: Fergus Printing Co., 1884. 134 pp. This is Volume II. of the *Chicago Historical Society's Collections.*

Mr. Long visited St. Louis and resided at Alton and Galena before 1827. The book is of great interest on account of its notes on the methods of travel and the extent of Illinois settlements at that date.

REYNOLDS, JOHN. *Belleville in January, 1854.* A 12-page pamphlet, printed without place, publisher, or date. In Library of Wisconsin State Historical Society.

Tells of the laying out of the city in the cornfield of George Blair, in 1814.

—— *A biographical Sketch.* (*Western Journal and Civilian,* XV., 100–114).

Gives glimpses of early travel and of pioneer life.

—— *The pioneer History of Illinois, containing the Discovery, in 1673, and the History of the Country to the Year 1818.* Belleville, Ill.: N. A. Randall, 1852. 2d ed., with portrait, notes and index, Chicago: Fergus Printing Co., 1887. 459 pp.

Contains much valuable biographical material, and describes the life of the early settlers in a clear way. Criticism: *Draper MSS.,* Z 13, 14.

ROOSEVELT, THEODORE. *The Winning of the West.* New York: G. W. Putnam's Sons, 1889–96. Vols. I.–IV. I., xiv.+352; II., 427; III., 339; IV., 363 pp.

Valuable, although bearing marks of haste in preparation. Criticism: *Am. Hist. Rev.,* II., 171.

SANBORN, EDWIN DAVID. *History of New Hampshire, from its Discovery to the Year 1830.* Manchester, N. H.: John B. Clarke, 1875. 422 pp.

Describes the unusually cold summer of 1816 and its effect upon western migration. The book is written in an extremely disconnected style, and is without index, references, or bibliography.

SERGEANT, THOMAS, Esq. *View of the land Laws of Pennsylvania. With Notices of its early History and Legislation.* Philadelphia: James Kay, Jr., and Brother. Pittsburgh: John I. Kay & Co., 1838. 13+203 pp.

Valuable for ascertaining the price at which Pennsylvania public lands, which competed with government lands in the West, were sold.

SHALER, NATHANIEL SOUTHGATE. *Kentucky. A pioneer Commonwealth.* Boston: Houghton, Mifflin & Co., 1885. viii.+433 pp.

Useful as giving an insight into the character of a neighboring state from which many of the early settlers of Illinois came. One of the best of the American Commonwealths series.

SHEA, JOHN GILMARY. *History of the Catholic Church in the United States, 1808-1843.* New York: John G. Shea, 1890. vii.+731 pp.

References to Illinois are very few, but are important. The volume is the third in the author's four-volumed History of the Catholic Church in the United States.

SIEBERT, WILBUR HENRY. *The Underground Rail Road from Slavery to Freedom; with an Introduction by Albert Bushnell Hart.* New York: The Macmillan Co., 1898. xiii.+iii.+478 pp.

Has notes of great interest on the U. G. R. R. in Illinois before 1830. Criticism: *Am. Hist. Rev.*, IV., 557.

SMITH, THEODORE CLARKE. *The Liberty and Free Soil Parties in the Northwest.* New York: Longmans, Green & Co., 1897. vii.+351 pp. *(Harvard Hist. Studies, VI.)*

A well-written book, but only the first chapter concerns the period before 1830. This chapter is, however, well worth attention.

STEINHARD, S. *Deutschland und sein Volk.* Gotha: Hugo Scheube, 1856-7. 2 vols. I., x.+658; II., 826 pp.

Pages 28-46 of volume II. are on the Germans in the United States and contain a few important facts, including statistics, for our period. The Vandalia (Ill.) settlement of 1820 is mentioned.

STEVENS, ABEL, LL. D. *History of the Methodist Episcopal Church in the United States of America.* New York: Phillips & Hunt, 1884. 4 vols. I., 423; II., 511; III., 510; IV., 522 pp.

The fourth volume of this history has interesting notes on Benjamin Young and Jesse Walker, respectively. These men came to Illinois as pioneer ministers; the former in 1804, the latter in 1806.

STRONG, MOSES M., A. M. *History of the Territory of Wisconsin, from 1836 to 1848. Preceded by an Account of some Events during the Period in which it was under the Dominion of Kings, States or other Territories, previous to the Year 1836. Madison, Wis.: Democrat Printing Co., State Printers,* 1885. 16mo. 637 pp.

A valuable book. Its chief interest for us is its sketches of early settlement in the Galena lead region.

SULTE, BENJAMIN. *Histoire des Canadiens-Français, 1608–1880. Montreal: Wilson & Cie.,* 1882–4. 8 vols. 8vo. About 160 pp. per vol. *Montreal: Granger Frères.* 40 parts, paper, $10; 4 vols, cloth.

Gives only slight attention to the French of Illinois. A popular work, but quite useful for a study of social institutions.

SUMMERS, THOMAS O. *Biographical Sketches of eminent itinerant Ministers distinguished, for the most Part, as Pioneers of Methodism within the Bounds of the Methodist Episcopal Church, South. Nashville, Tenn.: Southern Methodist Publishing House,* 1859. 374 pp.

Pages 48–56 give a character sketch of Jesse Walker and an idea of the character of the men to whom he preached in Illinois in 1807.

SWAYNE, WAGER. *The Ordinance of 1787 and the War of 1861. An Address delivered before the N. Y. Commandery of the Military Order of the Loyal Legion. New York: C. G. Burgoyne,* [c. 1893]. 90 pp.

Contains interesting notes on George Rogers Clark and on slavery in Illinois.

THOMSON, JOHN LEWIS. *Historical Sketches of the late War between the United States and Great Britain. Philadelphia: Thos. Desilver,* 1816. 359 pp. *5th ed.,* 1818.

Contains one of the earliest accounts of the massacre at Fort Dearborn, August 15, 1812. The account is short, but tolerably correct. The work was reprinted in 1887 [Philadelphia: J. B. Lippincott Co.], with a short account of the war with Mexico added. 656 pp.

THOMPSON, ZADOCK. *History of the State of Vermont, from its earliest Settlement to the Close of the Year 1832. Burlington: Edward Smith,* 1833. 12mo. 252 pp. *Reprinted with natural Hist. of Vt. and Gazetteer of Vt. Burlington: Zadock Thompson,* 1853. 8vo. 224+224+200+63 pp.

Describes the cold season of 1816–17.

THWAITES, REUBEN GOLD. *Early Lead-mining in Illinois and Wisconsin.* Pages 191–196 of *Am. Hist. Ass'n Rep't*, 1893. Washington: Government Printing Office, 1894.

Contains several interesting statements concerning the early history of the Galena region.

TUCKER, GEORGE. *Progress of the United States in Population and Wealth in fifty Years, as exhibited by the decennial Census.* Boston: Little & Brown, 1843. 12mo. 211 pp.

The fifty years were 1790–1840. Very useful for material concerning the relative growth of different sections of the country.

TURNER, FREDERICK JACKSON. *Middle West, The. International Monthly*, IV., 794–820 (1901).

The article has a few suggestions that are of value for our period.

—— *The Significance of the Frontier in American History.* Pages 199–227 of *Rep't of Am. Hist. Ass'n*, 1893.

Contains a valuable characterization of the French as colonizers.

VARNEY, GEORGE JONES. *A brief History of Maine.* Portland, Me.: McLellan, Mosher & Co., 1888. 336 pp.

Tells of the intense cold of 1816–17 and of the great Western exodus. A "Young People's History." Popular. Without references.

WALKER, EDWIN SAWYER. *History of the Springfield (Illinois) Baptist Association.* Springfield, Ill.: H. W. Rokker, 1881. 140 pp.

Tells of the organization of the United Baptist Church, of Springfield, on July 17, 1830, with eight members.

WALLACE, JOSEPH. *The History of Illinois and Louisiana under the French Rule, embracing a general View of the French Dominion in North America, with some Account of the English Occupation of Illinois.* Cincinnati: Robert Clarke & Co., 1893. vi.+433 pp.

Contains a great deal of material. Usually, though not always, correct.

WARDEN, DAVID BAILLIE. *A statistical, political and historical Account of the U. S. of N. A.; from the period of their first Colonization to the present Day.* Edinburgh: Archibald Constable & Co., 1819. 3 vols. 16mo. I., lxiv.+552; II., 571; III., 588 pp.

Pages 43-65 of Volume III. deal with Illinois exclusively. At the close of the chapter the author gives a bibliography for Illinois—five titles and two maps. A useful book.

WENTWORTH, Hon. JOHN. *Early Chicago. Two Lectures delivered April 11, 1875, and May 7, 1876, respectively.* 48 and 56 pp. Nos. 8 and 7 of *Fergus historical Series.* Chicago: Fergus Printing Co., 1876.

The critical supplemental notes are of especial interest.

WEST, MARY ALLEN. *A MS. Letter in the Illinois State Historical Library.*

Tells the story of the coming of James Moore and his party from Virginia in 1781.

Western monthly Magazine. Conducted by James Hall, Cincinnati, I., 73-83. *See* Peck, Rev. John Mason.

WHITE, EMMA SIGGINS. *Genealogy of the Descendants of John Walker of Wigton, Scotland, with Records and some fragmentary Notes pertaining to the History of Virginia, 1600-1902.* Tiernan-Dart Printing Co., 1902. xxx.+722 pp.

Valuable. Has original letters from Western emigrants. Suggests the great influx of people into Illinois in the third decade of the 19th century. Gives a good idea of the westward drift of population in the United States.

WHITON, JOHN MILTON. *Sketches of the History of New-Hampshire, from its Settlement in 1623 to 1833.* Concord: Marsh, Capen & Lyon, 1834. 222 pp.

Describes the great cold of 1816 and the great emigration to the West. An unimportant work, confessedly popular, and without references.

WILBUR, LA FAYETTE. *Early History of Vermont.* Jericho, Vt.: Roscoe Printing House, 1899-1903. 4 vols. I., 362; II., 419; III., 397; IV., 463 pp.

Pages 162-3 of Volume III. tell of the unusual cold of 1816-17 and quote Governor Galusha's reference to the impending famine. No references are given.

WILLIAMS, GEORGE WASHINGTON. *History of the Negro Race in America from 1619-1880.* New York: G. P. Putnam's Sons, 1882. 2 vols. I., x.+481; II., 611 pp. The two volumes are also issued as one.

Gives some statistics concerning slaves in Illinois and notes on Illinois slavery legislation. The author was a negro.

WILLIAMSON, WILLIAM DURKEE. *The History of the State of Maine; from its first Discovery, A. D. 1602, to the Separation, A. D. 1820, inclusive.* Hallowell: *Glazier, Masters & Co.*, 1832. 2 vols. I., iv.+696; II., 729 pp.

Tells of the unusual cold of 1816-17 and of the great movement toward the West. Strong in citation of authorities. Much above the average of State histories of its time.

WILSON, HENRY. *History of the Rise and Fall of the slave Power in America.* Boston: *James R. Osgood & Co.*, 1872-7. 3 vols. I., vii.+670; II., 720; III., 774 pp. *Houghton.* 3 vols.

Valuable material on slavery in Illinois. A strong work.

WINSOR, JUSTIN. *The westward Movement: the Colonies and the Republic west of the Alleghanies, 1673-98; with full cartographical Illustrations from contemporary Sources.* Boston: *Houghton, Mifflin & Co.*, 1897. 595 pp.

Criticism: *Am. Hist. Rev.*, III., 556.

WITHERS, ALEXANDER SCOTT. *Chronicles of border Warfare, or A History of the Settlement by the Whites, of North-western Virginia: and of the Indian Wars and Massacres, in that Section of the State.* Clarksburg, Va.: *Joseph Israel*, 1831. 319+iv. pp. Very rare. Same. New ed., edited and annotated by Reuben Gold Thwaites. Cincinnati: *Clarke*, 1895.

A few references are to events in Illinois. Criticism: *Am. Hist. Rev.*, I., 170.

YOUNG, WILLIAM T. *Life and public Services of General Lewis Cass.* 2d ed. Detroit: *Markham & Elwood*, 1852. 420 pp.

Tells of Gen. Cass' expedition to Illinois during the trouble with the Sauk Indians in 1827.

THE SETTLEMENT OF ILLINOIS.

INDEX.

A

Aboite river, 35.
Act creating Illinois county, 9, 15.
Act enabling Illinois to form a state government, 115.
Agricultural Society, formed, 168.
Agriculture, 130, 165. *See also* Farming, Fruits, etc.
Albemarle county, *Va.*, 153. 154.
Alton, founding of, 196, 204; land donations for church and school, 142.
Alvord, Clarence W., 5.
American Bottom, 130, 134, 157; map, *in pocket*.
American Fur Company, 157, 158.
American House, Springfield, 207.
Anarchy in Illinois, 40 *et seq.*: ended, 69.
Ancient Free and Accepted Masons, founded, 194.
Anderson, Robert, mention, 207.
Antanya, Michael, 67.
Anti slavery agitation. *See under* Slavery.
Anti slavery Society, Morgan Co., 183.
Arkansas Post, 63.
Arks, 125, 126; price of, 161. *See also* Flat-boats.
Assenisipia, mention, 46.
Augusta county, *Va.*, 15.
Austin, Móses, 196.

B

Bagargon, *Mr.*, elected magistrate, 61.
Baker, David J., 145.
Baltimore, 123, 160, 161.
Bandits, 155.
Bank of Cairo, 114.
Bank of Edwardsville, 207.
Bank of Mt. Carmel, 199.

Baptists, organized, 172; found Shurtleff college, 174; divided on slavery, 175.
Barbour, Philip, mention, 40.
Barges, 94, 129, 160.
Barter, 130. *See also under* Money.
Bates, Edward, 204.
Batteaux, 94.
Baynton, Wharton and Morgan, trading firm, 10.
Bears, 14, 173.
Beauchamp, William, 197, 198.
Beef, cost of, 164.
Bellefontaine, 51.
Bellevue, Iowa, terrorized by mob, 208.
Bentley, *Capt.*, 26.
Biddle, Nicholas, mention, 209.
Biggs, William, leg. coun., 113.
Birds, 14.
Birkbeck, Morris, founds English settlement, 124; method of fencing, 165.
Birkbeck's Settlement. *See* English Settlement, The.
Black Hawk, 81.
Black Hawk War, 146; mention, 207.
"Black Laws," 176, 186.
"Blue Laws," of Mt. Carmel, 200.
Blue Point, 157.
Bond, Shadrach, delegate to Congress, 113; governor of Illinois, 145, 208.
Books, 132.
Bosseron, *Maj.* F., 18, 24.
Bounty lands. *See* Military bounty lands.
Brady, ——, 38.
Brandy, price of, 97.
Brashears, *Capt.*, mention, 26.
Brick houses, 131.
Bridges, 114.
British at Michilimackinac attempt to divert Indian trade, 69; expeditions against Illinois settlers, 31-39, 107.

British Michilimackinac Company, 49.
Buffalo, 14.
Building, cost of, 168.
Burr, Aaron, mention, 203.
Butter, price of, 164.

C

Cahokia, attacked by British and Indians, 33; bounty lands, 57; commons, 72; court, 17; distress at, 25; population, 12.
Cahokia Indians, 53.
Cairo, Bank of, 114; dykes at, 114.
Calhoun, original name of Springfield, 207.
Calico, price of, 130.
Calvé, ——, trader, 33.
Canadian French settlers, 19.
Canal route ceded, 110.
Carbonneaux, Francis, 42-46.
Carlyle, eastern limit of frontier, 107; salt discovered, 18, 23, 171.
Carolinas, The, settlers from, 91.
Carondelet, *Baron* de, orders expulsion of Americans from Ft. Massac, 73.
Cartwright, Peter, journey to Baltimore, 1816, 123; personal traits, 191, 192; purchases land, 139; reasons for moving to Illinois, 166; representative from Sangamon Co., 191.
Cass, *Gov.* Lewis, averts Indian war, 135; protects Galena, 150.
Catholicism, slow increase of, 175.
Cattle, allowed to run at large, 20; raising of, 130. *See also* Live-stock.
Census of 1801, 88.
Cessions of land, by Indians, 44, 79-81, maps, 72, 104, 136; by individuals, 10, 24, 71, 196; by Virginia to United States, 45, 46; congressional, 57, 70, 72, 79.
Charleston, *Va.*, emigration from to Illinois, 190.
Chicago, in 1830, 190; massacre at, 109; platted, 142; post-office, 151; route to, 152; valuable port, 116.
Chicago Historical Society, 5, 11.
Chicago river, Indians cede tract six miles square at, 79.
Chickasaws, allies of Spain, 73.
Chippewa Indians, 134.
Cincinnati, trip from to Illinois, 1823, 154.

Clark, George Rogers, 14, 40, 45 *et seq.;* land granted to, 46; seizes Spanish goods, 54.
Clay, Henry, mention, 210.
Clergy, 174, 175, 196,
Climate, 95.
Clinton, De Witt, mention, 203.
Coal, in Illinois, 14, 131, 142, 165.
Cobbett, William, 160.
Coffee, price of, 130.
Coles, *Gov.* Edward, character, 210; emancipates slaves, 209; governor, 145, 208; message against slavery, 183; special envoy to Russia, 209; urges law to prevent kidnapping, 182.
College township, reserved by Ordinance of 1787, 101, 102.
Colleges, McKendree, 174; Shurtleff, 174.
Collot, *Gen.* [George Henry] Victor, "Journey in N. A.," 14, etc.; Map of the Country of the Illinois, *in pocket.*
Commerce in territorial period, 95, 96, 129.
Committee of Workingmen of Wheeling, *Va.*, 144.
Commodities, prices of, 49, 59, 130, 164.
Commons, Cahokia, 72.
Congress, delegate of N. W. Territory in, 76, 77; donates land, 142; early Illinoisians in, 146; memorialized:—by Galena, 150; by Illinois, 87, 100, 101, 138; petitioned, 53, 74, 75, 77, 78, 81, 86, 88.
Constitution of Illinois, provisions of, 117.
Constitutional Convention, 1824, 182, 183; votes for and against, chart of, 184.
Cook, Daniel P., non-resident proprietor of Springfield, 205; representative in Congress, 145.
Corn, price of, 96, 164.
Cotton, production of, in United States, 122, 129; raised in Illinois, 167, 168.
Counterfeiting, penalty for, 148.
Counties in Illinois, 1824, list of, 183.
Courts, 15, 17, 60, 62. *See also under* Illinois, Kaskaskia, Vincennes.
Cox, *Col.* Thomas, joint owner of Springfield, 206-208.
Crawford, William Henry, *Secretary of*

INDEX.

War, announces land policy, 109.
Crockett, David, mention, 205.
Croghan, George, description of Vincennes, 13.
Cruzat, *Spanish Commandant at St. Louis*, 39.
Cumberland Presbyterians, 143.

D

Dalton, *Capt.*, 34; elected magistrate, 61.
Dartmouth College, mention, 206.
Davis, Jefferson, mention, 207.
Deane, Silas, mention, 34.
Debtors, imprisonment of, 147.
Deer, 14.
Demoulin, Dumoulin, *or* De Moulin, John, 74.
Demunbrunt, Demunbrun, *or* De Munbrun, Thimothé, 22, 41.
Detroit, land office at, 80; mention, 190; threatened by de la Balme, 35, 36.
Dickinson College, mention, 210.
Dixon's ferry. *See* Ogee's ferry.
Dodge, *Capt.* John, 22-23, 26-27, 67.
Ducharme, *trader*, 33.
Ducoigne, ——, 68.
Duncan, Joseph, 145.

E

Easton, Joseph, emigrant from England, 1633, 203.
Easton, Rufus, founder of Alton, 203; political career, 204.
Edgar, John, career of, 174, 193, 194; correspondence concerning anarchy in Illinois, 67; land holdings of, 10, 101; letter to St. Clair, 85.
Edwards, Ninian, appointed governor of Illinois Territory, 111, 113, 145; in War of 1812, 107, 108; message of 1828, 149; on prices of public lands, 138; political career of, 210; wages offered by, 130.
Edwards county, Birkbeck's settlement in. *See* English Settlement.
Edwardsville, Bank of, 207; public lands at, 105, 137.
Ellery, Abm. R., mention, 203.
Emancipation. *See under* Slavery.
Emigration and immigration, 127, 176 *et seq.*; causes of: — from New England, 120, from the South, 121, 189; cost of, 124; food supply for emigrants, 119, 133; increase, 189; opposition to immigration, 91.
English Settlement, The, 124, 157, 161, 169; cost of transportation to, 160; ships produce to New Orleans, 154. *See also* Birkbeck, Morris; *also* Flower, George.
Enos, Pascal Paoli, joint proprietor of Springfield, 205, 206.
Enos, *Maj.-Gen.* Roger, 206.
Ernst, Ferdinand, mention, 167.
Extinguishment of Indian land titles, 77, 79, 81, 109, 144, 146.

F

Falls of Ohio, 30, 64, 65, 160, 162. *See also* Ft. Harmar; *also* Shippingport.
Farming methods, 168.
Federal Government owns land, 158.
Fencing, 165 n., 169.
Ferguson, Thomas, leg. coun., 13.
Ferries, 83, 114, 152.
Fever, 95. *See also under* Health.
Fever river, 134; lead mines at, 150.
Financial panic, 1819, 188-189.
Fisher, *Dr.* George, rep., 113.
Fisher, Myers, mention, 195.
Flat-boats, 94, 124, 125, 129, 154, 160. *See also* Arks.
Flax, 129.
Florida, Province of, 71.
Flour, price of, 49, 50, 94, 163, 164.
Flour-mills, 167; built by John Edgar, 193.
Flower, George, 124. *See also* English Settlement.
Food, scarcity, 21-23, 25, 28, 30; supply of, 133. *See also under* names of food products.
Fort Chartres, cannon from, 108; inhabitants, 12.
Fort Dearborn, massacre at, 109; mention, 190.
Fort Edwards, terminus of mail route, 151.
Fort Harmar, 64.
Fort Jefferson, 24, 25, 30.
Fort La Motte, mention, 107.
Fort Massac, 73, 79, 95, 107.
Fort Nelson, mention, 32.
Fort Russell, established, 108.

SETTLEMENT OF ILLINOIS.

Fort Stanwix, mention, 56.
Fort Wayne, Treaty of, 79.
Fox Indians, 33, 81.
Fox river, first flour-mill on, 167.
Franklin, Benjamin, mention, 34, 195.
Fredonian, mention, 197.
Free masons, organized, 194.
Freehold qualifications, 77, 112, 113.
Freeholders, housekeepers privileged as, 147.
Freight charges, 94, 124, 160 *et seq.*
French, Augustus C., 145.
French settlers, attitude toward Americans, 47-49; land holdings, 13, 18, 99; misled by La Balme, 34; offered free land by Spanish, 55; priests. emigrate from Illinois co., 68; towns, character of, 11.
French-Swiss from Lord Selkirk's colony reach Galena, 172.
Frontier, The, 48, 91, 106, 147, 206; Carlyle eastern limit of, 107.
Frontiersman, analysis of character of, 191, 201, 202.
Fruit, 129, 133, 168.
Fuel, scarcity of, 131.
Fulton county separated from Madison, 188.
Fur trade, 96. *See also* American Fur Company.
Furs, 130.

G

Gage, *Gen.* Thomas, 10.
Galena, 150-53; lead-mining, 172.
Gallatin county, saline, 170; slaves in, 180.
Game, 14, 51, 132.
Gamelin, Antoine, clerk of District Court, Post Vincennes, 60.
George, *Capt.* Robert, mention, 40.
Germain, *Lord* George, mention, 32.
Gibault, *Father* Pierre, mention, 68.
Governor and judges, 58, 62.
Grammar, John, rep., 113.
Grand Ruisseau, 52.
Granger, *Postmaster-General* Gideon, mention, 203.
Gratiot, Charles, 39.
Great Britain, King's proclamation, 1763, 10.
Great Western Road, 157.
Greene county, separated from Madison, 188.

Greenville, Treaty of, 79.

H

Hamilton, Alexander, 138; mention, 91.
Hamilton, *Gen.*, leads British against Vincennes, 15.
Hampden Sidney College, mention, 209.
Hamtramck, *Maj.* John F., at Kaskaskia, 53; petitioned for troops, 65.
Hancock, John, mention, 34.
Harmar, *Gen.* Josiah, 50; advice to French, 52; expedition from Vincennes to Kaskaskia, 51; on emigration from Illinois, 64; refuses request for troops, 69.
Harrison, Benjamin, 40; receives petition for General Assembly, 85.
Health, 27, 91, 95.
Henry, Mr., elected magistrate, 61.
Henry, Patrick, 209; instructions concerning Illinois County, 9.
Hinde, Thomas S., career in Illinois, 196, 197; description of Peter Cartwright, 192.
Hog raising, 14, 20.
Hogs, 144.
Honey, 129, 130, 133.
Hooker, *Rev.* Thomas, founder of Hartford, *Conn.*, 203.
Horse stealing, 65, 67, 69.
Hubbard, Adolphus Frederick, 210.
Hubbard, Gurdon Saltonstall, agent American Fur Company, 157.
Hubbard's Trail, extent of, 157.
Hunting, as occupation, 132.
Huron (Ouisconsin or Wisconsin) Territory, claims Galena, 150.

I

Iles, Elijah, career of, 205, 206.
Iles, Elizabeth Crockett, mention, 205.
Illinois:—
  Country, British in, 10 *et seq.;* climate, 14, 95; Collot's description of, 14; map, *in pocket;* conditions in 1787, 50, 51; development, 97, 98; enters second grade of territorial government, 85, 86; French population, 10, 12, 13, 30; French settlers offered free land by Spanish, 55; game in, 14, 51; governor and judges, 58; Indian owners of, 10 *et*

INDEX. 261

seq.; inhabitants of, 12, 13; immigration to, 91, 92; labor conditions in, 96, 97; population in 1767, 1772, 1788, 70; in 1790, 1800, 1810, 91, 97; racial conflicts in, 54, 55; rivers of, 92, 94; roads, 13, 14, 93, 94, 131; separation from Indiana, 85 *et seq.;* squatters in, 71.

County (1778-1783), Act creating, 9, 15; Act renewed, 25; Act dissolved, 31; anarchy, 40 *et seq.;* anomalous position, 18; bankrupt, 40; civil organization, 15; condition in 1780, 25, 26; courts, 15; extent of, 9, 10; French inhabitants dissatisfied, 30; hardships in early period, 21, 22; judges, election of, 17; military and civil authorities conflict, 25-27; military operations, 19, 22-24, 32-39; money scarce, 21; Spanish claims, 38.

Territory, books in, 132; boundaries, 90; cattle raising, 130; commerce in, 96, 129; delegates in Congress, 113; election of officials, 112; enters second grade of territorial government, 112; extent, 89; formed, 89-90; governor and judges, 111, 113; immigration to, 120, 121, 124, 126, 132; Indian troubles in, 106 *et seq.;* internal improvements proposed, 114; internal revenue, 1814, 128; judges for, 111; land office authorized, 103; land policy, 111; laws, 111, 112, 114; legislature, 100, 113; legislature southern in nativity, 112 n., 113; manufactures, 1810, 128, 129; newpapers in, 132; petitions for state government, 115; physical features, 86; population, 1810, 91; post-roads, 131; productductions, 129 *et seq.,* 133; qualifications for representative, 113; slavery, *see* general alphabet; suffrage in, 112; taxes, 133; transportation, 114, 129, 130.

State, admission proposed, 115, opposed, 118; agriculture in 1820, 165; "Black Laws," 176, 186; boundary, eastern, 90, northern, 115; cattle raising, 130; cessions of Indian lands, 134, 135; coal in, 14, 142, 165; constitution completed, 117; cost of living in, 130; counties, list of, 183; debtors, 147; election in 1822, 181; election laws, 1829, 148; emigration, *see* General alphabet; Enabling Act of 1818, 115; food supplies, 133; government southern in character, 145; governors, list of, 145; House of Representatives, mention, 185; in Congress, 118, 146; Indian agents, 134; Indian land claims, 134, 135; Indian traders, 134; Indian wars, 146, 207; internal revenue, 128; judicial circuit, 173; land, *see* general alphabet; laws, southern influence on, 186; manners and customs, 128 *et seq.,* 165; manufactures, 128; money, substitutes for, 130; New Englanders in, 146; newspapers, 132; northern boundary changed, 115; population required for admission, 116, 117; postal facilities in, 151, 158, 159; products of, 129, 167 *et seq.;* public lands, 136; salt springs legislation, 101; school tax, 148; senators and representatives, 145; settlement typical, 5; slavery, *see* general alphabet; southern influence in, 183, 184, 186; southern influence in, 183, 184, 186; taxation, 1828, compared with that of Kentucky, 149, 150; transportation, cost of, 150; facilities, 124, *see also* general alphabet; treasury receipts, 149; squatter population, 148; voting in 1829, 148.

Illinois and Michigan Canal, estimated cost of transportation by, 141; route ceded, 110; mention, 115.
Illinois Company, holdings of, 10, 44.
Illinois Herald, 132.
Illinois Intelligencer, 132, 140.
Illinois Land Company, 10 *et seq.*
Illinois river settlements, 134.
Illinois Navigation Company, 114, 115.
Illiteracy of French inhabitants, 13.
Immigration. *See with* Emigration.
Indentured servitude, 117, 176 *et seq.*
Indian agents, 134.
Indians, 11, 12; employed by British, 32; land cessions, maps: 1795-1801, 72; 1809-1818, 104; 1818-1830, 136; reservations, 134, 135; titles to land extinguished, 77, 79, 81, 109, 144, 146; traders, 134; tribes: Cahokias, 52; Chickasaws, 73; Chippewas, 134; Foxes, 33, 81; Kaskaskias. 12;

Kickapoos, 110; Menominees, 134; Mitchas, 52; Mitchigamias, 12; Ottawas, 135; Ouias, 29; Peorias, 12, 52; Piankashaws, 81; Potawatomies, 134; Sauks, 33, 81; Sioux, 31; Tamarois, 110; Winnebagoes, 135.
Indiana, population, 91, 181; route to, from North Carolina, 156; slavery, 185.
Indiana Territory, divided, 81, 88, 89; formed, 84.

J

Jacksonville, 156; English emigrants at, 189.
Jarrott's mill, 167.
Jefferson, Thomas, mention, 203, 204.
Johnson, *Capt.* elected magistrate, 61.
Johnson, *Col.* R. M., 163.
Jones, John Rice, career of, 195, 196; death, 196; mention, 68; with Clark, 54.
Jones, *Rev.* William, rep., 113.
Judges, election of, 17, 58, 111.
Judy, Samuel, leg. coun., 113.
Jurors paid, 58.
Jury, trial by, 60.
Justices of the peace, not paid, 23.

K

Kane, Elias K., 145.
Kaskaskia, bounty lands, 57; court, 17, 19; judicial district of, 44; land-office at, 103, 136, 137, 138, 143.
Kaskaskia Indians, 12.
Keel-boats, 125, 129; rates, 161.
Kenton, Simon, 179.
Kentucky, emigration to Illinois, 189; journey from, to Illinois, 1819, 155; mention, 21, 24, 32, 33, 189; population, 1790, 1800, 1810, 91, 93; 1820, 181.
Kentucky boats, 93, 94.
Kentucky Gazette, 189.
Kickapoo Indians, 110.
Kidnapping of negroes, 186.
King's proclamation, 1763, 10.
Knox county, 75 n., 86.
Kohos (Cahokia), mention, 27.

L

La Balme, *Col.* Augustin Mottin de, career of, 33 *et seq.*

Labor questions, 96, 97, 99, 130, 169.
Lafayette, *Marquis* de, entertained by John Edgar, 193; mention, 209.
Lake Michigan, advantages to Illinois of port on, 115, 116.
Land, Act of 1791, 72; canal, 141, 142; cessions by Indian tribes, 72, 104, 110, 136; cession by Virginia to U. S., 45, 46; church and school, 141, 142; classified for taxation, 84; cultivation of, 166; fertility of, 14, 165; form of holdings, 13, 38; French deeds to, 13; government entry of, 130; Kickapoo cession of, 1819, 134; military, 100; owned by Federal Government, 158; prices, 57, 80, 88, 92, 103-5, 136-8, 143; rental of, 166; Spanish donate to French, 55; tavern sites, 75; taxes on, 130; unoccupied in Kentucky, Ohio and Indiana, 98. *See also* Public lands.
Land-claims, 10; in Illinois, 140.
Land-companies, 10, 11.
Land-frauds, referred to Congress, 99, 100.
Land-grants, investigated, 57.
Land-holders, non-resident, mention, 140, 145.
Land-offices, 80; in Illinois, 44 *et seq.*, 103.
Land-titles, insecure, 51, 71; King's proclamation, 1763, 10.
Laws: "Black Laws," 176, 186; "Blue Laws," 200; territorial, 111-14.
La Valiniere, Pierre Huet de, mention, 68.
Lead, output of, 1823-1827, 151.
Lead region, rush to, 1826, 172.
Le Dru, removes to St. Louis, 68; signs petition, 66.
Le Grand, signature on land grant, 45.
Legras, *Col.* P., at Vincennes, 18.
Limestone beds at Alton, 204.
Lincoln, Abraham, in Black Hawk War, 207.
Linctot, 38 n., 39 n.
Live-stock, 27, 83, 169. *See also* Cattle.
Log canoes, 93.
Log houses, cost of, 168.
Long Prairie, 74.
Louis XVIII. of France, mention, 209.
Louisiana, emigration to, 86; province of, 91.
Louisiana Gazette, report of steamboat speed, 162.

INDEX. 263

Luzerne, *Chevalier*, 30, 36.
Lyon, Matthew, on price of lands, 88.

M

McCarty, Richard, 19, 20, 26, 27; killed, 29.
McDowell, William, 196.
McIlvaine, *Miss* Caroline M., 5.
McKendree College, opened by Methodists in 1828, 174.
McLean, John, 145.
McMaster, John Bach, 5.
Madison, *Governor of Kentucky*, 197.
Madison, James, mention, 209.
Madison, John, 196.
Madison county, population 1820, 1824, 1825, 132, 188.
Magistrates, 59 *et seq.*, 67.
Mail routes, 1825–1830, 158, 159.
Malaria, 91, 95.
Manufactures, 128, 129.
Maple sugar, 129.
Marietta, *O.*, 71.
Marriage, mixed, 51; without priest, 12.
Mary of the Incarnation, *Mother*, 11.
Maryland, settlers from, 91.
Mason and Dixon's line, 179.
Massachusetts, emigration to Illinois, 189.
Mechanics' lien, 149.
Menard, Pierre, leg. coun., 113, 208; Lt.-Gov., 145.
Menominee Indians, 134.
Methodist Episcopal Church, 174; mention, 191.
Meurin, *Father*, mention, 12.
Michigan, legislature meets in summer, 152.
Michilimackinac, British at, 32, 39, 46, 47, 69.
Miliet, *Mr.*, elected magistrate, 61.
Military bounty lands, 57.
Military organization, etc. *See under* Illinois.
Military Tract, land in, sold for taxes, 140.
Mills, 83, 167.
Miro, Estevan, *Governor of Louisiana and Florida*, proclamation of, 63, 71.
Mississippi river, navigation of, 21; settlement on hindered, 88.
Missouri, population, 82, 181; slavery in, 179, 180.
Missouri Compromise, 178.

Mitchigamia Indians, 12, 52.
Money, scarcity, 21, 22.
Monroe, *President* James, letter to Jefferson, 97; mention, 209.
Montgomery, *Lieut.-Col.* John, 15 *et seq.*
Morals. *See* Public morals.
Morgan, ——, member of trading company, 10.
Morgan, George, agent of Indiana Company, 56; land frauds, 56, 57.
Morgan county, anti-slavery society, 183; freehold rights to housekeepers, 147; separated from Madison, 188.
Morrison, William, landholdings of, 74, 100, 101.
Mount Carmel, Bank of, 199; donation of land for church and schools, 142; founding of, 196, 198; incorporation, 200.
Murray, Edward, 23.
Murray, William, mention, 10.

N

Negroes, 12, 64; punishment of, 179. *See also* Slavery.
New Design, founded, 91, 92, 95; mention, 83.
New England, immigrants from, 146.
New Jersey Land Company, 11.
New Madrid (L'Anse a la Graisse), 63 *et seq.*
New Orleans, flour market, 193; mention, 26.
New Orleans boats, 93, 94.
Newspapers:—*Illinois Herald*, 132; *Illinois Intelligencer*, 132, 140; *Kentucky Gazette*, 189; *Louisiana Gazette*, 162; *Shawnee Chief*, 132; *Western Intelligencer*, 132.
Non-resident landholders, 140, 145.
North Carolina, route from, to Indiana, 156.
Northwest Territory, bounties in, 84; congressional delegate seated, 76; divided, 76, 84, 85; enters second degree, 75; first sale of public land in, 75; judges, 62; laws, 83, 84; magistrates, 61; mention, 58; taxation, 83.

O

Ogee's (Dixon's) ferry, 152.
Oglesby, *Rev.* Joshua, rep., 113.

Ohio, emigration to, 76, 190; population, 91, 181; public land sale, 144.
Ohio Company, 71.
Ohio river, boundary of Illinois, 10; settlers, 88; settlers northwest of, 18, 19.
Ordinance of 1784, 46.
Ordinance of 1787, 40; amendments to, 115, 116; anti-slavery article, 176 *et seq.;* college township reserved by, 101; effect on Illinois country, 54, 55; violation of, 87.
Ottawa Indians, 135.
Ouia, town, 30.
Ouia (Wea) Indians, 29.
Ouisconsin (Wisconsin) Territory, Galena claimed by, 150.

P

Paget, M., mill built by, 193.
Palestine, sale of public lands at, 137.
Parker, Joseph, of Kaskaskia, 53, 54.
Peck, *Rev.* John M., Baptist minister, 124, 125, 192.
Peltry, debts paid in, 21, 43, 60.
Peoria, Indian agent at, 134; mention, 79.
Peoria Indians, 12.
Philips, Joseph, territorial secretary, 113.
Piankashaw Indians, 81.
Pierre, Eugenio, 38.
Pike county, separated from Madison, 188.
Pioneer clergy, 191 *et seq.*
Pirogues, 93, 94, 160.
Plums, at Smith's Prairie, 129.
Pollock, Oliver, 40.
Polypotamia, mention, 46.
Pope, Nathaniel, and the northern boundary, 115, 116; delegate in Congress, 113.
Population, 1788, 70; 1785-1799, 82; 1801, 88; 1790-1810, 91; 1818, 116; 1812, 113; 1820-1840, 187, 188; French, 1766-1777, 12.
Post routes. *See* Mail routes.
Post Vincennes, court regulations for, 59, 135. *See also* Vincennes.
Potatoes, price, 97, 164.
Potawatomie Indians, 134.
Prairie du Chien, inhabitants, 1801, 88.
Prairie du Rocher, bounty lands, 57; inhabitants, 1766-1777, 12; 1801, 88.

Prairies, 83, 86, 97, 109, 131, 156; fertility of, 165 *et seq.;* settlement, 130, 131.
Preëmption rights, 72, 75, 77, 78, 100, 102, 111, 113, 139, 144, 152; in various states, 102 *et seq.*
Presbyterians, at Galena, 175; Cumberland Presbyterians, 143.
Prices of commodities, 49, 59, 97, 130, 131, 164; of land, *see under* Land.
Priests, French, emigrate from Illinois, 68.
Pro-slavery agitation. *See under* Slavery.
Provisions, scarcity of, 21-23, 25, 28.
Public lands, donated for schools and internal improvements, 142; price of in various states, 103, 104, 105; proceeds of sales applied to roads and schools, 116; receipts from sale of, 143; sales in Illinois, 77, 81, 105, 106, 137, 143; sales in other states, 103, 104, 144; tax regulations of, up to 1818, 130.
Public morals, 28, 29.
Publications. *See* Books, Newspapers.

Q

Quebec, Bishop of, pastoral letter, 1767, 12.

R

Randolphs, The, mention, 209.
Randolph county, formed, 75 n., 83; slaves in, 180.
Rangers, volunteer for guard service, 108, 109.
Regulators of the Valley, 147.
Religious denominations, 172 *et seq.*
Reynolds, *Gov.* John, 145, 196.
Richland Creek, settlement, 78.
River craft, 93, 94, 126, 129.
Rivière du Chemin, fight at, 37.
Roads, 86, 116, 153 *et seq.;* Illinois settlements to Galena, 151; repairs, 158; Shawneetown to Birkbeck's settlement, 157; to Kaskaskia, Cahokia and St. Louis, 101, 102, 157; Vandalia to Springfield, 157. *See also under* Illinois; *also* Toll roads.
Rock river, 152.
Rock Spring Seminary (Shurtleff College) founded by Baptists in 1827, 174.

INDEX.

Rogers, *Capt.* ——, defense of, 28, 29.
Roosevelt, Theodore, "Winning of the West," 9.
Rush, Benjamin, mention, 195.

S

St. Clair, *Gov.* Arthur, 10, 64; at Kaskaskia, 69; establishes counties, 83; president of Congress, 54.
St. Clair, James, 74.
St. Clair, John Murray, 10, 193.
St. Clair, William, 74.
St. Clair county, divided, 83; formed, 75 n., 82.
St. Josephs, expedition against, 37, 38.
St. Louis, attacked by British, 33; population of, 1817, 132; Treaty of, 1804, 81.
St. Marie, Joseph, goods confiscated by Spanish, 63.
St. Philips, inhabitants of, 12.
St. Pierre, *Father*, leaves Cahokia, 68.
Ste. Geneviève, garrisoned by Spanish, 74.
Saline creek salt works, slave labor at, 117.
Saline river reservation, sale of, 142.
Saline spring in Gallatin county, 170, 171.
Salt, discovered at Carlyle, 1823, 171; legislation concerning, 101; prices of, 170 *et seq.*; works, New York, 153.
Sangamon county, emigration to, 1810-1825, 188; housekeepers as freeholders, 147; separated from Madison, 188.
Sauk Indians, 33, 81.
Schools, academic, funds given for, 199; common, established, 173; early, 173; land granted for, 116, 141, 142; teachers, 173, 174.
Scotch-Irish opposed to slavery, 92.
Selkirk, *Lord*, colony, 172.
Seminaries, location of, 174.
Servitude, indentured, 117, 176, 177, 179.
Shawnee Chief, 132.
Shawneetown, description, 1817, 125-7; land-office at, 103; road to Kaskaskia, 101, 102, 157; sale of public lands, 105, 137.
Shipping, 93, 94, 125, 129.
Shippingport, Falls of Ohio, mention, 162.

Short, Jacob, rep., 113.
Shurtleff College (Rock Springs Seminary) founded by Baptists in 1827, 174.
Sickness. *See under* Health.
Sioux Indians, 31, 32.
Skiffs, 93, 94.
Slave code, enacted in 1819, 179.
Slavery, 64, 65, 176 *et seq.*; abolition recommended by Coles, 185; antislavery article of Ordinance of 1787, 55, 177, 180; "Black Laws" of Illinois, 176, 186; children of slaves, 177; constitutional provisions, 178; decrease of, 187; effect on settlement, 177; freeing of slaves, 64, 65, 177, 179; French slaveholders, 55, 176, 177; importation of slaves authorized, 87; increase, 180, 181; indentured servitude, 117, 176 *et seq.*; legalization, 176; number of slaves, 1820, 1840, 187; Ordinance of 1787, 55, 176, 177, 180; whipping of slaves, 179.
Slave-trade, abolition of, 178.
Smith's Prairie, fruit at, 129.
Soulard, *Mr.*, 152.
Southern influence in Illinois, 145, 186.
Spain claims the Illinois country, 38; offers free land to Illinois settlers, 55, 71; refuses to allow navigation of Mississippi, 21.
Spanish, aggression upon United States, 73; trouble Illinois settlers, 21, 24.
Sprigg, *Judge* William, 111.
Springfield, called Calhoun when founded, 196; first store, 206; land-office at, 144; sales of public land, 137, 143; terminus of mail route, 158.
Squatters in Illinois, 50, 58, 72, 99, 148.
State Historical Society of Wisconsin. *See under* Wisconsin.
Steamboats, first on Ohio and Mississippi, 123; speed and rates of, 160, 162, 163.
Stephenson, Benjamin, delegate in Congress, 113.
Stuart, *Judge* Alexander, 111, 113.
Stuart, John T., mention, 207.
Suffrage, qualifications, 77, 78, 112-14, 117, 147, 148.
Sugar, maple, 129.
Supreme Court, U. S., decision of, 11.

SETTLEMENT OF ILLINOIS.

T

Talbott, Benjamin, leg. coun., 113.
Tallmadge, James, opposes admission of Illinois, 118, 179.
Tamarois, Indians, 110.
Tardiveau, Bartholomew, 51, 52, 55, 69.
Tavern-keepers (housekeepers) given freehold privileges, 147.
Tavern-sites, land ceded for, 75, 79.
Taxation, in N.-W. terr., 83; of land, 130, 133; of live-stock, 83.
Taylor, Zachary, mention, 207.
Tazewell, L. W., mention, 209.
Tea, price of, 130.
Teachers, salaries of, 174.
Tennessee, lands sold for taxes, 189.
Tennessee wagon, 155.
Thomas, *Judge* Jesse B., signs petition for retention of slavery in Illinois, 111, 178; territorial judge, 113, 145.
Timber, want of, 131.
Todd, *Col.* John, *Jr.*, 15, 16 *et seq.*
Toll roads, 157.
Tomahawk rights, 51.
Trading firms: Baynton, Wharton and Morgan, 10; British Michilimackinac Company, 49.
Trammell, Philip, rep., 113.
Transportation,
  cost: *via* canals, 141; *via* rivers, 124, 125, 126, 160;
  improvement in facilities, 157;
  land, 93, 126, 154–7, 161;
  water, 83, 92 *et seq.*, 114, 126, 129.
  See also River craft, Wagons.
Treaties:—Fort Wayne, 1803, 79; Greenville, 1795, 79; St. Louis, 1804, 81; Spain-U. S., commercial treaty, 73; Vincennes, 1803, 79; 1805, 81.
Trottier, F., 36.
Turbine wheel, 167.
Turner, Frederick Jackson, 5.
Turnpike, 93.

U

United States Supreme Court decision, 11.

V

Vandalia, mention, 188, 189; land-office at, 207; public lands sold, 137.
Vegetables, 168.
Vehicles, 152, 155, 156; emigrant wagons, 159, 164; Tennessee wagon, 155.
Vermilion saline, 142.
Vincennes, accept inducements of Morgan, 63; attack on, 32, 73; court, 17, 59; description of, 13; levy of troops at, 54; treaty, 1803, 79; treaty, 1805, 81. *See also* Post Vincennes.
Virginia, Augusta county, 15; Board of Commissioners for the Settlement of Western Accounts, 42–44; cedes Western lands to the United States, 45, 46; emigration from, to Illinois, 91, 92, 190, 201; legislation for protection of Illinois county, 9; military bounty lands, 46; money, 21, 23, 24.
Vote, August 2, 1824, 183; chart of, 184.

W

Wabash Land Company, 10 *et seq.*, 88.
Wabash Navigation Company, 200.
Wabash river, boundary line, 90, 154; expedition on, 41; landholders on, 10, 87, 88.
Wages, 96, 169.
Wagons, first, Galena to Chicago, 152. *See also* Vehicles.
War of 1812, 106 *et seq.*; mention, 118.
Water supply, 86.
Wayne county, separated from Illinois, 86.
Wea. *See* Ouia.
West, The, Commerce of, 96.
Western Christian Monitor, mention, 197.
Western frontier. *See* Frontier; also Wilderness.
Western Intelligencer, 132.
Western Territory, Ordinance for government of, 46.
Westward movement, 190.
Wharton, ——, member of trading firm, 10.
Wheat, price of, 164.
Wheeling, *Va.*, Committee of Workingmen, 144.
Wild animals, 14.
Wilderness, description of, 86; mention, 95. *See also* Frontier.
Wilderness Road, 93.
Wilkins, John, *British Commandant in Illinois*, 10.

Wilkinson, *Gen.* James, 204.
Williams, *Maj.*, 39.
Wilson, Alexander, rep., 113.
Winnebago Indians, 135, 151.
Winnebago war, 135, 146, 207.
Winston, Richard, 17, 18; sheriff at Kaskaskia, 26, 41, 61.
Wirt, William, mention, 209.
Wisconsin, southern boundary, 150.
Wisconsin, State Historical Society of, 11.
Wolves, 14; bounty for, 84, 148.

Wood, scarcity of retards settlement, 165.
Wyllys, *Maj.*, 69.

Y

Yorkshire, *England*, emigrants from, reach Jacksonville, 189.

Z

Zewapetas, 63.